Unequal Partners

Detail of "'Tom Tiddler's Ground.'—The Committee of Concoction," *Queen* 1, 16 (21 December 1861). By permission of the British Library, LD45.

UNEQUAL PARTNERS

Charles Dickens, Wilkie Collins, and Victorian Authorship

LILLIAN NAYDER

CORNELL UNIVERSITY PRESS

Ithaca & London

First published 2002 by Cornell University Press

Printed in the United States of America

Library of Congress Cataloging-in-Publication Data

Nayder, Lillian.
  Unequal partners : Charles Dickens, Wilkie Collins, and Victorian authorship / Lillian Nayder.
     p. cm.
  Includes bibliographical references (p.) and index.
  ISBN 0-8014-3925-6 (cloth : alk. paper)
    1. Dickens, Charles, 1812–1870—Authorship. 2. Literature publishing—Great Britain—History—
19th century. 3. Dickens, Charles, 1812–1870—Friends and associates. 4. English fiction—
19th century—History and criticism. 5. Collins, Wilkie, 1824–1889—Friends and associates.
6. Authorship—Collaboration—History—19th century. 7. Serial publication of books—History—
19th century. 8. Collins, Wilkie, 1824–1889—Authorship.   I. Title.
  PR4586.N39 2001
  823'.8—dc21

                                                                                    2001003445

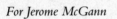
For Jerome McGann

Contents

Illustrations

The Collaborations of Dickens and Collins

1854   "The Seven Poor Travellers" (with Eliza Lynn, Adelaide Anne Procter, and George Augustus Sala), Extra Christmas Number, *Household Words* (14 December)

1855   "The Holly Tree Inn" (with William Howitt, Harriet Parr, and Adelaide Anne Procter), Extra Christmas Number, *Household Words* (15 December)

1856   "The Wreck of the Golden Mary" (with Percy Fitzgerald, Harriet Parr, Adelaide Anne Procter, and James White), Extra Christmas Number, *Household Words* (6 December)

1857   *The Frozen Deep,* first performed at Tavistock House on 6 January

        "The Lazy Tour of Two Idle Apprentices," *Household Words* (3–31 October)

        "The Perils of Certain English Prisoners," Extra Christmas Number, *Household Words* (7 December)

1858   "A House to Let" (with Elizabeth Gaskell and Adelaide Anne Procter), Extra Christmas Number, *Household Words* (7 December)

1859   "The Haunted House" (with Elizabeth Gaskell, Adelaide Anne Procter, George Augustus Sala, and Hesba Stretton), Extra Christmas Number, *All the Year Round* (13 December)

1860   "A Message from the Sea" (with Robert Buchanan or Henry F. Chorley, Charles Collins, Amelia B. Edwards, and Harriet Parr), Extra Christmas Number, *All the Year Round* (13 December)

Acknowledgments

I would like to thank Faith Clarke, the great-granddaughter of Wilkie Collins and Martha Rudd, for her kind permission to quote from unpublished letters and manuscripts written by Collins. I would also like to thank those libraries and archives that have allowed me to draw on material in their collections: the British Library; the Dickens House Museum; the Harry Ransom Humanities Research Center, University of Texas at Austin; the Mitchell Library; and the Pierpont Morgan Library. Bates College has provided me with research and publication grants, for which I am thankful.

Several people have provided me with encouragement and support while I worked on this book, and I am grateful to my colleagues at Bates College, especially Cristina Malcolmson and Carole Taylor, for their help. Andrew Gasson, chair of the Wilkie Collins Society, London, has generously supplied me with information about the collaborations of Dickens and Collins, and I am indebted to the work of Catherine Peters and Tamar Heller on the subject of Collins and his relationship to Dickens. I owe my greatest debts to Paul Cantor and Karen Chase, who introduced me to Dickens's fiction, and to Jerome McGann.

My husband, Matt Johnson, has shown great patience while I wrote and rewrote this book, as have our children, Nate and George: to them go love and thanks. I am also grateful for the encouragement I have received from my parents, Aileen and Leonard Grumbach, and from Ann and Jack Johnson.

Parts of chapter 2 were originally published in "Dickens and 'Gold Rush Fever': Colonial Contagion in *Household Words*," in *Dickens and the Children of Empire,* ed. Wendy S. Jacobson (New York: Palgrave, 2000), reproduced with permission of Palgrave. An earlier version of chapter 3 appeared as "The

Cannibal, the Nurse and the Cook in Dickens's *The Frozen Deep*," *Victorian Literature and Culture* 19 (1991): 1–24. A portion of chapter 4 was first published as "Class Consciousness and the Indian Mutiny in Dickens's 'The Perils of Certain English Prisoners,'" *Studies in English Literature, 1500–1900* 32, 4 (autumn 1992): 689–705. Portions of chapter 6 are adapted from "Robinson Crusoe and Friday in Victorian Britain: 'Discipline,' 'Dialogue,' and Collins's Critique of Imperialism in *The Moonstone*," *Dickens Studies Annual* 21 (1992): 213–31, with the permission of AMS Press, Inc. I thank the editors for allowing me to use this material.

Unequal Partners

Introduction

On 14 June 1870, Wilkie Collins was one of the twelve mourners who at-tended Dickens's private burial service at Poets' Corner, Westminster Abbey. His friendship of nearly twenty years secured him a place at the gravesite, where he stood with several of Dickens's family members and with Dickens's closest associates: John Forster, Frank Beard, Frederic Ouvry, and his own brother, Charles, who had married Dickens's daughter Kate in 1860. Yet Collins's in-clusion in this select group of mourners was more a sign of past than of present ties. Collins was "shocked and grieved" by Dickens's death,[1] but also distant enough to complain that the funeral set him behind on his novel *Man and Wife:* "The day of Dickens's funeral was a lost day to me," he told his agent William Tindell two days later: "I am backward with the proofs of the book—and, as they are not at all intelligently read, they take a long time."[2]

Mourning his "lost day" rather than his lost friend in his letter to his agent, Collins fails to register much feeling at Dickens's death. Yet his concern with his publishing schedule seems oddly apt, since it represents a legacy left to him by Dickens. Indeed, it was Dickens who taught Collins the value of a day's work—by proving that novel writing could be a lucrative, middle-class profes-sion and by demonstrating just how profitable fiction could be when it was se-rialized and mass produced. At the same time, Dickens also taught Collins to look to his own interests, since the profits of his literary labors were not his

1. Letter to Catherine Beard, 8 June 1870, in *Suzannet Dickens Collection Catalogue,* ed. Michael Slater (London: Sotheby Parke Bernet, 1975), p. 144; quoted by Catherine Peters, *The King of Inventors: A Life of Wilkie Collins* (Princeton, N.J.: Princeton University Press, 1991), p. 319. Subsequent references to *The King of Inventors* are cited parenthetically in the text.

2. Autograph letter signed (ALS) to William F. Tindell, 16 June 1870, Mitchell Library; quoted by Peters, *King,* p. 320.

alone. Introducing Collins to the "factorylike conditions" governing the Victorian writing profession,[3] Dickens paid Collins by the column for his work in *Household Words* and then hired him as a staff writer at five guineas a week, while making more than a thousand pounds each year as the journal's editor and part owner.[4] Insisting that the writings of his contributors appear anonymously, under a masthead that read "Conducted by Charles Dickens," Dickens marketed his own name rather than theirs. With his essays, short stories, and novels strictly quantified in length, duration, and value, and serialized under Dickens's name, Collins came to see that fiction writing could be considered both a middle-class profession and a form of alienated labor. His literary works were part of a commodity system in which worth is measured by sales and in which an author's name is itself a marketable asset.[5] With some truth, Collins imagined himself as both a successful professional and as a wage slave in his working relationship with Dickens, as a brilliant young writer tutored by the "inimitable" Charles Dickens and as a resentful and exploited hand.

In expressing regret over a workday "lost" to Dickens's funeral, Collins recognizes his own market value, while also revealing the distance that had come to separate him from Dickens by 1870. Collins's subdued remarks to Tindell about Dickens's death contrast sharply with the excitement he expressed at keeping company with the "Great man" in the early 1850s, soon after they met. "Forward all my letters to 'care of Charles Dickens Esqre,'" Collins told his mother in September 1852, while staying with Dickens in Dover, and regaled her with the details of their daily routine:

> We breakfast at 10 minutes past eight—after breakfast Dickens goes into his study, and is not visible again till two, when he is available for every pleasant social pur-

---

3. Mary Poovey, *Uneven Developments: The Ideological Work of Gender in Mid-Victorian England* (Chicago: University of Chicago Press, 1988), pp. 104–5.

4. With his half-share in *Household Words* and his annual salary of five hundred pounds as editor, Dickens made between £1,163 and £1,652 per year from the periodical from 1851 to 1859. By breaking with Bradbury and Evans and becoming his own publisher in 1859, Dickens made considerably more from *All the Year Round* than he had from *Household Words*. See Robert L. Patten, *Charles Dickens and His Publishers* (Oxford: Clarendon Press, 1978), appendix D, p. 464. Even before meeting Dickens, Collins was impressed by his money-making abilities. As he informed R. H. Dana in 1849, Dickens "made *four thousand guineas* by his last year's Christmas book—(The Battle of Life)—a five shilling publication, (!) which everybody abused, and which, nevertheless, everybody read." ALS to R. H. Dana, 12 January 1849; Morris L. Parrish Collection, Princeton University Library. *The Letters of Wilkie Collins*, ed. William Baker and William M. Clarke, 2 vols. (London: Macmillan, 1999), 1:54.

5. As Anne Lohrli notes, Collins was the only writer other than Dickens to have his name published in *Household Words*—in advertisements for his novel *The Dead Secret*, serialized from January to June 1857. See "Wilkie Collins and *Household Words*," *Victorian Periodicals Review* 15, 3 (fall 1982): 118–19. Similar advertisements acknowledging Collins's authorship of *The Woman in White*, *No Name*, and *The Moonstone* appear in *All the Year Round*.

pose that can be imagined, for the rest of the day—Dinner at 1 / 2 past 5—and bed between 10 and eleven—Such is the life here—as pleasant a life by the seaside as it is possible to lead.

I shall get to work tomorrow, and finish and correct my book [*Basil*] in a week, I hope—If good ideas are as infectious as bad, the end of the novel—written in *this* house—ought to be the best part of it—Dickens anticipates a fortnight of the very hardest work to make up for the time lost in our last trip. The visitors here are getting used to him now. But when he first came, they used to wait to waylay him every morning—and have a good long stare at the "Great man" as he went to his bath![6]

Nearly forty years old when he met Collins in 1851, Dickens was the famous writer and editor of *Household Words,* while Collins, at twenty-six, had published one novel and was working on another, hopeful that Dickens's "good ideas" would prove "infectious" and that Dickens's industriousness would provide a model for his own. Collins was to learn—by working with, and for, the "Great man" over the next seventeen years—that Dickens's influence was constraining as well as inspiring and that comparisons between them usually worked to his own disadvantage. Collins clearly benefited from his association with Dickens and his employment as staff writer and collaborator, yet also chafed under Dickens's control, and believed that Dickens sometimes got the credit that was due to subordinates.

In the complex dynamic that developed between them, Collins increasingly felt the need to resist Dickens's authority and claim his work as his own. Appropriately, the last letters that they exchanged, in January 1870, centered on the question of literary ownership, as Collins asked Dickens to formally acknowledge his legal right to collect and reprint the work that had appeared in *Household Words* and *All the Year Round,* and Dickens complied: "At your request I can have no hesitation in stating . . . that the copyright in any of your novels, tales, and articles which have appeared in the periodicals entitled Household Words and All the Year Round was never purchased by the proprietors of those Periodicals, they having merely purchased from you the right of first publishing the same therein."[7] Bothered by the official tone of their exchange, Dickens included a personal note along with his "formal letter," yet

6. ALS to Harriet Collins, 9 September 1852. The Pierpont Morgan Library, New York. MA 3150.32. *The Letters of Wilkie Collins,* 1:89.

7. Charles Dickens to Wilkie Collins, 27 January 1870, *The Letters of Charles Dickens,* ed. Walter Dexter, 3 vols. (Bloomsbury: Nonesuch Press, 1938), 3:762; subsequent references to *Letters* are cited parenthetically in the text. For letters written through 1867, I rely on the Pilgrim edition of *The Letters of Charles Dickens,* ed. Madeline House, Graham Storey, and Kathleen Tillotson, 11 vols. to date (Oxford: Clarendon, 1965–); subsequent references to the Pilgrim edition are cited parenthetically in the text.

one that registers as effectively as any legal document could his sense of distance from Collins: "I don't come to see you because I don't want to bother you. Perhaps you may be glad to see me by-and-bye. Who knows?" (*Letters,* 3:762).

As Catherine Peters observes, Dickens's note suggests that the breach between the two writers was due to Collins rather than himself (*King,* 312). Yet Dickens's letters and behavior indicate that the feeling was mutual, as he complained to friends of Collins's unorthodox sexual relationships and expressed his discomfort with the more radical elements of Collins's writing.[8] Although Dickens created a scandal by separating from his wife Catherine in 1858 and devoting himself to the young actress Ellen Ternan, he adamantly denied the adulterous affair and was put off by Collins's willingness to publicly flaunt convention in his relationships with his two mistresses, Caroline Graves and Martha Rudd, supporting both women but marrying neither. Equally troubled by Collins's willingness to give political offense to middle-class readers, Dickens often "tone[d] down" what he felt Collins's writings "put too prominently forward" (Pilgrim, 8:623) and set both himself and his subeditor, W. H. Wills, as watchdogs over Collins's articles in the hope of rendering them less "offensive to the middle class" (Pilgrim, 8:669). "Don't go to press with Wilkie's paper . . . without my seeing it," Dickens characteristically warned Wills on 10 November 1858, expressing his distrust of Collins's political satire, the *Household Words* article "Doctor Dulcamara, M.P." (Pilgrim, 8:702).

Since the publication of John Forster's biography (1872–74), which relegates Collins to the margins of Dickens's life, critics have disagreed over how to formulate the relationship between the two writers and how to judge their relative importance to one another. Some have taken their cue from Forster and minimized Collins's significance, describing the younger novelist as "the indispensable companion of [Dickens's] . . . frivolous hours,"[9] while others have taken the relationship more seriously, whether to celebrate or bemoan its effects. "When Dickens gave himself up to plot his spontaneity disappeared," J. W. T. Ley complained in 1924: "And in all this I trace the Wilkie Collins influence, which, from an artistic point of view, has always seemed to me the most unfortunate happening in Dickens's life."[10] "From Dickens's death to the present day," Robert P. Ashley counters, "militant Dickensians lost no opportunity to bewail the Dickens-Collins relationship and to belittle Collins's achievement. . . . The fact that Collins seems to have influenced Dickens as much as Dickens influenced Collins made the younger novelist . . . guilty of a kind of heresy."[11]

---

8. See, for example, Dickens's letter to Esther Elton Nash, 5 March 1861 (Pilgrim, 9:388–89).

9. Una Pope-Hennessy, *Charles Dickens* (New York: Howell, Soskin, 1946), p. 291.

10. J. W. T. Ley, "Wilkie Collins's Influence upon Dickens," *Dickensian* 20 (1924): 65–66.

11. Robert P. Ashley, "Wilkie Collins and the Dickensians," *Dickensian* 49 (1953): 64.

Recent approaches to the relationship have proved to be more productive, as critics consider it in more theoretical and less partisan ways. Defining herself against an older generation of critics who haggle over the respective literary merits of the two writers, Sue Lonoff discusses their mutual indebtedness in her thoughtful essay on the subject, while Jerome Meckier places their rivalry in the context of Victorian literary history, as one in "a series of revaluative responses and replies" among competing Victorian realists.[12] While most critics who have written on the subject represent Collins as the beneficiary in the relationship, both Lonoff and Meckier speak of the psychological and artistic benefits that Dickens derived from Collins. Lonoff argues that Collins enabled his literary mentor to "nurture" a young writer and hence "to allay his fears of declining authority, potency and vigor," while Meckier suggests that Collins provided Dickens with "creative stimulus" by challenging his artistic preeminence.[13]

This book, like the studies by Lonoff and Meckier, considers the ways in which both Dickens and Collins benefited from their collaborations. Yet it also considers the inequities built into their working relationship at *Household Words* and *All the Year Round*, which both men clearly recognized and that Collins sometimes accepted but increasingly came to resist. It does so by placing their relationship in the context of the Victorian publishing industry and examining the material aspects of their literary labors. At the same time, this book considers their collaborations in the larger context of Victorian labor disputes and political unrest, to which their stories explicitly and self-consciously respond. Examples of unrest and rebellion—among English workers, colonized natives, and Englishwomen anxious for independence—often serve as the subjects of the collaborative stories and allow Dickens and Collins to examine and mediate their own disputes. Their often-conflicting ways of representing this material reveal their political differences as well and help to account for the growing distance between them.

Focusing on the stories that Dickens and Collins coauthored for *Household Words* and *All the Year Round*, their variants of the melodrama *The Frozen Deep* (1856–74), and their novels about empire—*The Moonstone* (1868) and *The Mystery of Edwin Drood* (1870)—this book shows how their collaborative works

12. See Sue Lonoff, "Charles Dickens and Wilkie Collins," *Nineteenth-Century Fiction* 35 (September 1980): 150–70; and Jerome Meckier, *Hidden Rivalries in Victorian Fiction: Dickens, Realism, and Revaluation* (Lexington: University Press of Kentucky, 1987), p. 2.

13. Lonoff, "Dickens and Collins," 160; Meckier, *Hidden Rivalries*, p. 2. In the most recent essay on the collaborative relationship, which focuses on "The Wreck of the Golden Mary," Anthea Trodd considers Dickens's ambivalence about collaborating with other writers and views Collins as a lackey of sorts, assigned the busy work of plot development. See "Collaborating in Open Boats: Dickens, Collins, Franklin, and Bligh," *Victorian Studies* 42, 2 (winter 1999–2000): 201–25.

represent and reconfigure the relationship between the two men while also tracing Collins's efforts to establish his autonomy as a novelist famous in his own right. In the collaborative works that date from the 1850s, Collins and Dickens imaginatively resolve their conflicts by taking on such roles as seagoing officers in the merchant marine, Arctic explorers in search of the Northwest Passage, and idle apprentices on holiday. Casting Dickens and Collins as captain and first mate in "The Wreck of the Golden Mary" (1856), for example, and as fellow apprentices vacationing together in "The Lazy Tour of Two Idle Apprentices" (1857), these works idealize their relationship by altering its basis and its terms. They obscure the uncomfortable contract negotiations that took place between them in the mid 1850s as well as Collins's discontent as Dickens's staff writer and subordinate, while also revealing Collins's willingness to compromise with and emulate his senior.

At the same time, their adventure stories bring them together in roles and under circumstances that strengthen their mutual allegiance by defining them against troublesome others whose differences in race, class, and gender outweigh their own. Emphasizing Collins's status as a professional rather than a hired hand, Dickens makes him part of the management team in "The Wreck of the Golden Mary." Assigning him the role of first mate, John Steadiman, from whose point of view Collins writes, Dickens pits him against a potentially mutinous crew of common sailors, a miser modeled on the stereotypical Jew, and an unruly female who cannot be controlled by the officers and men—the *Golden Mary* herself. In the face of such dangers, the captain and mate join forces, their interests one and the same. In *The Frozen Deep,* Richard Wardour and Frank Aldersley, played on the stage by Dickens and Collins respectively, overcome their rivalry by recognizing their common enemy in a savage Highland woman who threatens them both. By the 1860s, however, such strategies have lost much of their efficacy, as Collins proves increasingly willing to stake out his own more radical position and write at cross purposes with Dickens.

In privileging male bonds and defining themselves and their fictional personae against unruly others, Dickens and Collins resemble the male collaborators discussed by Wayne Koestenbaum and Jeffrey Masten—Beaumont and Fletcher, Wordsworth and Coleridge, and Rider Haggard and Andrew Lang, for example—and this book, like Masten's, considers the ties among male collaboration, conceptions of authorship, and the patriarchal.[14] But because the

14. See Wayne Koestenbaum, *Double Talk: The Erotics of Male Literary Collaboration* (New York: Routledge, 1989); and Jeffrey Masten, *Textual Intercourse: Collaboration, Authorship, and Sexualities in Renaissance Drama* (Cambridge: Cambridge University Press, 1997).

collaborative works of Dickens and Collins were produced under strikingly different circumstances than the early modern dramas discussed by Masten, my analysis diverges from his. If the collaborations of Beaumont and Fletcher undermine post-Enlightenment conceptions of authorial autonomy and textual property, as Masten argues, those of Dickens and Collins show how, by the 1850s, the idea of authorship had become inseparable from that of private property, even as their market relations, their editorial and publishing practices, and their ideological aims undermined romantic myths of the creative and solitary genius. Significantly, both Dickens and Collins were outspoken advocates of international copyright law, and each believed that his originality should be legally recognized and protected. If collaborative authorship in Dickens's journals prevented readers from recognizing Collins's originality and name, he would be compensated with his staff salary and his association with the "Great man."[15]

For the nineteenth- and twentieth-century collaborators discussed by Koestenbaum, the property rights and the integrity of the author seemed clear. But in foregrounding the psychoanalytic dimensions of male collaboration and its relation to "homosexual desire," Koestenbaum avowedly "stint[s]" the historical and examines neither "methods of textual production" nor the construction of authorship.[16] By contrast, my discussion of Dickens and Collins considers the material grounds of authorship and collaboration, as each writer attempts to produce and profit from what he considers his own property.

While enabling the collaborators to stage and mediate their own differences, the works they coauthored also allow them to address and partly defuse certain political issues that Dickens, in particular, found troubling. Dickens developed the collaborative stories in response to problems of army recruitment during the Indian Mutiny, allegations of cannibalism among the members of Sir John Franklin's Arctic expedition, and demands among Englishwomen for equal rights, among other topical concerns of the 1850s and 1860s. They were largely designed to discredit expressions of labor unrest and resentment among English workers as well as attempts to gain legal rights and employment for women.

15. For discussions of the conception of the author and the relation between ideas of literary originality and copyright law, see Mark Rose, *Authors and Owners: The Invention of Copyright* (Cambridge, Mass.: Harvard University Press, 1993); and *The Construction of Authorship: Textual Appropriation in Law and Literature,* ed. Martha Woodmansee and Peter Jaszi (Durham, N.C.: Duke University Press, 1994). For discussions of Dickens, Collins, and their support of international copyright, see Alexander Welsh, *From Copyright to Copperfield: The Identity of Dickens* (Cambridge, Mass.: Harvard University Press, 1987); and Sundeep Bisla, "Copy-Book Morals: *The Woman in White* and Publishing History," *Dickens Studies Annual* 28 (1999): 103–49.

16. Koestenbaum, *Double Talk,* pp. 8, 9.

Using a variety of defensive strategies to allay these "social problems," the stories unite angry workers with their leisured superiors by invoking the more threatening specter of female emancipation, or by placing Englishmen in imperial outposts during native revolts, where, regardless of their class differences, they must band together against those Dickens represents as murderous savages.

With each collaborative work, Dickens initially conceived of the story and then asked Collins, sometimes with other writers, to contribute to it, most often for the Extra Christmas Number of *Household Words* or *All the Year Round*.[17] Having formulated the story's premise and aims, Dickens would provide Collins with a plotline and cast of characters and often assign him a point of view from which to write. Generally, Dickens asked Collins to write a specific chapter or narrative portion while writing his own separate sections, but for *The Frozen Deep* he had Collins draft the play and then thoroughly revised it.

As a young man anxious to succeed as a professional writer, impressed by Dickens's genius and fame, and delighted by Dickens's attentions, Collins willingly accepted his subordinate position in their collaborative relationship, at least at the outset. In some sense, the tone of their relationship, in its first years, was set by the circumstances under which they first met—rehearsing for a production of Bulwer-Lytton's comedy, *Not So Bad As We Seem,* in which Collins took the role of Smart, valet to Lord Wilmot, played by Dickens. But as a writer who had contributed to periodicals known for their "Red republicanism"[18] (such as the *Leader*) before coming to *Household Words,* Collins held views that were considerably more radical than those of Dickens, and he did not always keep them in check. Although Collins sometimes sounds as wary of class unrest, women's rights, and native insurrection as his senior collaborator, he proves more willing to challenge the status quo than Dickens does. Hoping to succeed as a middle-class professional yet troubled by his perception of working-class injuries, gender inequities, and imperial wrongdoing, Collins not only complies with but works against Dickens from nearly the start of their collaborations.[19]

17. Harry Stone discusses the evolution of the Christmas Numbers in *Charles Dickens' Uncollected Writings from "Household Words," 1850–1859,* 2 vols. (Bloomington: Indiana University Press, 1968), 2:523–24. Deborah A. Thomas describes their subjects and lists their contributors. See *Dickens and the Short Story* (Philadelphia: University of Pennsylvania Press, 1982), pp. 140–53.

18. Kirk Beetz, "Wilkie Collins and *The Leader,*" *Victorian Periodicals Review* 15, 1 (spring 1982): 25.

19. In her study of Adelaide Anne Procter, a frequent contributor to the Christmas Numbers, Gill Gregory sees a similar dynamic in Procter's relationship to Dickens. In a chapter on Dickens's "editorial authority," Gregory argues that Procter "challenges implicitly [Dickens's] authoritative voice through her choice of themes and tropes and in her resistance to the narrative frameworks devised by Dickens," representing excluded figures who "exist in tension with, and at times in direct opposition to, [Dickens's] narrative resolutions and conclusions." See *The Life and Work of Adelaide Procter: Poetry, Feminism and Fathers* (Aldershot, U.K.: Ashgate, 1998), p. 192.

Their working relationship began in April 1852, when Dickens accepted "A Terribly Strange Bed" for *Household Words,* paying Collins £7.10.0 for it. In February 1853, Dickens rejected Collins's second submission, "Mad Monkton," which he found potentially offensive to readers in its treatment of hereditary insanity. But soon afterward, he accepted "Gabriel's Marriage" instead. Between April 1852 and September 1856, when he offered Collins a salaried position on his staff, Dickens published thirteen of his works, two of which appeared in collaborative Christmas Numbers, "The Seven Poor Travellers" (1854) and "The Holly Tree Inn" (1855).[20]

Instead of immediately accepting Dickens's salaried job offer, Collins hesitated. Chapter 1 considers the reasons for his delay, examining the editorial and business practices of *Household Words,* the compromises required of its contributors, and the constraints that were placed on them. Negotiating his contract with Dickens, Collins asked to write a long work of fiction for the journal, resisting the market formula imposed on him at *Household Words,* where he was expected to write short essays or short stories in four parts. Objecting to the anonymity required of those whose works were published under Dickens's name, Collins expressed the discontent felt by such writers as Elizabeth Gaskell and George Augustus Sala, who came to believe that Dickens unfairly profited from the labors of unnamed subordinates. To these writers, it appeared that Dickens had created a class system in which contributors were the servants or hands and Dickens himself was the master.

Nonetheless, these class differences are imaginatively overcome in the work on which Dickens and Collins collaborated soon after their negotiations of September 1856. Chapter 2 focuses on "The Wreck of the Golden Mary," in which Dickens writes as Captain Ravender, who embodies an ideal of responsible and selfless social authority, and Collins writes as his faithful first mate,

---

20. By mid-September of 1856, when Dickens offered the salaried position to Collins, the latter had already been paid nearly £250 for his literary labors at *Household Words.* For "A Terribly Strange Bed," Dickens paid £7.10.0, and for "Gabriel's Marriage," £5.15.6 for each of its two chapters. In 1854, when Collins first collaborated on a Christmas Number, he received £10 for "The Fourth Poor Traveller." Dickens published "Sister Rose" in April 1855 and "The Yellow Mask" in July 1855, both in four installments. Collins earned £40 for the first story and £33 for the second. His "Cruise of the Tomtit" was published in December 1855, as was "The Ostler," his contribution to the 1855 Christmas Number. For these, Dickens paid £10 and £16.16.0, respectively. In March 1856, Collins received £50 for the five installments of "A Rogue's Life." In June, Dickens accepted "Laid Up in Two Lodgings," paying Collins £7.7.0 for the first chapter and £6.6.0 for the second. "The Diary of Anne Rodway" appeared in July, and "My Spinsters" in August; Collins earned £20 for the first and £6.6.0 for the second. Dickens published "My Black Mirror" on 6 September and "To Think, or Be Thought For?" on 13 September, paying Collins £6.16.6 and £5.5.0, respectively. These figures come from W. H. Wills's Office Book for *Household Words,* edited and annotated by Anne Lohrli. See *"Household Words": A Weekly Journal, 1850–1859, Conducted by Charles Dickens* (Toronto: University of Toronto Press, 1973).

John Steadiman. Inspired to compose the story, in part, by reports of labor unrest among common sailors in the British merchant marine, Dickens designs "The Wreck of the Golden Mary" to displace and obscure class conflict. He accomplishes this by idealizing social relations on board ship; by sending his mariners to California, where mutinies were commonplace, and attributed to "gold-rush fever" rather than exploitation and discontent; by identifying the underlying threat to the captain's authority in the emancipated woman and the miser instead of the common sailor; and by casting Collins as "steadiman," a devoted rather than a resentful subordinate.

For his part, Collins generally plays along, helping to construct this conservative social idyll and emphasizing the first mate's dedication to his captain. Although the miserly Mr. Rarx is never identified as a Jew in the story, Collins develops the anti-Semitism implicit in Dickens's portrait of this figure, highlighting his economic and sexual deviance and contrasting his ideas of wealth and women with those of Christian Englishmen. In effect, Collins uses the alleged pathology of the Jew to demonstrate the health of the English class system and of a patriarchal culture that treats its women properly, as a natural and renewable sexual resource rather than a treasure to be hoarded. Yet in his account of the shipwreck, which is partly based on the experience of Bligh and the *Bounty,* Collins recognizes class unrest among the sailors as well as the potentially mutinous behavior of first mates and strips Captain Ravender of his authority.

Collins more fully develops the theme of mutiny in *The Frozen Deep,* the focus of chapter 3. As an instance of collaboration, this melodrama differs from the other works I discuss because it exists in a number of different versions, some written solely by Collins. First formulated by Dickens as an elaboration on his series of *Household Words* articles about Sir John Franklin and his lost Arctic expedition, *The Frozen Deep* consists of Collins's initial draft of the play, written in 1856 at Dickens's request; Dickens's revised version of Collins's draft, used in the 1857 performances; and Collins's subsequent revisions of 1866 and 1874. Responding to allegations of cannibalism among the lost explorers, a charge that carried with it the implication of class warfare, Dickens and Collins approach their subject in notably different ways.

In his *Household Words* articles on the lost Arctic explorers, Dickens denies the charges that they fed on each other, emphasizing their unity and honor as British imperialists. If any of them were, indeed, murdered, he suggests, the blame must rest with savage Eskimos rather than common sailors. Collins, too, defuses the threat of social cannibalism in his draft of *The Frozen Deep:* not simply by denying it but by making it the subject of his dark comedy. His melodrama includes scenes in which the cook on the expedition—aptly named John

Want—jokes about the failing health of his officers as he makes bone soup, predicting that he will be the last survivor. More menacing than Want, however, is a second working-class cannibal who figures prominently in Collins's draft, presumably on Dickens's instructions: a Scottish housekeeper first conceived of by Dickens. A former wet nurse and a Highlander, she conflates the threat of class unrest with the dangers posed by native rebellion and female nature. Drawing on stereotypes of the "devouring mother" and the barbarous Scot in his portrait of Nurse Esther, Collins redefines the threat of cannibalism in his draft, while also suggesting that both the nurse and the cook have good reason to feel hungry. Lending force to Nurse Esther's point of view, despite her status as a barbarous Highland woman, he endows her with the prophetic powers of second sight, casting her as a visionary who sees more than the civilized English characters who disparage her. At one and the same time, Collins invokes and questions ideas of the primitive in his portrait of Esther.

Once Collins completed his draft, Dickens heavily revised it, making Esther a more barbarous figure and removing signs of class strife among the explorers. Severing the class connection established by Collins between the nurse and the cook and discrediting Esther's claims to visionary power, Dickens foregrounds her racial otherness. Revising Dickens's version of *The Frozen Deep,* in turn, in 1866 and 1874, Collins restores the theme of class conflict, eliminates the figure of the female savage, and gives new credibility to the female visionary. He uses the story to examine what had become, by the 1870s, his most explicit literary theme—the problem of gender inequities.

More clearly than any other collaborative work, *The Frozen Deep,* as revised over nearly twenty years, reveals the divisions between Dickens and Collins. Yet such tensions subtly inform their collaborative stories of 1857, the subject of chapter 4. Written in the same year in which Dickens serialized *The Dead Secret,* the first of Collins's novels to appear in Dickens's periodicals, "The Lazy Tour of Two Idle Apprentices" elides the distinction between the staff writer and the literary conductor, as both become "apprentices" to "lady Literature." This wishful representation is part of a larger strategy at work in the story: the attempt to obscure class divisions in England, which were made painfully clear during the Indian Mutiny when working-class men proved reluctant to join the army, defend the empire, and fight for the national honor.

In "The Lazy Tour," Dickens and Collins counter these divisions by imagining the working class as an idle one and by representing Collins himself as the apprentice Idle, who somehow makes a living, though he performs little or no work. In "The Perils of Certain English Prisoners," the 1857 Christmas Number, they achieve a similar end by sending resentful English privates to a colony off the coast of Honduras, loosely based on British India, in which the natives rebel. Coming to see their social superiors as their allies and fellow countrymen, the English privates overcome their feelings of class resentment and fight side by side with gentlemen against their *real* enemies, the mutinous savages.

In both of these stories, Collins seems to carry out Dickens's orders, yet his compliance proves incomplete. Although Collins imagines himself as a man of leisure and as Dickens's fellow apprentice in "The Lazy Tour," this fantasy conflicted with his knowledge that he was performing literary labors for Dickens's profit as well as his own, and his narrative includes an interpolated tale critical of the power of capital and the division between the laboring and the leisure classes. In "The Perils," Collins follows Dickens's plotline yet substantially alters his tone, satirizing the figures of British authority whom Dickens defends and suggesting that working-class privates may have more in common with colonized natives than with their own officers.

Between 1858 and 1861, Collins collaborated with Dickens on four Christmas Numbers, stories to which Elizabeth Gaskell, Adelaide Anne Procter, and other writers contributed as well: "A House to Let" (1858); "The Haunted House" (1859); "A Message from the Sea" (1860); and "Tom Tiddler's Ground" (1861). From 1859 to 1862, Dickens serialized two more of Collins's novels—*The Woman in White* (1859–60) and *No Name* (1862–63). In 1862, with his market value rising, Collins resigned from Dickens's staff, having attained a position of fame and affluence comparable to that of Dickens. He did not contribute to another Christmas Number until 1867, when he and Dickens coauthored "No Thoroughfare."

This story, which is the focus of chapter 5, proved to be their last collaboration, and its treatment of male partnership and the theme of legitimacy helps to explain why. A story about illegitimate sons, unwed mothers, and maternal claims, "No Thoroughfare" fails to unite its central male characters as the earlier collaborations had. Despite the threat of female autonomy, the male partnership of illegitimate sons that forms at the outset of the story quickly dissolves and is replaced by male relationships characterized by inequities and resentment, with Dickens most closely aligned with the "fatherly" notary in the story, whose job is to authenticate and legitimate. Suggesting the collaborators' own inability to form a true partnership, "No Thoroughfare" testifies to the inequities that still divide them, as Dickens continues to grant legitimacy to the work of his coauthor, despite Collins's rise to fame and relative fortune. Divided in their political sympathies as well, the collaborators write at cross purposes in "No Thoroughfare," their differences in outlook most clearly revealed by Collins's re-creation of the story for the stage. Adapting the 1867 Christmas Number for its run at the Adelphi Theatre during Dickens's absence in America, Collins transforms its "swarthy" and murderous villain into a tragic hero, anticipating his treatment of the Hindu priests in *The Moonstone,* serialized in *All the Year Round* immediately after "No Thoroughfare."

After losing this final contest for control of a collaborative story's meaning, Dickens decided to bring the Christmas Numbers to an end. His last and unfinished novel, *The Mystery of Edwin Drood,* can be understood in the context of his decision to abandon collaboration—as an attempt to reclaim and control the subject of race relations and empire, particularly as Collins develops it in *The Moonstone.* Chapter 6 considers the interplay between their two novels.

Set in India and England, and written during the tenth anniversary of the Indian Mutiny, *The Moonstone* returns to the subject of "The Perils" but approaches it more critically, dramatizing the crimes committed in the name of empire and representing devout Hindus as victims rather than victimizers. Developing analogies between forms of domination, Collins compares the British theft of a sacred Hindu diamond to the symbolic violation of the English heroine by the gentleman she plans to marry, and the sepoy rebellion to working-class unrest at home. Like Collins, Dickens acknowledges the crimes of the empire in *Edwin Drood*—most notably in his portrait of the Landlesses, a brother and sister newly arrived in England from Ceylon, who recall the Hindus of *The Moonstone,* and point to the disinheritance of colonized peoples. Yet Dickens also foregrounds their innate ferocity and displaces criminality from West to East. In *The Moonstone* Collins calls attention to the crimes of "the Honourable John"—the East India Company—whose profits depended on the colonial production of opium and its unlawful sale to the Chinese. But in *Edwin Drood,* Dickens associates opium consumption with eastern "contagion" rather than with British drug trafficking. Although Dickens draws analogies between the English working class and the eastern races, he does so to suggest that its members threaten the empire at home, through their racial degeneration. Dividing Collins's "dark" and "lithe" heroine into two female figures, one English and one eastern, Dickens pointedly rejects a comparison between oppressed Englishwomen and colonized Indians and reinstates the familiar image of Mutiny lore: the Englishwoman threatened by oriental desire.

Dickens's death in June 1870 gave Collins the final word in this exchange, and he described *Edwin Drood* as a "last laboured effort, the melancholy work of a worn-out brain."[21] The acerbic tone of Collins's remark may well have been sharpened by the context in which he wrote it—in the margins of Forster's *Life of Dickens.* Represented by Forster as a minor figure in Dickens's life, or relegated, at best, to the position of a literary apostle, Collins was left to

21. "Wilkie Collins About Charles Dickens. (From a Marked Copy of Forster's 'Dickens')," *Pall Mall Gazette* (20 January 1890): 3.

contend with his secondary status after nearly twenty years of collaboration. Thus it comes as no surprise that Collins took offense when asked by the publisher Frederic Chapman in 1873 to identify his own contributions to "No Thoroughfare"—so that they could be omitted from future editions of Dickens's works:

> It is impossible for me to indicate correctly my share in the Acts jointly written (I. and IV.),—we purposely wrote so as to make discoveries of this difficult, if not impossible. I inserted passages in his chapters and he inserted passages in mine. I can only tell you that we as nearly as possible *halved* the work. We put the story together in the Swiss chalet at Gad's Hill, and we finished the Fourth Act side by side at two desks in his bedroom at Gad's Hill.[22]

Having once struggled to have his work recognized as his own at *Household Words,* Collins is now forced to the exigency of merging his writing with Dickens's. Although his extant manuscript indicates that he could have distinguished his "share in the Acts jointly written" from that of Dickens, he refuses to do so. As his letter to Chapman goes on to suggest, his refusal is due to the bitter knowledge he has gained from Dickens's publishers: that while "everything connected with [*Dickens's*] writing is part of the literary history of England," his own is not.[23] Indeed, Collins's contribution to "The Perils" is still omitted from the Oxford Illustrated edition of the *Christmas Stories,* which reprints it without its crucial middle section, as a narrative "in two chapters" rather than three.[24]

Despite Collins's claims in his letter to Chapman, his contributions to the collaborative works can, more often than not, be clearly distinguished from those of Dickens. However, such attributions have value not simply because they demonstrate or disprove Collins's literary merit but because they illuminate the complex dynamics of his working relationship with Dickens and remind us that the stature of the "inimitable" novelist was secured, at least in part, by certain editorial practices that worked to the disadvantage of his subordinates.

22. Wilkie Collins to Frederic Chapman, 11 May 1873, quoted in Frederic G. Kitton, *The Minor Writings of Charles Dickens* (London: Elliot Stock, 1900), p. 173.

23. Ibid.

24. Charles Dickens, "The Perils of Certain English Prisoners," in *Christmas Stories,* Oxford Illustrated Dickens, 21 vols. (1956; reprint, Oxford: Oxford University Press, 1987), 11:192. Unlike the Oxford edition, the Everyman, edited by Ruth Glancy, retains Collins's portion of "The Perils." Glancy also includes Collins's portions of "The Wreck of the Golden Mary," "A House to Let," "A Message from the Sea," and "No Thoroughfare" but omits his contributions to the Christmas Numbers of 1854, 1855, 1859, and 1861. See Charles Dickens, *The Christmas Stories,* ed. Ruth Glancy (London: J. M. Dent, 1996).

CHAPTER I

Professional Writers and Hired Hands:

Household Words and the Victorian Publishing Business

In October 1864, Collins's seventh novel, *Armadale,* was about to begin its monthly serialization in the *Cornhill,* published by Smith & Elder. Writing to his mother, Collins tells her of the favorable responses the novel has received. "Dickens has read my proofs," he explains, "and is greatly struck by them":

> He prognosticates certain success. Miss Hogarth could not sleep till she had finished them—and (to quote quite another sort of opinion) Mr. Smith tells me that the *Printers* are highly interested in the story. I set great store by getting the good opinion of these latter critics—for it is no easy matter to please the printers, to whom all books represent in the first instance nothing but weary hard work.[1]

Noting that book production means something quite different to working-class printers than it does to middle-class authors, publishers, and readers, Collins acknowledges the largely invisible labor required to manufacture literary commodities. Playing on the class divisions within the Victorian publishing industry, he refers to the printers as difficult "critics" whose approval he particularly values, yet whose opinions are "quite another sort" than those of Dickens, Georgina Hogarth, and George Smith. While his tone seems somewhat facetious, his letter raises serious questions about the kinds of work performed in the Victorian publishing industry and the relationship between manual and intellectual labor. If, as Collins himself suggests in his articles and

---

1. Autograph letter signed (ALS) to Harriet Collins, 19 October 1864. The Pierpont Morgan Library, New York. MA 3150.86. My transcription differs slightly from that in *The Letters of Wilkie Collins,* ed. William Baker and William M. Clarke, 2 vols. (London: Macmillan, 1999), 1:251–52.

letters, novelists can be said to "manufacture" literature out of "raw material,"[2] and can be compared to a seamstress, their intellectual property resembling the "lovely frock" she produces on her own sewing machine,[3] is the work of novel writing to be understood as a craft or as an industry? What are an author's claims to books that he or she writes yet that are also manufactured? How can we define the class status of novelists whose earnings are often substantially higher than those of the printers, yet whose literary labor is, in its own way, alienated and standardized?

As historians and critics have noted, authorship became a middle-class profession in the nineteenth century. Writers could now earn a living without depending on other sources of income, or on the system of aristocratic patronage that operated in the 1700s.[4] While some professional Victorian writers lived in poverty, the majority did not.[5] Their incomes depended on the popularity of their works but also on the types of publishing agreements they negotiated, and these varied widely—from the sale of an author's copyright for a fixed sum to a profit-sharing agreement that was dependent on sales. Whatever the particular arrangements the writers made, their profession was made possible by technical innovations that dramatically lowered publishing costs, by the serialization of fiction in cheap monthly numbers and in weekly and monthly periodicals, and by the development of a mass reading public willing to purchase or borrow newly affordable literary commodities.

But while Victorian writers could consider themselves middle-class professionals, their literary labor and the conditions under which it was performed connected them to the printers with whose "weary hard work" Collins commiserated. Earning a weekly salary of five guineas as a staff member at *Household Words,* more than three times the average weekly wage received by printers and binders,[6] Collins secured his position as an up-and-coming middle-class professional in 1856. But because he contributed to a mass-produced periodical owned by Dickens, W. H. Wills, John Forster, and Bradbury and Evans, his writing profited a group of investors to which he did not belong; was strictly regulated in its length, form, and time of delivery; and appeared under Dickens's name rather than his own. For such reasons, Norman N. Feltes de-

2. [Wilkie Collins], "A Shy Scheme," *Household Words* 17 (20 March 1858): 315.

3. ALS to James Payn, 26 November [1869]; Harry Ransom Humanities Research Center, the University of Texas at Austin.

4. See Robert L. Patten, *Charles Dickens and His Publishers* (Oxford: Clarendon Press, 1978), and John Sutherland, *Victorian Novelists and Publishers* (Chicago: University of Chicago Press, 1976).

5. See Nigel Cross, *The Common Writer: Life in Nineteenth-Century Grub Street* (Cambridge: Cambridge University Press, 1985), p. 5.

6. Geoffrey Best, *Mid-Victorian Britain: 1851–1875* (New York: Schocken Books, 1972), p. 95.

scribes the Victorian novelist as simply another "hand" subject to capitalist control. "The writer's work was produced in a journal within relations of production analogous to those prevailing in a textile mill," Feltes argues, and "fiction writers entered their pages as hand-loom weavers entered a factory."[7] In similar terms, Mary Poovey speaks of the "factorylike conditions" under which Victorian literature was written and represents the author as "one instance of labor, an interchangeable part subject to replacement in case of failure or to repair in case of defect": "The conditions by which novels were serialized made absolutely clear the extent to which 'literature' was part of the market economy and literary work was alienated labor," she argues.[8]

Dickens himself worked as a literary hand for much of his early career, exploited by Richard Bentley and others, and acutely aware that the profits of his labors were not his alone. Although he became increasingly skilled at negotiating contracts, he did not earn more from his writings than his publishers did until 1847, with *Dombey and Son*,[9] and he remained sensitive to the inequities between publishers with capital and writers without it. "You and I know very well that in nine cases out of ten the author is at a disadvantage with the publisher because the publisher has capital and the author has not," he told Forster in November 1866, objecting to a pamphlet advocating the payment of royalties instead of advances:

> We know perfectly well that in nine cases out of ten money is advanced by the publisher before the book is producible—often, long before. No young or unsuccessful author (unless he were an amateur and an independent gentleman) would make a bargain for having that royalty, to-morrow, if he could have a certain sum of money, or an advance of money. . . . I make bold to say—with some knowledge of the subject, as a writer who made a publisher's fortune long before he began to share in the real profits of his books—that if the publishers met next week, and resolved henceforth to make this royalty bargain and no other, it would be an enormous hardship and misfortune because the authors could not live while they wrote. (Pilgrim, 11:270)

For writing to remain a middle-class profession, Dickens argues, publishers must make it possible for authors to "live while they wr[i]te," even if they refuse "to share in the real profits."

7. Norman N. Feltes, *Modes of Production of Victorian Novels* (Chicago: University of Chicago Press, 1986), pp. 63–64.

8. Mary Poovey, *Uneven Developments: The Ideological Work of Gender in Mid-Victorian England* (Chicago: University of Chicago Press, 1988), pp. 104–5.

9. Patten, *Charles Dickens*, pp. 18, 10.

When he launched *Household Words* in 1850, Dickens was careful to stipulate that he would receive half the net profits of the weekly periodical; the other half was divided among Bradbury and Evans, the journal's publishers, who received a one-quarter share, and Wills and Forster, who each received one-eighth. In addition, Dickens was paid an annual salary of £500 as editor, and Wills an annual salary of £416 as subeditor. Although Bradbury and Evans were responsible for printing *Household Words* and managing the warehousing, accounting, and advertising for the journal, Dickens negotiated contracts with contributors and had editorial control over their fiction and essays. When Dickens broke with Bradbury and Evans in 1859 and established *All the Year Round* in place of *Household Words,* he became, in effect, both editor and publisher: "Dickens was now an unfettered bookseller, and manuscript buyer in the market with other publishers," John Sutherland notes.[10] Chapman and Hall served as agents for the new journal, but it was printed by the firm of Charles Whiting, and Dickens and Wills were its sole proprietors. "To an extent unusual, perhaps unprecedented," Robert Patten observes, "Dickens was his own publisher. He had taken his assertion of his own rights and the exercize of his own power as a writer about as far as they could possibly go."[11]

Determined not to be exploited or controlled by his publishers, Dickens turned publisher himself, and critics have long argued that he exercised his power with the best interests of his fellow authors in mind. As his letters to Wills and others make clear, Dickens paid very careful attention to matters of style in his periodicals, sought to improve the stilted or awkward prose of contributors, and offered advice on the structure and pacing of serialized fiction. Writing in the 1940s, Gerald Grubb emphasized these elements of Dickens's editing and praised him for his ability to "develop" Collins, to "train" Gaskell, and to "guide" Bulwer-Lytton.[12] In his more recent study, Sutherland characterizes *All the Year Round* as a "writing workshop" and imagines "the ferment of ideas about fiction that were current there." While recognizing Dickens's tendency to flaunt his power by paying some authors much more highly than others for narratives of equal length, Sutherland speaks of Dickens as a "fellow labourer" at the journal, drawing on the self-representations he provided to prospective contributors (Pilgrim, 9:93). Noting that well-respected novelists such as Bulwer-Lytton published in *All the Year Round,* a twopenny weekly, Sutherland argues that Dickens "liberated" them from the six shilling quarterly, "perform[ing] a general service to the profession of novel-writing."[13]

10. Sutherland, *Victorian Novelists,* p. 169.
11. Patten, *Charles Dickens,* p. 271.
12. Gerald G. Grubb, "Dickens' Editorial Methods," *Studies in Philology* 40 (1943): 100.
13. Sutherland, *Victorian Novelists,* pp. 186, 170, 169, 187.

Most recently, however, critics interested in Dickens's relationships with in-dividual contributors—particularly Elizabeth Gaskell—have questioned the idea of his "service to the profession," foregrounding his political rather than his sty-listic concerns and arguing that writers often felt constrained and exploited when working for him.[14] Such feelings were due to Dickens's party line on cer-tain issues, which he expected his writers to support, but also to the editorial policies of his periodicals, which served his interests more clearly than their own. Although *Household Words* and *All the Year Round* were cheap periodicals, they did not necessarily "liberate" their contributors as a result. Indeed, Dickens conceived of both weeklies as vehicles for middle-class opinion and values, and while he encouraged writers to embrace "the spirit of reform," he did not per-mit them to express views that he felt might put off middle-class readers.[15] Henry Morley, one of Dickens's first staff writers, contributed dozens of arti-cles and poems to *Household Words* and *All the Year Round* over the course of his career, yet he found Dickens and Wills "too much afraid of offending sub-scribers" and preferred working with John Forster at the *Examiner* as a result.[16]

Dickens allowed for a range of opinion in his periodicals, but he carefully monitored that range, defining and defending its boundaries. If a work Dickens was serializing became too politically daring for his tastes, he might edit the man-uscript or manipulate the context in which it appeared to alter its political significance. His treatment of Gaskell's "Lizzie Leigh" provides a case in point. As Elsie Michie explains, when Gaskell suggested that prostitutes could be re-deemed and remain within mainstream English society, Dickens followed up her installments with letters promoting emigration, undermining Gaskell's view: "The whole issue [of *Household Words*] appeared to argue in favor of Dickens's position that emigration was the solution to the problem of prostitution."[17]

While Dickens helped to determine how readers constructed the meaning of his contributors' works, at times he also received credit for authoring them because they were published anonymously, under the masthead "Conducted by Charles Dickens." Writing to Gaskell on 31 January 1850, inviting her to

14. As Hilary M. Schor notes, Gaskell represented herself as "a slave to production" at *Household Words* and Dickens as "the demanding taskmaster" to be resisted. See *Scheherezade in the Marketplace: Elizabeth Gaskell and the Victorian Novel* (Oxford: Oxford University Press, 1992), p. 142.

15. "I don't know how it is but she gets so near the sexual side of things as to be a little dangerous to us," Dickens warned Wills of Eliza Lynn, telling his subeditor to look out for "Bawdry" portions of her fiction (Pilgrim, 7:432, 8:16). While Gerald Grubb commends Dickens for keeping *Household Words* "clean" and protecting "the sensibilities of his readers," these policies significantly narrowed the artistic and political parameters of the journal. See Grubb, "Dickens' Influence as an Editor," *Studies in Philology* 42 (1945): 811, 813, 822.

16. Henry Shaen Solly, *The Life of Henry Morley, L. L. D.* (London: Edward Arnold, 1898), p. 163.

17. Elsie B. Michie, *Outside the Pale: Cultural Exclusion, Gender Difference, and the Victorian Woman Writer* (Ithaca, N.Y.: Cornell University Press, 1993), pp. 87–88.

contribute to his new periodical, Dickens outlined his policy of anonymous publication, claiming that "no writer's name will be used—neither my own, nor any others—every paper will be published without any signature; and all will seem to express the general mind and purpose of the Journal, which is, the raising up of those that are down, and the general improvement of our social condition" (Pilgrim, 6:22). However, "the general mind and purpose" of *Household Words* were clearly "Charles Dickens's Own," one of the titles he considered for the periodical, and his name as well as references to his novels appeared throughout.[18] Having shaped the meaning of Gaskell's "Lizzy Leigh" by manipulating its context, Dickens was mistakenly identified as its author in America, by publishers who assumed that the leading story of *Household Words* must be his. Thus while Gaskell initially believed that anonymity "would give her 'free swing,'" she found that "*Household Words* was less a place of freedom . . . than one where she lost control of her writing."[19]

Other writers made the same discovery—Collins included. When Collins's "Sister Rose," serialized in *Household Words* in April 1855, was reprinted by Peterson in Philadelphia later that year, it was published as a work "by Charles Dickens."[20] So, too, was the fiction of George Augustus Sala. Sala's first *Household Words* article, "The Key of the Street" (6 September 1851), appeared in France in the early 1850s under Dickens's name, in the collection *Nouveaux Contes de Charles Dickens*,[21] and Dickens continues to receive credit for Sala's fiction. "As recently as 1971," Ruth Glancy observes in her notes to Dickens's *Christmas Stories*, "*The New York Times* published Sala's contribution to the 1851 Christmas number 'What Christmas Is in the Company of John Doe,' and attributed it to Dickens."[22]

Clearly, Dickens was not simply "raising up . . . those that are down" in *Household Words* but running a business in which the profits and renown were

18. As Harry Stone notes, *Household Words* "achieve[d] its cohesiveness . . . through assimilation to a Dickensian vision of life. The featuring of Dickens' name on the masthead and on the running heads, the suppression of all other by-lines and signatures, the accommodation of all views . . . to those Dickens held, the stylistic adherence to his notions of fancy, drama, and compression—all would create a coherent identity. While employing a diversity of writers, . . . *Household Words* would seem to speak with a single voice" (*Charles Dickens' Uncollected Writings from "Household Words," 1850–1859*, 2 vols. [Bloomington: Indiana University Press, 1968], 1:14). As Hilary Schor expresses the point, Dickens's "imprint was everywhere" in *Household Words*, "his voice was pervasive," and "his initial vision of the journal (as a shadow that would go inside the homes of others . . .) suggests his desire precisely to intrude, silently, but potently" (*Scheherezade*, 92).

19. Michie, *Outside the Pale*, pp. 87–88.

20. Andrew Gasson reproduces the cover of the Peterson edition of "Sister Rose" in *Wilkie Collins: An Illustrated Guide* (Oxford: Oxford University Press, 1998), p. 140.

21. P. D. Edwards, *Dickens's 'Young Men': George Augustus Sala, Edmund Yates and the World of Victorian Journalism* (Aldershot, U.K.: Ashgate, 1997), p. 12.

22. Ruth Glancy, ed., *Christmas Stories* (London: J. M. Dent, 1996), p. 838.

primarily his. Thus Douglas Jerrold declined to contribute to *Household Words* when Dickens asked him to. Although Dickens told Jerrold that "the periodical is anonymous throughout," Jerrold read him the masthead and then countered, "*mon*onymous throughout."[23] A magazine proprietor himself, Jerrold understood that an author's name was a marketable commodity and that the anonymity on which Dickens insisted not only denied writers their artistic due but compromised their financial success in the long run.[24] When Collins published his very first story, "The Last Stage Coachman," in Jerrold's *Illuminated Magazine* in 1843, it appeared under his own name rather than Jerrold's.

Not only were Dickens's contributors required to publish anonymously; they encountered strict stipulations about the structure, length, and content of their fiction and essays; were forced to submit to the editorial authority of Dickens; and occasionally became embroiled in disputes over copyright and permission to reprint their works.[25] Writing to Edmund Yates in January 1857 of his efforts to publish *A Journey Due North* in book form, Sala complained of Dickens's "ungenerous refusal" to let him reprint a small portion of his articles, comparing Dickens to Shylock.[26] He returned to the charge in his *Life and Adventures*. "As the law of copyright then stood," he explains, "I had absolutely no remedy," since "the proprietor of a periodical had the power of putting an embargo on the republication of contributions, unless a special agreement to the contrary had been made."[27] "Confound it! I gave him malt for his meal. . . . I wrote nearly three hundred articles for *Household Words;* and I was such a dullard, so maladroit, so blind to my own interests, that [until 1857] . . . I never sought his permission to republish one of those papers."[28]

Although Sala feels "maladroit" in his negotiations with Dickens, women writers were placed at a particular disadvantage at *Household Words,* their authorship treated as illegitimate by virtue of their gender. Inviting Geraldine

23. Frederic B. Perkins, *Charles Dickens: A Sketch of His Life and Works* (New York: Putnam, 1870), p. 88; quoted by Edgar Johnson, *Charles Dickens: His Tragedy and Triumph,* 2 vols. (New York: Simon and Schuster, 1952), 2:704.

24. While he generally idealizes Dickens's relations with his staff members, Frederic G. Kitton concedes that anonymous publication had "evil consequences" for the young writers at *Household Words,* "whose literary and commercial prospects" were damaged, and whose contributions "were attributed to Dickens, and sometimes reprinted with his" (*The Minor Writings of Charles Dickens* [London: Elliot Stock, 1900], p. 114).

25. Grubb discusses the "quantitative" restriction placed on contributors and the structural formulas Dickens promoted in his periodicals in "Dickens' Pattern of Weekly Serialization," *ELH* 9 (June 1942): 141–56.

26. Quoted by Edwards, *Dickens's 'Young Men,'* p. 37.

27. George Augustus Sala, *The Life and Adventures of George Augustus Sala,* 2 vols. (New York: Scribner's, 1895), 1:311.

28. Ibid., 1:310. Edwards discusses this conflict in *Dickens's 'Young Men,'* expressing some "doubts" about Sala's account (pp. 35–38).

Jewsbury to contribute to *Household Words* in February 1850, Dickens draws an analogy between his periodical (and the anonymity it required of authors) and the London Foundling Hospital, where women left their infants with no name. While granting Jewsbury the right to republish her work ("the power of re-claiming [her] own children, after a certain time," as he puts it), Dickens im-plicitly compares her to an unwed mother who leaves her child at the foundling; in this way, Dickens suggests that *he* rather than *she* gives legitimacy to her literary "offspring" (Pilgrim, 6:44). As the work of Gaskell scholars makes clear, Dickens promoted the sexual double standard at *Household Words* and as-sociated the professional female author with the "public" or fallen woman.[29] If Gaskell or Jewsbury were to insist on receiving publicity or demand a higher rate of pay, they would compromise their status as proper ladies. Comparing Gaskell with Jerrold and Collins in this regard, Michie argues that the men were able to negotiate effectively with Dickens or to pursue their own literary en-terprises, while Gaskell could not. Refusing to write for Dickens, Jerrold ran his own periodicals, and Collins was "compensated" with a salaried position at *Household Words,* but Gaskell continued writing for Dickens on his own terms until she left for the *Cornhill.*[30]

There can be no doubt that Collins, as a male writer, possessed considerable advantages over Gaskell and other women novelists in his dealings with Dickens, who sometimes paid women less than men for comparable labors and used his periodicals to ridicule the idea of women's rights and professional am-bition.[31] As Henry Solly notes, the difficulties posed by demanding women au-thors became a theme with Dickens and Wills, who told Morley "how they were bothered by contributors, especially ladies, objecting to alterations."[32] This theme recurs in the letters and collaborative works of Dickens and Collins, who made use of sexual stereotypes to elide their own differences, joining to-gether against troublesome females—women writers, in particular.[33] Writing to

29. Addressing Gaskell as "Scheherezade," Schor argues, Dickens conflates her storytelling abilities with her powers of seduction (*Scheherezade,* 3); referring to her "literary vows of temperance or absti-nence," Dickens implies that Gaskell is a wayward woman when she agrees to write for him (Michie, *Outside the Pale,* p. 85).

30. Michie, *Outside the Pale,* pp. 88–89.

31. As Sutherland notes, Dickens paid Bulwer-Lytton "£1,500 for an eight-month story" and Gaskell "£400 for the same length of narrative at exactly the same period. Who today would agree with that ratio?" (*Victorian Novelists,* 169).

32. Solly, *Life of Henry Morley,* p. 161.

33. Tamar Heller observes that, after reading *Basil* (1852), Dickens praised Collins by contrasting him to "the conceited idiots who suppose that volumes are to be tossed off like pancakes" (Pilgrim, 6:824)—presumably referring to incompetent woman writers who had best remain in the kitchen. See *Dead Secrets: Wilkie Collins and the Female Gothic* (New Haven, Conn.: Yale University Press, 1992), pp. 90–91.

Collins about Dinah Mulock on 24 March 1855, for example, in response to a letter of Collins's own, Dickens complains of her attempt to retain control over "A Ghost Story," just published in *Household Words:*

> You have guessed right! The best of it was that she wrote to Wills, saying she must particularly stipulate not to have her proofs touched, "even by Mr. Dickens." That immortal creature had gone over the proofs with great pains—had of course taken out the stiflings—hard-plungings, lungeings, and other convulsions—and had also taken out her weakenings and damagings of her own effects. "Very well," said the gifted Man, "she shall have her own way. But after it's published show her this Proof, and ask her to consider whether her story would have been the better or the worse for it." (Pilgrim, 7:575–76)

Ridiculing the literary "convulsions" of the woman writer, whose "weakenings and damagings" of the story require his correction, Dickens discredits Mulock's desire for autonomy. Promoting his superior, masculine knowledge, he makes her the subject of a private joke between men.[34]

In his turn, Collins writes "A Petition to the Novel-Writers" for *Household Words,* in which he directs his "remonstrance to the lady novelists especially," who have transformed "our dear, tender, gentle, loving old Heroine" into "her modern successor": "the impudent young woman" whom Collins calls "the Man-Hater" and who is clearly a figure for the lady novelist herself.[35] Developing this disparaging portrait in a second *Household Words* article, "A Shy Scheme," Collins criticizes what he represents as the "self-conceit" of glib women who push men from the literary marketplace, despite their presumably inferior talents. Referring to these writers as "Eve's daughters," Collins compares them to unruly women who propose marriage rather than accepting the "secondary privilege of giving the answer."[36]

But while Collins joked with Dickens about Mulock and disparaged "lady novelists," he was himself subject to some of the same terms imposed on the woman writer at *Household Words.*[37] Despite the sense of solidarity that Collins

34. It might be objected that Dickens was correct in his judgment of Dinah Mulock Craik, most of whose novels are now forgotten. Yet so, too, are many novels of Bulwer-Lytton, whose writing Dickens praised. As these two examples remind us, judgments of literary value are shaped by social assumptions and prejudices, and subject to striking revisions. Thirty years ago, Collins himself was in much the same position as Dinah Mulock Craik is today, with many of his works out of print.

35. Wilkie Collins, "A Petition to the Novel-Writers," *Household Words* 14 (6 December 1856): 481–85; *My Miscellanies*, vol. 20 of *The Works of Wilkie Collins*, 30 vols. (New York: AMS Press, 1970), pp. 76, 79–80.

36. [Collins], "A Shy Scheme," 314–15.

37. Solly makes this point about Dickens's male contributors, implying that their manhood was compromised by Dickens's editorial control; told by Wills not to object to changes made in his articles and poems, Morley "suffered in silence" (*Life of Henry Morley,* 161).

established with Dickens by joking about the incapacity of female authors and the threat they pose, he was well aware of his own differences with the conductor of *Household Words,* even as he helped to imaginatively elide them. Although his subordination to Dickens was different in kind and degree from Mulock's or Gaskell's, it was evident nonetheless, and cast in terms of class difference at the outset of their acquaintance, as seen in the two men's performance in Bulwer-Lytton's *Not So Bad As We Seem.*

Bulwer-Lytton's 1851 comedy was written and performed to benefit the Guild of Literature and Art, a newly formed organization of which Dickens served as vice president. Dickens hoped the guild would "entirely change the status of the Literary man in England" (Pilgrim, 6:259) by promoting the economic self-sufficiency of professional writers, who would provide mutual assistance, aided by insurance and pension plans. Serving as benefactor, Bulwer-Lytton agreed to provide a site for guild houses on his estate in Hertfordshire.[38] Setting his play in the 1740s, Bulwer-Lytton promotes the guild and argues for its necessity by dramatizing the plight of a Grub Street author, David Fallen, a literary genius who has spent much of his life in poverty. Fallen has been humiliated by his aristocratic patron, the duke of Middlesex, who treats him like a beggar, leaves him in the hall "among porters and lackeys," and invites him to eat with his servants rather than himself.[39] Forced to compromise his principles and write pamphlets for both the Whigs and Tories to survive, Fallen ultimately demonstrates his moral integrity by refusing to sell a scandalous manuscript left in his possession, although doing so would injure his former patron and earn him a small fortune. Exposing the pitfalls of aristocratic patronage for the literary man, Bulwer-Lytton's play includes passages that look ahead to the 1850s, when writers have gained their independence as middle-class professionals esteemed by the English reading public. As Lord Wilmot, played by Dickens, tells Fallen, "Oh, trust me, the day shall come, when men will feel that it is not charity we owe to the ennoblers of life—it is tribute! When your Order shall rise with the civilisation it called into being; and, amidst an assembly of all that is lofty and fair in the chivalry of birth, it shall refer its claim to just rank among freemen" (88).

But while the actors in the play—themselves Victorian men of letters—claim their "just rank" as middle-class professionals and members of the guild, their

38. Dickens explained the aims of the guild in his *Household Words* article "The Guild of Literature and Art" (3 [10 May 1851]: 145–47). For an insightful discussion of the guild, Dickens's role in its history, and the reasons for its failure, see Cross, *Common Writer,* pp. 70–76.

39. Sir Edward Bulwer-Lytton, Bart., *Not So Bad As We Seem; or, Many Sides to a Character. A Comedy in Five Acts* (London: Chapman and Hall, 1851), pp. 87–88; subsequent references to *Not So Bad As We Seem* are cited parenthetically in the text.

script reinscribes the hierarchical relationships that Bulwer-Lytton and the guild presumably dismantle. The play reveals, for example, that the "plebeian" Hardman, who claims to be a self-made man, has only risen to a position of authority because of the secret patronage of Sir Geoffrey Thornside and Lord Wilmot, who has bribed the prime minister on Hardman's behalf; and far from leveling the class differences among its characters, the play reinvents them—by self-consciously staging the system of patronage currently in place among some of the writers in the cast, with Dickens as Lord Wilmot, the son of an earl, Douglas Jerrold as his low-born "double," Softhead, and Collins as his valet, Smart. Replacing the "chivalry of birth" with that of genius and originality, the play foregrounds the literary "nobility" of Dickens, referred to in the script as one "who defies imitation," while such contributors to *Household Words* as R. H. Horne and Charles Knight are cast as inferiors or hangers-on—those who, at best, merely imitate the inimitable (138). Playing the part rejected by Wills, who may have been unwilling to appear as Dickens's servant and lackey, Collins performed a host of menial tasks for his "master." The play opens in Lord Wilmot's apartment in St. James, with Smart mixing Wilmot's chocolate and singing his praises as a "fine gentleman" who speaks ill of himself yet does only good to others (3–4).

Although Bulwer-Lytton rather than Dickens or Collins wrote the parts of Lord Wilmot and his valet, Dickens was responsible for the casting of the play, claiming the part of Wilmot for himself and arranging for Collins ("a very desireable recruit") to play Smart (Pilgrim, 6:257–58, 310). Collins's role as Smart preceded his employment at *Household Words* by a year, yet the comedy set the tone for his relationship with Dickens in its earliest period, with the young writer often playing the role of Dickens's respectful and admiring subordinate.[40] Despite Dickens's interest in the Guild of Literature and Art and the "esprit de corps" it was to spread among writers (*Not So Bad,* 134), the first stories on which he and Collins collaborated—the 1854 and 1855 Christmas Numbers of *Household Words*—reinforce rather than diminish the sense of their class differences.

Dickens began issuing Extra Christmas Numbers in 1851 and continued to do so through December 1867, with the appearance of "No Thoroughfare" in *All the Year Round.* The Christmas Numbers were published as separate issues of thirty-six pages, initially priced at three pence, and proved to be especially popular, sometimes doubling circulation figures for the journal.[41] Initially a series of narratives written by eight or nine different contributors, the stories were

40. Hence Collins's biographer, Nuel Pharr Davis, refers to Collins as Dickens's "valet" in the title of his chapter on their early friendship. See *The Life of Wilkie Collins* (Urbana: University of Illinois Press, 1956), p. 89.

41. Patten, *Charles Dickens,* p. 243; Pilgrim, 7:495.

DRAMATIS PERSONÆ.

𝔐en.

THE DUKE OF MIDDLESEX,	⎫ *Peers attached to the Son of James II.,*	⎫ MR. FRANK STONE.
THE EARL OF LOFTUS,	⎭ *commonly called the First Pretender.*	⎭ MR. DUDLEY COSTELLO.

LORD WILMOT, *a Young Man at the Head of the Mode more than a Century ago, Son to* LORD LOFTUS . . . . . ⎱ MR. CHARLES DICKENS.

MR. SHADOWLY SOFTHEAD, *a Young Gentleman from the City, Friend and Double to* LORD WILMOT . . . . . ⎱ MR. DOUGLAS JERROLD.

MR. HARDMAN, *a Rising Member of Parliament, and Adherent to* SIR ROBERT WALPOLE . . . . ⎱ MR. JOHN FORSTER.

SIR GEOFFREY THORNSIDE, *a Gentleman of Good Family and Estate*   MR. MARK LEMON.

MR. GOODENOUGH EASY, *in Business, Highly Respectable, and a Friend of* SIR GEOFFREY . . . . ⎱ MR. F. W. TOPHAM.

LORD LE TRIMMER,	⎫	⎡ MR. PETER CUNNINGHAM
SIR THOMAS TIMID,	⎬ *Frequenters of Will's Coffee House* . .	MR. WESTLAND MARSTON.
COLONEL FLINT,	⎭	⎣ MR. R. H. HORNE.

MR. JACOB TONSON, *a Bookseller* . . . . MR. CHARLES KNIGHT.

SMART, *Valet to* LORD WILMOT . . . . MR. WILKIE COLLINS.

HODGE, *Servant to* SIR GEOFFREY THORNSIDE . . . . MR. JOHN TENNIEL.

PADDY O'SULLIVAN, *Mr. Fallen's Landlord* . . . . . MR. ROBERT BELL.

MR. DAVID FALLEN, *Grub Street Author and Pamphleteer* . . MR. AUGUSTUS EGG, A.R.A.

LORD STRONGBOW, SIR JOHN BRUIN, COFFEE-HOUSE LOUNGERS, DRAWERS, NEWSMAN, WATCHMEN, &c., &c.

𝔚omen.

LUCY, *Daughter to* SIR GEOFFREY THORNSIDE . . . . MRS. COMPTON.

BARBARA, *Daughter to* MR. EASY . . . . MISS ELLEN CHAPLIN.

THE SILENT LADY OF DEADMAN'S LANE.

Date of Play.—THE REIGN OF GEORGE I.

Scene.—LONDON.

Time supposed to be occupied, From the noon of the first day to the afternoon of the second.

Dramatis Personae, Edward Bulwer-Lytton, *Not So Bad As We Seem*. London: Chapman and Hall, 1851.

given more coherence by Dickens from 1854 onward, when he began to unify and link the various narratives by constructing a framework for them, having first provided prospective contributors with instructions that included an abstract of the story and an overall theme. Of the seventeen Christmas Numbers that Dickens published, Collins contributed to nine, two of which were written solely by him and Dickens—"The Perils of Certain English Prisoners" in 1857 and "No Thoroughfare" in 1867.

In her reading of the Christmas Numbers, Deborah Thomas argues that they reveal the importance of "fellow feeling" for Dickens.[42] As she notes, Dickens hoped the stories would "strike the chord of the season" (Pilgrim, 6:809), and their collaborative nature, like their recurring pretense of oral narration, suggests that they celebrate communal effort and feeling, looking back to a time before Victorian modes of literary production separated authors from editors and publishers, and writers from readers. Like the amateur theatricals he staged at Tavistock House, and which he compared to "writing a book in company" (Pilgrim, 8:256), the Christmas Numbers highlight Dickens's desire to be part of a creative community. Yet they also demonstrate his need to wield the authority within any such community and set himself apart from and above his collaborators.

In constructing the scenarios for the Christmas Numbers, Dickens often uses the relationships among the characters to self-consciously represent and justify his authority over his contributors, whose debt and subordination to their editor become unspoken subjects in the stories. In "The Seven Poor Travellers," for example, the 1854 story to which Sala, Adelaide Anne Procter, and Eliza Lynn as well as Collins contributed, Dickens assumes the part of the benevolent gentleman whose narrative opens the story, and who treats six poor travelers to a Christmas eve dinner in Rochester. By contrast, Collins's character—one of those treated—is "a shabby-genteel personage in a threadbare black suit" who, Dickens tells us, doesn't look as if he ever "belonged to . . . a profession."[43] The persona Dickens assigns to Collins calls the professional status and the middle-class respectability of the young writer into question while the one Dickens constructs for himself bolsters his image as the generous patron.[44]

42. Deborah A. Thomas, *Dickens and the Short Story* (Philadelphia: University of Pennsylvania Press, 1982), p. 66.

43. Charles Dickens, "The Seven Poor Travellers," in *Christmas Stories*, ed. Glancy, pp. 62, 79.

44. As Gill Gregory notes, "Dickens is identified with . . . the founder of the 'Richard Watts' charity" and "the metaphorical 'rich'ness of the editor and proprietor is contrasted with the poverty of his contributors or 'travellers'" (*The Life and Work of Adelaide Procter: Poetry, Feminism and Fathers* [Aldershot, U.K.: Ashgate, 1998], p. 214).

In the next Christmas Number, "The Holly-Tree Inn," Dickens draws similar distinctions between his fictional persona and that of Collins. "The Ostler shall be yours," Dickens tells Collins in October 1855, writing him from Boulogne about his part in the upcoming story, to which William Howitt, Procter, and Harriet Parr also contributed (Pilgrim, 7:721). A social idyll of sorts, "The Holly-Tree Inn" highlights the class differences among its characters while exempting the have-nots from any feelings of class injury or discontent. As in "The Seven Poor Travellers," Dickens writes as the gentleman, a guest snowed in for a week at the inn, while his fellow writers take the parts of working-class figures: Procter is the barmaid, Parr the poor pensioner, Howitt the landlord, and Collins the ostler. Complaining to Collins in December 1855 that he found the work of the other contributors "disappointing," Dickens explains his decision to adopt a working-class persona as well, writing as Cobbs, the "boots" at the inn (Pilgrim, 7:762). Ostensibly a working-class tale, Cobbs's narrative centers on the virtues of the gentleman who once employed him, and Dickens describes it as "a Fairy Story" of sorts (Pilgrim, 7:762). In effect, it is a fantasy about employee satisfaction and a worker's devotion to masters who treat their servants well. When Cobbs gives notice to his boss, he does so because of his own restlessness and not because he has "anythink to complain of."[45]

As a contributor to "The Holly-Tree Inn," Collins supports Dickens's social fantasy, attributing the sufferings of the poor working man, Isaac Scatchard, to an unruly woman rather than to class inequities or inadequate wages. In Collins's narrative, Scatchard is turned down for a job despite "the excellent written testimonials, as to character, which he was able to produce." When he has work, his employers are "not punctual payers of wages."[46] Nonetheless, Scatchard exhibits "phlegmatic patience" and "quiet civility" in the face of his hardships (108). The anger we expect him to feel is expressed, instead, by the ghostly and bitter "lady," Rebecca Murdoch, who is mysteriously drawn to Scatchard. Appointing a meeting with him in "Fuller's Meadow" (116–17), and hence associating herself with the Victorian feminist of that name, Rebecca Murdoch seems oddly powerful and genteel despite her impoverished circumstances. "For all its poverty-stricken paleness," for example, her skin appears "as delicate as if her life had been passed in the enjoyment of every social comfort that wealth can purchase" (116). As such tensions suggest, Collins uses his feminist figure to displace the problem of class injury. Unwisely marrying Miss Murdoch, only to have her assume his rights, defy his commands, and "almost

45. Charles Dickens, "The Boots," "The Holly-Tree Inn," in Christmas Stories, ed. Glancy, p. 110.
46. Wilkie Collins, "The Ostler," in Mad Monkton and Other Stories, ed. Norman Page (Oxford: Oxford University Press, 1994), pp. 106–7; subsequent references to "The Ostler" are cited parenthetically in the text.

deprive him of his powers of speech" (116), Scatchard is attacked as he lies in bed. In her "delicate, lady's hand," his wife wields a large clasp knife that she claims as "her own especial property" (123), and that resembles those that "labouring men use" (110, 125). This working-class weapon, placed in a lady's hands, and in her husband's bedroom, transforms working-class violence into a menacing exhibition of female strength and autonomy.

In using the threat of female autonomy to displace class conflict in his fiction, Collins won Dickens's approval—not only in their early collaborations with other writers but also in the four-part stories that he contributed to *Household Words*. In fact, one such story, "The Diary of Anne Rodway," so impressed Dickens that it led him to collaborate solely with Collins on some works of fiction for the periodical.

The unspoken appeal of "Anne Rodway," serialized in June 1856, lay in its ability to redefine the heroine's sense of class injury as a woman's dissatisfaction with her lot, only to domesticate her. At the beginning of the story, Anne Rodway, an impoverished needlewoman, questions class privilege: "The clergyman said in his sermon . . . that all things were ordered for the best, and we are all put into the stations in life that are properest for us. I suppose he was right, being a very clever gentleman . . . but I think I should have understood him better if I had not been very hungry at the time, in consequence of my own station in life being nothing but Plain Needlewoman."[47] Yet the grounds of Anne's discontent soon shift, as she becomes a female detective who violates gender boundaries.

Anne takes up detective work after the death of Mary Mallinson, a fellow needlewoman who suffers a fatal head injury in the street. The authorities blame Mallinson's death on her employers, who "unkindly let her go home alone, without giving her any stimulant," after she faints from overwork (141). Suspecting foul play, Anne investigates, yet her discoveries defend rather than challenge the class system. Anne finds that Mary's employers are not to blame for her death; the needlewoman did not collapse from exhaustion in the street but was assaulted by a drunken, working-class man. Anne's investigation disproves allegations of class injury and relegates domestic violence to the working class. At the same time, it leads her to discover her "proper place" as a woman, as her fiancé Robert takes over her role as sleuth, kindly forcing her back to the private sphere: "I wanted to go with Robert . . . but he said it was best that he should carry out the rest of the investigation alone; for my strength and resolution had been too hardly taxed already" (156). Told by Robert that she is "to work at home for the future" (163), Anne proves grateful to her male

47. Wilkie Collins, "The Diary of Anne Rodway," in *Mad Monkton and Other Stories,* ed. Page, p. 129; subsequent references to "Anne Rodway" are cited parenthetically in the text.

protector rather than resentful of his privileges: "Oh, I hope I shall live long after I am married to Robert! I want so much time to show him all my gratitude!" (157–58).

Filled with "strong admiration" for Collins's tale of wifely subordination and gratitude, and struck by its "genuine power and beauty" (Pilgrim, 8:161), Dickens initially told Wills to "pay Eighteen Guineas" for it but then decided to pay Collins an extra pound, since "it is very specially good":

> P.S. I re-open this . . . to say that you had best give Collins £20—in a handsome note, stating that I had told you that I saw such great pains in his story and so much merit, that I wished to remove it from ordinary calculations. I have a floating idea in my mind that after Little Dorrit is finished . . . he and I might do something in Household Words together. He and I have talked so much within the last 3 or 4 years about Fiction-Writing, and I see him so ready to catch at what I have tried to prove right, and to avoid what I thought wrong, and altogether to go at it in the spirit I have fired him with, that the notion takes some shape with me. . . . The advance in any case is not a large one, and if I were asked, in reference to the claims of this little Diary, to say who else could have done that about the Dead Girl, I confess I should find it very difficult (putting your conductor out of the question), to name the man.
>
> I write this in the confidence of your knowing that I am not a Literary Bounderby, and not misunderstanding me. (Pilgrim, 8:159)

In this letter, Dickens constructs and reconstructs his tie to Collins, both recognizing and obscuring their market relations. Although Dickens removes "Anne Rodway" "from ordinary calculations," he acknowledges that literary merit has a market price and rewards Collins with bonus pay. In 1856, Dickens was conscious of the rising market value of Collins's fiction and warned Wills "not [to] shave close" in their offers of payment. "I think, in such a case as that of Collins's the right thing is to give £50," Dickens tells him on 1 April 1856, in regard to A Rogue's Life: "I know of offers for stories going about—to Collins himself for instance—which make it . . . desirable that we should not shave close in such a case" (Pilgrim, 8:80).

Distinguishing himself from "a Literary Bounderby"—presumably one who exploits others and takes credit for their work—Dickens defends his business practices. But at the same time, he represents the value of Collins's story and the basis of their relationship as a matter of artistry and literary ethics (the "right" and "wrong" of "Fiction-Writing") rather than money, with Collins as an eager pupil "fired" with Dickens's spirit and "ready to catch at" his mentor's ideas and beliefs. Having Wills conduct the business of Household Words and give Collins and others their pay, Dickens distanced himself from market relations. As their 1856 contract negotiations make clear, however, Collins saw Dickens as an entrepreneur as well as an artist and understood that in producing "the strongest thing for H. W." (Pilgrim, 8:159), he was profiting a group of investors.

Writing to his subeditor on 16 September, two months after the publication of "Anne Rodway," Dickens describes Collins as an "industrious and reliable" contributor and explains his decision to offer the young writer a salaried position. Asking Wills to open negotiations with Collins, he outlines the terms that the subeditor is to offer. Although Dickens describes Collins as "very suggestive" and "exceedingly quick to take [his] notions," his instructions to Wills anticipate resistance or refusal on Collins's part. As if to answer the objections that his contributor is likely to raise, he is careful to list, for Wills's use, the benefits that will accrue to Collins as a staff member. "I have been thinking a good deal about Collins," Dickens tells Wills,

> and it strikes me that the best thing we can just now do for H.W. is to add him on to [Henry] Morley, and offer him Five Guineas a week. . . . I don't think we should be at an additional expense of £20 in the year by the transaction.
>
> I observe that to a man in his position who is fighting to get on, the getting his name before the public is important. Some little compensation for its not being constantly announced is needed, and that I fancy might be afforded by *a certain engagement*. If you are of my mind, I wish you would go up to him this morning, and tell him this is what we have to propose to him today, and that I wish him, if he can, to consider beforehand. You could explain the nature of such an engagement to him, in half a dozen words, far more easily than we could all open it together. And he would then come prepared.
>
> Of course he should have permission to collect his writings, and would be handsomely and generously considered in all respects. I think it would do him, in the long run, a world of good; and I am certain that by meeting together—dining three instead of two—and sometimes calling in Morley to boot—we should knock out much new fire.
>
> What it is desirable to put before him, is the regular association with the work, and the means he already has of considering whether it would be pleasant and useful to him to work with me, and whether any mere trading engagement would be likely to render him as good service. (Pilgrim, 8:188–89)

Here, Dickens develops a clever negotiating strategy, one that anticipates and dispels Collins's doubts, eliding his status as a hired hand. Appealing to Collins's ambition as a man "fighting to get on," Dickens distinguishes his offer from "any mere trading engagement." Collins is not being offered a trade but a middle-class *profession,* complete with job security. To make the point more convincing, Dickens obscures his own position as Collins's publisher and employer—as one who will profit from the literary labors of his prospective staff member. Under the pretense that his subeditor is far better at explaining business matters than he is, Dickens removes himself from the labor negotiations that he initiates and directs. He is there simply to "knock out much new fire." If anyone will benefit from the offer he has to make, Dickens argues, that person is Collins and not himself. Although Collins's name will not be brought "before the public," the position at *Household Words* "would do him, in the long run, a world of good," "be pleasant and useful to him," and "render him . . . good service." While noting that the owners of *Household Words* will "be at an additional expense," albeit a minor one, if Collins accepts his offer, Dickens fails to acknowledge the much greater benefit that he receives through the sole association of the periodical—and of Collins's writings—with the name "Charles Dickens," itself a marketable commodity, and the only one placed "before the public" by *Household Words*.

Despite the promise of "handsome" and "generous" treatment, and the list of benefits that were to accrue to him as a staff member, Collins initially rejected Dickens's proposal. By the fall of 1856, he was considerably less willing than he had once been to play the role of Dickens's devoted and grateful servant, whether in Bulwer-Lytton's comedy or such works as "The Seven Poor Travellers." His novel *Hide and Seek,* published by Richard Bentley in 1854, had met with modest success, and he saw his market value rising. Thus it is not surprising that a new sense of bargaining power informs his response to Dickens's job offer.

In particular, Collins objected to the restrictions placed on his writing at *Household Words*—the stipulation that he produce brief essays or short stories in four weekly parts—and to the dissociation of his name from his own published work—a "confusion of authorship" that, in Collins's view, characterized Dickens's periodical (Pilgrim, 8:189).[48] In a second letter to Wills, Dickens reveals the grounds of Collins's objections when he attempts to refute them. Although he asserts that any "confusion of authorship" in the periodical will enhance Collins's literary reputation rather than detract from it, Dickens modifies the initial terms of his offer, warning Wills not to "conclude anything *un*favourable with Collins":

> I think him wrong in his objection, and have not the slightest doubt that such a
> confusion of authorship (which I don't believe to obtain in half a dozen minds out

---

48. Here, Dickens quotes from Collins's objections in a letter of his own to W. H. Wills, dated 18 September 1856. With four or five exceptions, Collins's letters to Dickens do not survive, since Dickens purposely destroyed them.

of half a dozen hundred) would be a far greater service than dis-service to him. This I clearly see. But, as far as a long story is concerned, I see not the least objection to our advertising, at once, before it begins, that it is by him. I *do* see an objection to departing from our custom of not putting names to the papers in H.W. itself; but to our advertising the authorship of a long story, as a Rider to all our advertisements, I see none whatever.

Now, as to a long story itself, I doubt its value to us. And I feel perfectly convinced that it is not one quarter so useful to us as detached papers, or short stories in four parts. But I am quite content to try the experiment. The story should not, however, go beyond six months, and the engagement should be for twelve. (Pilgrim, 8:189)

In commenting on Collins's "skillful negotiations" with Dickens in 1856, critics represent his employment as a staff member at *Household Words* as a sign of empowerment—the moment in which he forced Dickens to "capitulate" to his own demands and joined "the Gentleman's Club" of literary professionals.[49] Indeed, in his negotiations with Dickens, Collins won a number of concessions; he would finally be allowed to write a "long story" for *Household Words,* the novel *The Dead Secret,* and his authorship would be acknowledged in riders to the periodical, although not in the serialized installments themselves.

Yet in becoming Dickens's staff member, Collins did not simply join the ranks of professional writers. He also gave up his connection to the *Leader,* became affiliated solely with *Household Words,* and made his subordination to Dickens official, as one of the "satellites" of "Jupiter," as a contemporary reviewer put it.[50] While Collins forced Dickens to make a number of concessions, some were required on his part as well. Collins was permitted to write a novel for the periodical, for example, but he did so on Dickens's terms, altering his plans for *The Dead Secret* to fit a six-month run, and plagued by fears that the "good things" about it would be attributed to Dickens. In April 1856, Collins read a "sketch of the plot of [his] new novel to Dickens," he told his mother, "and even *he* could not guess what the end of the story was, from the beginning." "Keep all this a profound secret from everybody," he warns her, "for if my good natured friends knew that I had been reading my idea to Dickens— they would be sure to say when the book was published, that I had got all the good things in it from him."[51] Indeed, after *The Dead Secret* was serialized in

49. Heller, *Dead Secrets,* p. 92; Davis, *Life of Wilkie Collins,* p. 192; Heller, *Dead Secrets,* p. 88.

50. "Tom Tiddler's Ground: Extraordinary Proceedings in Wellington-Street," *Queen* 1, 16 (21 December 1861): 313.

51. ALS to Harriet Collins, 5 April 1856. The Pierpont Morgan Library, New York. MA 3150.50. *The Letters of Wilkie Collins,* 1:155.

Household Words, reviewers made this very claim, despite the riders announcing Collins's authorship: "Our readers will easily recognize who is the Gamaliel at whose feet Mr. Collins must have sat," the *Saturday Review* asserted.[52]

But for the moment, the advantages of joining Dickens's staff outweighed the disadvantages in Collins's thinking, and the story on which they began working soon after completing their contract negotiations helps to explain why. Having offered Collins a position he meant to be understood as "professional," Dickens cast Collins in the role of John Steadiman, the first mate in the 1856 Christmas Number, "The Wreck of the Golden Mary." Thus in the fall of 1856, Collins could imagine himself as a member of Dickens's management team—as an officer rather than a common sailor, a salaried and professional writer rather than a wage slave and hired hand. While placed in a hierarchical relationship with his "captain," Collins was nonetheless represented as his most immediate subordinate and right-hand man, ready to assume command if and when his captain should falter.

Despite this idealized portrait of their relationship, however, tensions between them remained. Their differences are both acknowledged and displaced in "The Wreck of the Golden Mary," by means of a cast full of troublesome figures. The angry workers, the independent women, and the miser in the Christmas Number all express, in the discredited form of the other, the resentment and desires that Collins harbored as Dickens's subordinate, while also serving to define him as Dickens's fellow officer, fellow Englishman, and social ally.

52. Unsigned review, *Saturday Review* (22 August 1857): 188; *Wilkie Collins: The Critical Heritage,* ed. Norman Page (London: Routledge & Kegan Paul, 1974), p. 72. In Acts 22:3, Gamaliel (A.D. 50) is the elder responsible for educating Paul.

CHAPTER 2

Collins Joins Dickens's Management Team:
"The Wreck of the Golden Mary"

Less than two weeks after telling Wills not to "conclude anything *un-favourable* with Collins" (Pilgrim, 8:189), and two months before Collins officially became a salaried staff writer at *Household Words*,[1] Dickens sent his "scheme" for the upcoming Christmas Number to prospective contributors. The sixth in Dickens's annual series, "The Wreck of the Golden Mary" was a collaborative undertaking but only in a limited sense. Although several writers contributed to the story, Dickens formulated its plotline and defined its aims. The story was to center on the wreck of an English trading ship en route to Australia, Dickens explained, which "got foul of an Iceberg," and on the hero-ics of the captain, "a cool man with his Wits about him," who got his men and passengers into an open boat before the ship sank. Steering the boat and cheer-ing his companions, who took turns rowing, the captain would encourage them to tell stories to keep them "from dwelling on the horrors of their condition." These stories did not have to relate directly to the narrators, Dickens said, and could be told in either the first or third person, since "the whole narrative of the Wreck will be given by the Captain to the Reader in introducing the sto-ries. Also, the final deliverance of the people." As he did in "The Seven Poor Travellers" and "The Holly-Tree Inn," Dickens would take the central and au-thoritative role in the new story, that of the heroic captain, while reserving the roles of passengers and crew members for his subordinates at *Household Words*:

> There are persons of both Sexes in the boat. The writer of any story may suppose
> any sort of person—or none, if that be all—as the Captain will identify him if need

1. That is, when Dickens began to publish Collins's works without paying him for them individu-ally—the first example of which was "A Petition to the Novel-Writers," published on 6 December 1856.

be. But among the Wrecked there might naturally be The Mate, The Cook, the Carpenter, the Armourer (or Worker in Iron), the Boy, the Bride Passenger, the Bridegroom passenger, the Sister passenger, the brother passenger, the mother or father passenger or son or daughter passenger, the child passenger, the Runaway passenger, the old Seaman, the toughest of the crew, etc etc. (Pilgrim, 8:195)

As published on 6 December 1856, "The Wreck of the Golden Mary" tells the story of the officers, crew, and passengers on board the *Golden Mary,* a newly built merchant vessel of three hundred tons that sets sail in 1851, bound from Liverpool to San Francisco. The ship is manned by Captain William George Ravender, First Mate John Steadiman, and Second Mate William Rames, in addition to a crew of eighteen, and carries twenty passengers. Among these passengers, four are characterized in detail: Mrs. Atherfield, "a bright-eyed, blooming young wife who was going to join her husband in California"; her three-year-old daughter Lucy, the couple's only child, who is affectionately nicknamed "The Golden Lucy" on the voyage out; Miss Coleshaw, a thirty-year-old spinster "going out to join a brother"; and Mr. Rarx, an "old gentle-man . . . who was always talking, morning, noon, and night, about the gold discovery."[2] Taking out cargo to "the diggers and emigrants in California," which is to be exchanged for gold (2), the ship collides with an iceberg off Cape Horn after more than two months at sea. The ship quickly sinks, but all those on board escape the wreck on two boats. In spite of the hardships they endure, most survive. After spending nearly thirty days in open boats, they are picked up by an English brigantine. Transferred to a California coasting vessel, they arrive at their destination soon after their rescue at sea.

Dickens and Collins wrote most of "The Wreck of the Golden Mary," but Percy Fitzgerald, Harriet Parr, Adelaide Anne Procter, and James White contributed to it as well. Of the story's three sections, Dickens wrote the first, narrated by Ravender and entitled "The Wreck." The second, "The Beguilement in the Boats," consists of stories told by the Armourer (Fitzgerald); Poor Dick (Parr); the Supercargo (Fitzgerald); the Old Sailor (Procter); and the Scotch Boy (White). These serve as interpolated tales in a larger frame narrative provided by Steadiman, whose part Collins authored. Steadiman also narrates the third and final section of the story, "The Deliverance," which was written by Collins.

2. [Charles Dickens], "The Wreck," "The Wreck of the Golden Mary," *Household Words* (6 December 1856), Extra Christmas Number, p. 3; subsequent references to "The Wreck of the Golden Mary" are cited parenthetically in the text. Dickens's portion of the story, pp. 1–10, is entitled "The Wreck," and Collins's portion, which begins on p. 11, is interrupted by the interpolated tales (pp. 13–29), for which Dickens wrote introductory paragraphs. Collins's narrative resumes as "The Deliverance," pp. 30–36.

Although "The Wreck of the Golden Mary" generally follows Dickens's rudimentary scheme, it diverges from his original outline in a number of ways, some of which bear on Collins's role in the story. As in Dickens's initial scheme, "The Wreck of the Golden Mary" describes the collision of an English trading vessel with an iceberg and celebrates the heroics of her captain, who keeps his head and saves his passengers and crew. It contains five interpolated narratives, most related in the first person, which the captain and mate solicit to lift the spirits of the survivors. Yet the characters are headed for California rather than Australia, and they are most clearly imperiled by the unruly behavior of the miserly passenger, Mr. Rarx. After the wreck, they divide into two boats rather than escaping on one, with the longboat commanded by the captain and the surfboat by the first mate. The mate assumes some of the narrative functions assigned to the captain in Dickens's scheme as well. While Ravender narrates that part of the story entitled "The Wreck," Steadiman introduces the interpolated tales and narrates "The Deliverance." As in the sketch, the story places members of both sexes on the ship, but the wife, mother, and daughter figures are separated from their male relations, who remain on shore.

These changes serve Dickens's aims in the story and help to reveal his reasons for undertaking it. "The Wreck of the Golden Mary" was written in response to what Victorians termed "The Blue-Jacket Agitation"—the problem of labor unrest among sailors in the British merchant marine, itself a recurring subject in *Household Words*—and formulated during Dickens's contract negotiations with Collins, who voiced some dissatisfaction with the terms initially offered to him at the journal. The story expresses Dickens's concerns about disgruntled and demanding workers, including his own, and enables him to imaginatively resolve them. By sending his mariners to California instead of Australia, by identifying the miser as a primary threat to their well being, by granting female figures a troubling degree of autonomy, and by casting Collins as a devoted first mate who shares the captain's responsibilities, Dickens redefines and defuses the threat posed to capital and management by a discontented and insubordinate labor force.

I

Critics have long recognized the metaphoric resonance of shipwreck for Dickens, who uses this image to represent social disorder and class revolution in his fiction. As William J. Palmer observes, "Shipwrecks form, in [Dickens's] different novels, images of . . . utter social and political chaos leading to social apocalypse."[3] But in the 1850s, shipwreck had a literal meaning for Dickens as well and was represented in *Household Words* as the tragic result of the greed of ship owners and the incompetence of captains and officers, who unnecessarily placed the lives of their men at risk.

Dickens became interested in the treatment and discontent of common sailors in the British merchant marine because of the uproar triggered by the adoption of the Mercantile Marine Act in 1851. As the London *Times* reported on 6 March 1851, and *Household Words* recounted two weeks later, a deputation of merchant seamen, angered by the workings of this legislation, had appeared before the president of the Board of Trade in London on 5 March. The men had gone to state their grievances and to ask that portions of the statute be suspended. Although the board's president reminded these men that the act was designed "to benefit and improve their condition," they protested that it did not. Presenting their memorial to the board—a written statement of "the causes of discontent and dissatisfaction extensively felt by master mariners and seamen of the united kingdom"—they argued that the act deprived them of what little power they had previously exercised and further restricted their rights and liberties. Under the guise of encouraging their moral and professional improvement, the act imposed fines and penalties for misbehavior and increased "the arrogance, oppression, and injustice of ships' officers," who levied these fines. In their view, the scrutiny to which they were now subjected threatened "to destroy [their] manly characters . . . and reduce to the condition of slaves their class, who for ages past have helped to maintain the freedom and glory of this country." By allowing the captain to report on the character of his men in the ship's logbook, and hence to determine whether or not they received another berth, the act endowed him with "unconstitutional" powers. The seamen had hoped that the act would allow them to respond to their captain's allegations in the logbook, by inserting their own account of his charges against them, but it did not. "When an entry was made in the log against a man," the sailors told the board, "the man should have it read over to him, . . . have the power of entering his defence, and the names of parties who could speak in his behalf."[4]

Identifying himself as one such party, Dickens quickly began publishing articles on "The Blue-Jacket Agitation," the first on 22 March 1851 and the sec-

3. William J. Palmer, "Dickens and Shipwreck," *Dickens Studies Annual* 18 (1989): 59–60.

4. "The New Mercantile Marine Act: Deputation to the Board of Trade," *Times* (London), 6 March 1851, 5. Captain A. G. Course provides a useful analysis of the social history of the British merchant marine, the legislation affecting "poor Jack" in the nineteenth century, and the sailors' attempts at unionization in the 1850s. See *The Merchant Navy: A Social History* (London: Frederick Muller, 1963), pp. 214–39.

ond two weeks later. By the time *Household Words* ceased publication in 1859, nearly twenty articles that bear on the merchant marine and "the life of poor Jack" appeared in it.[5] Supporting the seamen's cause, Morley's "We Mariners of England" (26 February 1853) and "The Life of Poor Jack" (21 May 1853) argue that common sailors have valid reasons to complain about officers and ship owners. Describing the dangers to which the men are exposed, many of which are unnecessary, Morley's articles criticize the poor judgment of captains and mates, and the greed of middle-class ship owners. More concerned with profits than safety, owners fail to make repairs yet "lie snug from censure" when sailors are killed and ships wrecked as a result: "The world is very slow to connect a respectable citizen of Liverpool with a wreck happening in the Bermudas, while he sat at tea in his own parlour, innocently happy with his wife and family."[6] All-too-often, ships and their instruments take the blame for disasters caused by irresponsible officers and owners:

> Can any blame by any possibility attach to any human creature? No. Obviously it must be laid upon the compasses. And this is a convenient thing, because there is no fine payable by compasses, and they are case-hardened against imprisonment. . . . We have great consideration for the feelings of a captain as a captain, of an owner as an owner, and generally of the gentlemen hidden behind the compasses. We regret, therefore, that this matter should be of a solemn kind that will not bear the consideration of those feelings any more. There must be . . . not only moral and sentimental, but material and legal motives for the utmost care on the part of all who send or take men down to the sea in ships. ("Modern Human Sacrifices," 563)

But while this article calls for "defined responsibilities and no evasion" (563) and insists that officers and owners be held legally liable for the fate of their men, others published by Dickens do not. In their least sympathetic moments, these articles associate the sailors with primitive peoples and characterize them as ignorant and undisciplined workers who prefer "low lodging-houses and . . .

---

5. See, for example, "The Preservation of Life from Shipwreck" (3 August 1850), "Lives and Cargoes" (29 March 1851), "The Sailor at Home" (10 May 1851), "Life and Luggage" (8 November 1851), "The 'Merchant Seaman's Fund'" (13 December 1851), "A Sea-Coroner" (13 March 1852), "Sailors' Homes Afloat" (19 February 1853), "We Mariners of England" (26 February 1853), "The Life of Poor Jack" (21 May 1853), "Voices from the Deep" (31 December 1853), "Modern Human Sacrifices" (11 February 1854), "Jack and the Union Jack" (25 February 1854), "The Learned Sailor" (1 July 1854), "When the Wind Blows" (24 March 1855), "Wrecks at Sea" (11 August 1855), "Red Rockets" (21 June 1856), and "Hovelling" (7 February 1857).

6. [Henry Morley], "Modern Human Sacrifices," *Household Words* 8 (11 February 1854): 562; subsequent references to "Modern Human Sacrifices" are cited parenthetically in the text.

low taverns" to the well-run Sailors' Homes in which religious instruction and reading material are provided.[7] Generally speaking, Dickens proved a reluctant champion of maritime labor, and the articles that he published about the British merchant marine usually endorse the act to which the sailors objected, suggesting that the time has come for "the meshes of law" to draw around "that noble animal," "the nautical leviathan."[8] While the sailors find the new rules and regulations irritating and restrictive, they are necessary nonetheless and will ultimately work to the men's advantage: "Doubtless, a coat and trousers would be an intolerable restraint to a Tahitian at first, but by-and-by he would value these articles as he progressed in civilisation" ("The Blue-Jacket Agitation," 40).

When Dickens dramatizes life in the British merchant marine in "The Wreck of the Golden Mary," he acknowledges the problem of labor unrest within it but does so only indirectly and proves as evasive in his treatment of shipwreck as those who blame the compasses for it in "Modern Human Sacrifices." In his portion of the Christmas Number, Dickens's mariners set sail on 7 March 1851, in the wake of the maritime labor dispute reported in the *Times* and in *Household Words*. Drawing on the iconography of social revolution, he describes their wreck off Cape Horn and compares the experience of Captain Ravender to that of Captain Bligh, set adrift after the mutiny on the *Bounty*. In the process, however, Dickens deflects blame for working-class unrest away from sailors, officers, and ship owners alike.

He does so, most obviously, by placing his mariners in a historical context in which labor unrest is both safely explained and discredited. In the lawless days of the California gold rush, sailors were expected to desert their vessels as soon as they reached port, regardless of the treatment they received. More subtly, Dickens displaces the problem of labor unrest by redefining the nature of the social threat posed in the story. Rather than staging a mutiny among English sailors, he focuses on the troubles caused by the greed of the "ungovernable" Mr. Rarx (9), a miser whom he models on the stereotypical Jew without labeling him as such, and whose desire to hoard gold poses both economic and sexual dangers to the community.[9] At the same time, Dickens feminizes the un-

7. [George Augustus Sala], "Cheerily, Cheerily!" *Household Words* 6 (25 September 1852): 28. See also [James Hannay], "The Sailors' Home," *Household Words* 2 (22 March 1851): 612–15.

8. [James Hannay], "The Blue-Jacket Agitation," *Household Words* 3 (5 April 1851): 39; subsequent references to "The Blue-Jacket Agitation" are cited parenthetically in the text.

9. For recent discussions of Dickens's representations of Jews and the question of his anti-Semitism, see Murray Baumgarten, "Seeing Double: Jews in the Fiction of F. Scott Fitzgerald, Charles Dickens, Anthony Trollope, and George Eliot," in *Between "Race" and Culture: Representations of "the Jew" in English and American Literature,* ed. Bryan Cheyette (Stanford, Calif.: Stanford University Press, 1996), pp. 44–61; Jonathan H. Grossman, "The Absent Jew in Dickens: Narrators in *Oliver Twist, Our Mutual Friend,* and *A Christmas Carol,*" *Dickens Studies Annual* 24 (1996): 37–57; and Deborah Heller, "The Outcast as Villain and Victim: Jews in Dickens' *Oliver Twist* and *Our Mutual Friend,*" in *Jewish Presences*

ruly labor force on the *Golden Mary,* transforming the threatened mutiny of sailors into a potential rebellion of women who aspire to become sea captainesses and sail the ship of state.[10] Casting Collins, his own disgruntled subordinate, as a faithful first officer who gains his own command after the wreck, Dickens imaginatively resolves his own labor dispute at *Household Words.* He encourages his new staff member to define himself against unruly women and Jews, and to consider himself an officer and a manager of labor rather than a hired hand.

For his own part, Collins generally plays along, accepting his role as the devoted yet professional subordinate and displacing the threat of labor unrest by developing Dickens's implicitly anti-Semitic depiction of the miser. Yet Collins also exhibits resistance to Dickens's scheme, more fully acknowledging the threat of class unrest than his senior collaborator and ultimately depriving the captain of his authority. While John Steadiman finds the market value of his services rising at Collins's conclusion of the story, the unemployed Captain Ravender does not.[11]

II

When "The Wreck of the Golden Mary" is read in its original format, as an issue of *Household Words,* what is most striking about the story is the way in which Dickens dissociates it from the political context in which it first appeared—the ongoing discussion of the conflict between discontented merchant

---

in *English Literature,* ed. Derek Cohen and Deborah Heller (Montreal: McGill-Queen's University Press, 1990), pp. 40–60.

10. In recent years, a number of critics have discussed Dickens's treatment of gender, his feminine ideal, and his own relationships with women. See, for example, Michael Slater, *Dickens and Women* (London: J. M. Dent, 1983); Patricia Ingham, *Dickens, Women and Language* (Toronto: University of Toronto Press, 1992); David Holbrook, *Charles Dickens and the Image of Woman* (New York: New York University Press, 1993); and Gail Turley Houston, *Consuming Fictions: Gender, Class, and Hunger in Dickens's Novels* (Carbondale: Southern Illinois University Press, 1994).

11. In her discussion of "The Wreck of the Golden Mary," Anthea Trodd overlooks the threat of labor unrest that informs the story—unrest at sea and at the *Household Words* office. Focusing on Dickens's mixed feelings about collaboration, she argues that he uses the idealized images of the "jolly Tar" (217) and "the collective moral authority of the British seafaring community" to "validate" his "collaborative enterprise" (202), although these very images were called into question by the contemporary events that partly inspired the story. At the same time, Trodd overlooks Collins's resistance to Dickens's authority, depicting him as a wholly compliant subordinate who wrote the section of the story with which Dickens chose not to be bothered, developing his "plot-oriented skills": "It was Collins's deputed job to rescue the open boats tossing in the sea where Dickens had left them . . . filling in the portions of narrative, the 'business part' of the stor[y], in which Dickens had lost interest" (220). See "Collaborating in Open Boats: Dickens, Collins, Franklin, and Bligh," *Victorian Studies* 42, 2 (winter 1999–2000): 201–25.

sailors and their officers. Whether they support or criticize maritime labor, such articles as "The Blue-Jacket Agitation," "We Mariners of England," and "Sailors' Homes Afloat" represent the sailors as resentful and dissatisfied workers who believe that "the advantages got out of new laws are ten to the owners and the captain against one to the man before the mast."[12] "We are not too stupid to make comparisons," the seaman who narrates "Sailors' Homes Afloat" asserts, contrasting the splendors of his officers' lodgings to the squalor of his own.[13] Angered by greedy ship owners and privileged yet abusive officers, the men depicted in these articles threaten to desert their ships and organize a labor strike. "Do[ing] the work of an elephant upon the keep and lodging of a pig,"[14] they demand to be used like men and appear to be preparing for a violent insurrection: "the devil-*may*-care look of the tar [is] changed to a devil-*does*-care expression," readers are warned. "We've been still enough," one sailor explains, "but still water's deep; and if you sound far enough, you'll find the devil at the bottom!" ("The Blue-Jacket Agitation," 38).

In "The Wreck of the Golden Mary," these mutinous depths are largely unsounded. Idealizing class relations among ship owners, officers, and sailors, Dickens disavows the social unrest exposed in the articles surrounding his story. Unlike the greedy ship owners described in "Modern Human Sacrifices," the owner of the *Golden Mary* is generous and humane: "a wiser merchant or a truer gentleman never stepped," Captain Ravender explains in Dickens's narrative (2). The captain himself is strikingly different from the rash and power-hungry officers sometimes described in *Household Words*. Despite recurring portraits of imprudent and inefficient captains who carelessly forfeit the lives of their men, Ravender is both prudent and efficient, and Dickens sets him apart from his irresponsible cohorts. "In my opinion," Ravender explains in Dickens's narrative,

> a man has no manly motive or sustainment in his own breast for facing dangers, unless he has well considered what they are, and is able quietly to say to himself, "None of these perils can now take me by surprise; I shall know what to do for the best in any of them; all the rest lies in the higher and greater hands to which I humbly commit myself." On this principle I have so attentively considered (regarding it as my duty) all the hazards I have ever been able to think of, in the ordinary way of storm, shipwreck, and fire at sea, that I hope I should be prepared to do . . . whatever could be done, to save the lives entrusted to my charge. (2)

12. [Henry Morley and Samuel Rinder], "Sailors' Homes Afloat," *Household Words* 6 (19 February 1853): 529.

13. Ibid.

14. [Henry Morley], "The Life of Poor Jack," *Household Words* 7 (21 May 1853): 286.

Similarly idealized, though in very different terms, Dickens's common sailors are neither the victimized beasts of burden nor the "louts" and "skulking lubbers" portrayed elsewhere in *Household Words* ("Modern Human Sacrifices," 562). Carefully selected by the captain and first mate, the crew contains "none but good hands" (3), Dickens writes, men who are "as smart, efficient, and contented, as it was possible to be" (5). Manned by this idealized crew, the *Golden Mary* sets sail in a fair wind, bound on a voyage that promises well: "And so, in a good ship of the best build, well owned, well arranged, well officered, well manned, well found in all respects, we parted with our pilot at a quarter past four o'clock in the afternoon of the seventh of March, one thousand eight hundred and fifty one, and stood with a fair wind out to sea" (3).

But as this departure date suggests, the threat of labor unrest underlies Dickens's idealizations, despite his efforts to obscure it. Dickens assures us that the sailors prove "good men and true" when faced with danger, following orders and "fall[ing] towards their appointed stations" as the ship begins to sink (6). Yet the very fact that the ship founders suggests otherwise, and a number of details in the story reveal what Dickens disclaims—the connection between his shipwreck narrative and class rebellion. Subtle signs of unrest and rebellion are apparent in Dickens's narrative, despite Ravender's insistence that the men are as "contented as it was possible to be."

After the shipwreck, for example, the men constantly moan at their oars, yet Captain Ravender wishfully interprets this moaning as an inarticulate expression of contentment: he hears the sailors "moaning all the time in the dismallest manner," Dickens notes, but "almost always got the impression that [they] did not know what sound [they] had been making" and "thought [they] had been humming a tune" (8). In turn, this wishful image of the men happily humming as they work is undermined by the captain's admission that he "had more than one rough temper with [him] among [his] own people" and has placed these men in his boat so that he will "have them under [his] eye" (8). Perhaps most significantly, Dickens refers to Captain Bligh and the mutiny on the *Bounty*, treating Bligh's experience as a prototype for Ravender's own. Concerned that his companions in the longboat may be troubled by fears of cannibalism, itself a well-known metaphor for class warfare, Ravender recounts Bligh's story to reassure them that starving castaways rarely devour each other (9). However, he does so by recounting a tale of mutiny at sea, thus qualifying the reassuring moral of his story. Furthermore, the notorious fact that Bligh was cast adrift during a mutiny led by his first mate Fletcher Christian underscores the potential for rebellion among Ravender's officers as well as his crew.

Clearly, then, Dickens cannot entirely repress the social anxieties that underlie "The Wreck of the Golden Mary." But he can displace and discredit them—by sending his mariners to a uniquely lawless region, in the company of self-sufficient Englishwomen and an ungovernable miser.

III

Although Dickens's preliminary scheme of the 1856 Christmas Number identifies Australia as the destination of his characters, the *Golden Mary* sets sail for California in the story itself. At first glance, this change seems unimportant, since California and Australia were both common destinations of the trading vessels that left English ports in the 1850s and served as equally remote places to which troublesome relations could be shipped. "Captain, there's my nephew," says a character in Dickens's introduction to Parr's interpolated tale: "I want to ship him off to Australia, to California, or anywhere out of the way" (18).

However, in March 1851, when the *Golden Mary* sets sail, California differed from Australia in one crucial way: gold had been discovered there. "There was gold in California—which, as most people know, was before it was discovered in the British colony of Australia," Ravender explains in Dickens's narrative (1). In sending his mariners to California, Dickens sends them to the gold regions and thus supplies them with a simple, apolitical reason for insubordinate behavior: gold-rush fever.[15] As the owner of the *Golden Mary* warns the captain in Dickens's opening pages, mutinous behavior is only to be expected among men en route to California, even when they are well treated and well paid: "Ravender, you are well aware that the lawlessness of that coast and country at present, is as special as the circumstances in which it is placed. Crews of vessels outward-bound desert as soon as they make the land; crews of vessels homeward-bound, ship at enormous wages, with the express intention of murdering the captain and seizing the gold freight; no man can trust another, and the devil seems let loose" (2). Because of these "special . . . circumstances," the behavior that is fueled by class resentment in "Sailors' Homes Afloat" becomes a symptom of gold-rush fever in "The Wreck of the Golden Mary"—an explanation that Dickens's original readers were prepared to accept by an extensive series of articles published on the gold rush in *Household Words*. These articles represent gold-rush fever as an infection to which *all* people are vulnerable, regardless of their class sympathies, their living conditions, and their wage, and that produces in otherwise contented workers the delusion that they

---

15. For an extended analysis of this "disease" and the political use to which Dickens puts it, see Lillian Nayder, "Dickens and 'Gold-Rush Fever': Colonial Contagion in *Household Words*," in *Dickens and the Children of Empire,* ed. Wendy S. Jacobson (New York: Palgrave, 2000), pp. 67–77.

are being exploited by those with capital and denied their fair share of wealth.[16] Invoking this mechanism of disease in his narrative, Dickens obscures the genuine causes of discontent among men in the merchant marine.

While the concept of gold-rush fever serves Dickens's ends in "The Wreck of the Golden Mary," so, too, does a second element of the California gold rush—the prostitute with the "heart of gold."[17] Drawing on this female stereotype from gold-rush literature and lore, Dickens redefines the nature of rebellion and desertion in the Christmas Number. Associating the *Golden Mary* herself with the emancipated woman of the 1850s, and then conflating her work in the public domain with prostitution, Dickens transforms a class threat into a sexual one. Displacing the sailors' desertion of their ship with a wife's desertion of her home and family, he traces the social ills plaguing those on board the *Golden Mary* to what he suggests is their sexual source. Like Margaret Fuller and Thomas Wentworth Higginson, Americans whose support for women's rights is itself the subject of *Household Words* articles,[18] Dickens locates the struggle for female emancipation and professional employment in a maritime context but ridicules their idea that "sea captainesses" belong at the helm of oceangoing vessels. Dickens uses the *Golden Mary* to expose the dangers of women's professional ambition and sexual autonomy, which in his view threaten to wreck the ship of state.

16. See, for example, [Richard H. Horne], "A Digger's Diary," *Household Words* 6 (29 January 1853): 457–62; and [Sidney Laman Blanchard], "A Musician in California," *Household Words* 4 (18 October 1851): 94–96. *Household Words* articles describing the California gold rush include: "The Golden City" (29 June 1850); "A Woman's Experience in California" (1 February 1851); "The Short Cut to California" (15 March 1851); "A Lynch Trial in California" (20 September 1851); "From California" (8 April 1854); "Mr. Wittlestick" (4 November 1854); "Tinder from a Californian Fire" (24 February 1855); "The First Vigilance Committees" (15 November 1856); and "Civilisation in California" (13 March 1858). Dickens also published an extensive series of articles on the Australian gold rush once it was underway. Here, too, the symptoms of gold rush fever are exhibited among the miners, but their behavior is kept in check by the vigilance of the British government, which adopts measures to maintain order and prevent certain types of workers (sailors and agricultural laborers, in particular) from deserting their posts: "No [digging] licenses were granted to any one who could not produce a certificate of discharge from his last service" ([Henry Morley], "The Harvest of Gold," *Household Words* 5 [22 May 1852]: 213).

17. The articles Dickens published on the gold rush obliquely refer to this female figure; see [Richard H. Horne], "A Digger's Diary," *Household Words* 8 (3 September 1853): 6–11, esp. 8; [William Howitt], "Gold-Hunting. In Two Parts. Part the First," *Household Words* 13 (24 May 1856): 448–54, esp. 452; and [Eliza Lynn], "Civilisation in California," *Household Words* 17 (13 March 1858): 301–4, esp. 301–2. For brief discussions of the stereotype, see Mary Murphy, "The Private Lives of Public Women: Prostitution in Butte, Montana, 1878–1917," in *The Women's West*, ed. Susan Armitage and Elizabeth Jameson (Norman: University of Oklahoma Press, 1987), pp. 193–205, esp. p. 193; and Anne M. Butler, *Daughters of Joy, Sisters of Misery: Prostitutes in the American West, 1865–90* (Urbana: University of Illinois Press, 1985), p. 75.

18. See, for example, [T. M. Thomas], "Margaret Fuller," *Household Words* 5 (24 April 1852): 121–24.

In the 1850s, arguments over the rights and employment of women were voiced with increasing frequency, as questions about their status became especially pressing. Women's movements in America and England challenged the concept of the separate spheres and the idea that wives and daughters were naturally designed to manage the domestic realm. This challenge was justified, in part, by data from the 1851 census, which revealed a paucity of eligible bachelors in Great Britain and suggested that "redundant" women would have to enter the work force whether they wished to or not.[19]

These issues made their way into the columns of *Household Words,* in articles disparaging "the Rights of Women" and "Bloomerism," and invoking stereotypical conceptions of female nature to defend the sexual status quo.[20] While these articles express little concern over the employment of working-class women, they voice pity for middle-class widows and spinsters forced to support themselves, and indignation at wives and mothers who, in the name of emancipation, willingly leave the domestic sphere: "Homes [are] deserted" and "children . . . given to a stranger's hand, . . . while the Emancipated Woman walks proudly forward to the goal of the glittering honours of public life, her true honours lying crushed beneath her, unnoticed."[21] Like Mrs. Jellyby, who tends to her philanthropic business instead of the needs of her family in *Bleak House* (1852–53), the professional women depicted in *Household Words* are negligent wives and mothers, absurd figures who desert their families and violate their own nature by assuming the roles of men.

Among the most absurd of these women, as Dickens's journal portrays them, are those who seek employment at sea. Not content with "teaching, preaching, voting, [and] judging," Betsy Miller and her cohorts aspire to become sea captains or to command men-of-war, "prefer[ring] quarter-decks . . . to a still home and a school-desk":

> Imagine a follower of a certain Miss Betsy Millar [*sic*], who for twelve years commanded the Scotch brig, Cloetus—imagine such a one at the head of one's table, with horny hands covered with fiery red scars and blackened with tar, her voice

---

19. As Dickens knew, the 1851 census showed that over 2 million women in Great Britain had already joined the work force. Sala's "Numbers of People" (*Household Words* 10 [21 October 1854]: 221–28) underscored "the disparity between the sexes" reported in the census (223) and reprimanded bachelors for not marrying.

20. These articles include Dickens's own "Sucking Pigs" (*Household Words* 4 [8 November 1851]: 145–47), in which he ridicules Bloomerism, women's missions, and the idea of female M.P.s as "nonsense" associated with America. "That great country . . . is not generally renowned for its domestic rest," Dickens claims, and has "yet to form itself for its best happiness on the domestic patterns of other lands" (146).

21. [Eliza Lynn], "Rights and Wrongs of Women," *Household Words* 9 (1 April 1854): 159.

hoarse and cracked, her skin tanned and hardened, her language seasoned with nautical allusions and quarter-deck imagery, and her gait and step the rollicking roll of a bluff Jack-tar. She might be very estimable as a human being, honourable, brave, and generous, but she would not be a woman. . . . What man (moderately sane) would prefer a woman who had been a sea captain ten or twelve years, to the most ordinary of piano-playing and flower-painting young ladies? Mindless as the one might be, the rough practicality of the other would be worse; and help-less as fashionable education makes young ladies, Heaven defend us from the vir-ile energy of a race of Betsy Millars![22]

Betsy Miller, the daughter of a ship owner from Saltcoats, did indeed command the British vessel *Cloetus* in the 1840s and 1850s, sailing among various Scottish and Irish ports.[23] Articles about Miller had appeared in the Glasgow *Post* in 1852, and in the next year Thomas Wentworth Higginson discussed her in *Woman and Her Wishes*. As Higginson points out, Miller accomplished what Margaret Fuller set forth as an "extreme instance" of woman's capabilities: "When Margaret Fuller, in answer to a question from one who wished to set limits to the sphere of women, answered 'Let them be sea-captains, if you will,' she did not forsee that Captain Betsey Miller, of the bark Cloetus, would ere-long be doing [that] very thing." "If Miss Miller can walk the quarter-deck," Higginson argues, then "energetic women will make their way into the avo-cations suited to them, and the barrier once broken down, others will follow."[24]

On a first reading of "The Wreck of the Golden Mary," Dickens's attack on emancipated women and, more particularly, on the female "Jack-tar," appears to have little bearing on the story. The female characters who have gone to sea on board the *Golden Mary* are passengers rather than sea captainesses and seem as idealized in their own womanly way as the officers and sailors who man the ship. Although Mrs. Atherfield and Miss Coleshaw assume control of the cap-tain's quarters, they do not claim their rights as emancipated women in doing so. Instead, they perform their womanly duties in the ship's domestic sphere, under the direction of the "fatherly and protecting" captain: "I gave them their places on each side of me at dinner, Mrs. Atherfield on my right and Miss Coleshaw on my left; and I directed the unmarried lady to serve out the break-fast, and the married lady to serve out the tea. Likewise I said to my black stew-ard in their presence, 'Tom Snow, these two ladies are equally the mistresses of

22. Ibid., 158.

23. According to A. G. Course, Captain Betsy Miller was "reported to be a very capable seaman and master, weathering rockbound shores in heavy gales when other vessels were shipwrecked" (*The Merchant Navy*, 221).

24. Thomas Wentworth Higginson, *Women and Her Wishes; an Essay: Inscribed to the Massachusetts Constitutional Convention* (Boston: Robert F. Wallcut, 1853), p. 9.

this house, and do you obey their orders equally;' at which . . . they all laughed" (4). While the emancipated woman demands equal rights, Dickens speaks of Mrs. Atherfield and Miss Coleshaw as "equally the mistresses of this house" and gives them "equal" authority over Tom Snow, conceding only that the women are equal to each other and superior to the black steward.

In Dickens's narrative, Mrs. Atherfield and Miss Coleshaw are separated from their menfolk and headed for a land characterized in *Household Words* as a "Utopia" for "emancipated females"—California, in particular, as a place where "a woman . . . can earn as much, or more than a man."[25] Nonetheless, neither woman seeks autonomy or a working wage. Though separated from her husband, Mrs. Atherfield hopes to be reunited with him in the West and remains a devoted mother and wife, a "little gentle woman" (9). Miss Coleshaw, although a thirty-year-old spinster, eventually reveals her reasons for emigrating in Dickens's narrative. She is not planning to join a brother, as she first tells Ravender, but is "on [her] way to marry a disgraced and broken man, whom [she] dearly loved when he was honorable and good" (10)—and hoping to mend a man's fortunes rather than seek her own.

However, the women represented in the interpolated tales of the Christmas Number more clearly threaten the status quo and develop the theme of female independence. Each of the five interpolated stories that Dickens selected from an overabundance of submissions addresses the problem of female autonomy, often associating it with betrayal.[26] In Procter's Old Seaman's ballad, for example, a shipwrecked sailor returns home only to find that his beloved wife has married one of his friends. In Parr's tale, Dick Tarrant is ruined when his cousin Amy marries his rival. Sister Jean deserts her father and brother in the story written by White, and a woman accused of sorcery is thrown overboard in Fitzgerald's narrative of the Supercargo. In Fitzgerald's second contribution, the Armourer's tale, Mary Arthur bewitches the blacksmith, encourages his advances, and then "ma[kes] him know his place" (16), rejecting him in favor of the local squire. Rejected, in turn, by the gentleman, Mary Arthur plots his murder, framing the blacksmith for her crime. With eyes that shoot fire "like a pair of stars" (14), Mary Arthur recalls the cruel woman of Petrarchan tradition, but she is also modeled on the emancipated woman of the 1850s. Educated in London, she manages "The Joyful Heart," an inn that darkly parodies the

25. [Lynn], "Rights and Wrongs," 158; [Miss Harrold and W. H. Wills], "Chip: A 'Ranch' in California," *Household Words* 3 (9 August 1851): 471.

26. On 15 December 1856, Dickens told Marguerite Power that he could not accept her submission to *Household Words* because he had on hand "a considerable residue of stories written for the Christmas No.—not suitable to it—and yet available for the general purposes of Household Words" (Pilgrim, 8:239).

domestic joys of the private home. Conflating Mary's public work with prostitution, Fitzgerald describes her as sexually transgressive, "a nice [i.e. lewd] girl," "a false, hollow jade" (16).

In Dickens's own narrative, the female character who most closely resembles Mary Arthur is the *Golden Mary* herself. At the beginning of the story, the captain explains that he is a single man. Years ago, he was engaged to a woman named Mary, but "she was too good for this world and for [him], and . . . died six weeks before [their] marriage-day" (1). But while Ravender describes himself as a bachelor, Dickens implies that he is, in effect, a married man—not simply because he cherishes the memory of his dead fiancée but because the *Golden Mary* has replaced her in his affections. As the narrator puts it in "Sailors' Homes Afloat," quoting a maritime ditty, "they're afloat, they're afloat on the fierce rolling tide, the ocean's their home, and the bark is their bride."[27]

When Ravender first sees the *Golden Mary,* her allure is immediately apparent to him. In a scene that resembles a marriage ceremony, the ship takes the place of her dead namesake in the captain's affections:

> I told [the ship owner] I had nearly decided [to accept his job proposal], but not quite. "Well, well," says he, "come down to Liverpool to-morrow with me, and see the Golden Mary." I liked the name (her name [i.e. his fiancée's] was Mary, and she was golden, if golden stands for good), so I began to feel that it was almost done when I said I would go to Liverpool. On the next morning but one we were on board the Golden Mary. . . . I declare her to have been the completest and most exquisite Beauty that ever I set my eyes upon.
>
> We had inspected every timber in her . . . when I put out my hand to my friend. "Touch upon it," says I, "and touch heartily. I take command of this ship, and I am hers." (2)

A beautiful and dutiful bride to her commander, the ship is a kind mother to her passengers as well; she is described in precisely the same terms as Mrs. Atherfield and carries her "children" in "her lap" (4).

Initially, the *Golden Mary* appears to merit the devotion of her family members. "The ship did her duty admirably" (5), Ravender remarks, praising her obedience. Nonetheless, her function and design make inevitable her violation of Dickens's feminine ideal. Unlike Mrs. Atherfield and Miss Coleshaw, the *Golden Mary* is built for work in the public domain and is far from monogamous, since any sailor on board can consider her his "bride." The wife idealized in *Household Words* is weaker than her husband, "anchored" by her trust

27. [Morley and Rinder], "Sailors' Homes Afloat," 531–32.

in and dependence on him.[28] But the *Golden Mary* is "a very fast sailer," controlled with difficulty by her crew (4), and clearly the dominant partner in her union(s).

Having empowered the *Golden Mary,* Dickens dramatizes the near fatal consequences of doing so. Betraying the trust placed in her by the passengers and crew, she deserts her husband(s) and children on the high seas. Transforming the ship from an ideal and obedient wife into an emancipated woman and, finally, into a fallen one, Dickens equates her independence with sexual promiscuity. Drawing on the sexual associations of shipwreck, a metaphor for prostitution as well as class disorder, Dickens uses the sinking vessel as an image for the fallen woman in the Christmas Number.[29] Although the captain naively asserts that "golden stands for good" when he compares the ship to his dead fiancée, Victorian readers were no doubt aware that the term "golden," as applied to women, has a double meaning and describes both virgins and whores. When, for example, Rosa Dartle confronts the fallen Emily in *David Copperfield* and accuses her of prostituting herself, she mockingly describes her as "true gold."[30] Invoking the image of the "prostitute with the heart of gold" in the Christmas Number, Dickens strips the *Golden Mary* of the sentimentalized virtues associated with this figure and suggests that she is a forgery of sorts, a cheap imitation of the captain's virgin bride.

Described as an "exquisite Beauty" by the captain (2), the *Golden Mary* resembles the prostitutes who appear in their "frills" and "finery" in *Household Words* articles on the gold rush.[31] She is gaudily dressed up by Lucy Atherfield, who treats the ship as a "doll," "tying ribbons and little bits of finery to the belaying pins" (4). After the collision, the disorderly conduct of the ship confirms our suspicions of her character. "Reeling" and "lurching" like a drunkard, she recalls the vessels described comically elsewhere in Dickens's journal, "outward-bounders" who had "been taking a parting glass" and "were rolling, and staggering, and . . . winking their port-holes at each other, and flirting their blue-peters in the air, in a way that no respectable, steady-going vessels would think of doing."[32] Indecent in her behavior, the *Golden Mary* enables Dickens

---

28. [W. H. Wills], "One of Our Legal Fictions," *Household Words* 9 (29 April 1854): 257–58.

29. In *David Copperfield* (1849–50), the prostitute Martha considers drowning herself by the water's edge, and Hablot Browne's illustration of the scene places the degraded woman next to "the rotting skeleton of a boat," an emblem of the disease and decay associated with prostitution. See Lynda Nead, *Myths of Sexuality: Representations of Women in Victorian Britain* (Oxford: Basil Blackwell, 1988), p. 127.

30. Charles Dickens, *David Copperfield,* ed. Trevor Blount (1966; reprint, Harmondsworth: Penguin, 1980), p. 789.

31. See, for example, [Louisa Anne Meredith], "Shadows of the Golden Image," *Household Words* 15 (4 April 1857): 316.

32. [John Capper], "Off to the Diggings," *Household Words* 5 (17 July 1852): 407.

to displace the class tensions among the men in his story with the conflict between a loose woman and her husband(s). Before the sailors have a chance to desert their ship, the ship deserts the sailors, abandoning them on the high seas. As Captain Ravender recounts in Dickens's narrative, "We could hardly have felt more shocked and solitary than we did when we knew we were alone on the wide ocean, and that the beautiful ship in which most of us had been securely asleep within half an hour was gone" (6–7).

In abandoning her captain, crew, and passengers, the *Golden Mary* deserts her proper place but also evades her proper use—as a sexual resource to be "mined." Indeed, the central motif of the Christmas Number, that of the "golden" woman, depends on the analogy between the precious metals of mother earth and the riches of female sexuality, a connection realized by means of the "Golden Lucy," who testifies to the wealth of her mother's womb.[33] Yet the failure to exploit Mary's "golden" resources in the story is due not only to female rebellion but also to the deviant form of manhood that Mr. Rarx, the miser, embodies. Although Rarx treasures the gold that the female figures embody, he does so for the wrong reasons: to hoard and worship it rather than mine and coin it. His character enables Dickens to displace class conflict in yet another way—by foregrounding the dangers posed to patriarchy and social order by what he implicitly represents as the deviance of the Jew.

Introduced by Dickens as a human predator of sorts—"an old gentleman, a good deal like a hawk if his eyes had been better and not so red"—Mr. Rarx is "always talking, morning, noon, and night, about the gold discovery. But, whether he was making the voyage, thinking his old arms could dig for gold, or whether his speculation was to buy it, or, to barter for it, or to cheat for it, or to snatch it anyhow from other people, was his secret. He kept his secret" (3). Two years before Dickens composed this passage, a writer for the *Jewish Chronicle,* citing the example of Fagin, asked "why Jews alone should be excluded from 'the sympathizing heart' of this great author."[34] Anxious to defend

33. In a host of articles Dickens published about mining, the mineral riches of the earth are sexualized and exploited, and compared to the reproductive wealth of womankind. "Mines are spoken of in the feminine gender," one such article explains: "'Oh! she's a wonderful mine! Mr. Moneyman, of Exeter, is getting his nine thousand a-year out of her.' Or, 'I'm afraid she's almost knocked'—(up)" ([Edmund Saul Dixon], "If This Should Meet His Eye," *Household Words* 4 [13 March 1852]: 598). In Morley's "Change for a Sovereign" (*Household Words* 5 [5 June 1852]: 279–80), Mother Earth appears as a subservient yet generous woman who freely serves gold to the men sitting at her table (280). As G. J. Barker-Benfield explains in discussing Victorian medical and religious tracts, precious minerals serve as "common images for . . . woman's and the continent's body," "link[ing] them together as areas viewed by men as exploitable in the same way, and as expressions of man's mastery over his own resources." See "The Spermatic Economy: A Nineteenth-Century View of Sexuality," in *The American Family in Social-Historical Perspective,* ed. Michael Gordon, 2d ed. (New York: St. Martin's Press, 1978), p. 382.

34. Quoted by Baumgarten, "Seeing Double," p. 50.

himself against charges of anti-Semitism, yet eager to invoke its cultural power in the face of class unrest, Dickens draws on anti-Semitic stereotypes in his portrait of Mr. Rarx but without any direct acknowledgment. As Jonathan H. Grossman notes in discussing "the possibility of Scrooge's Jewishness," critics ought not to "see . . . a veiled Jew or a racist portrait in every [Dickens] character with stereotypical Jewish traits," since Christian figures with such traits might be intended to subvert anti-Semitic stereotypes.[35] But while Mr. Rarx, like Scrooge, is never labeled a Jew, Dickens emphasizes his disbelief in Christ and the Resurrection (9) while also endowing him with stereotypically Jewish traits: an obsession with gold, a predilection for shady financial practices, and the aberrant sexual desires associated with hoarding one's treasure rather than making productive use of it.

Like the "anti-Semite's Jew" described by Judith Halberstam, Mr. Rarx is both a sexual and an economic parasite and refuses to let his wealth circulate as it should.[36] His deviance is common knowledge in Dickens's narrative: "Old Mr. Rarx was not a pleasant man to look at, nor yet to talk to, or to be with," Ravender asserts, "for no one could help seeing that he was a sordid and selfish character, and that he had warped further and further out of the straight with time" (4). More specifically, Mr. Rarx seems anxious to possess a "golden" girl instead of a grown woman and thus appears a pedophile rather than a husband and father, his perversity as great a problem for patriarchy as the autonomy of women who claim their sexual resources as their own. Having described the "astonishing interest" Mr. Rarx takes "in the child"—an interest that is neither welcome nor paternal—Dickens envisions them in a romantic triangle of sorts: "If the Golden Mary felt a tenderness for the dear old gentleman she carried in her lap, she must be bitterly jealous of the Golden Lucy" (4).

In the Christmas Number, Collins rather than Dickens develops the sexual implications of such passages, when representing the delirium of Mr. Rarx. For his own part, Dickens chooses to explain Mr. Rarx's attraction to Lucy as a spiritual offense, dropping what he may have seen as an overly provocative approach to the subject. Puzzled by the miser's interest in the young girl—his way of "look[ing] at her and touch[ing] her, as if she was something precious to him" (4)—Dickens's Ravender discovers its cause. Defined against the Christians who place their faith in "His merciful goodness," Mr. Rarx proves to be an idolatrous descendant of the Israelites who worshipped the Golden

35. Grossman, "The Absent Jew," 51, 55 n. 13.

36. Judith Halberstam, "Technologies of Monstrosity: Bram Stoker's *Dracula*," *Victorian Studies* 36, 3 (spring 1993): 337, 346. Halberstam discusses the sexual and economic "parasitism" of the Jew as represented in the Victorian discourse of anti-Semitism, as does Sander L. Gilman in *The Jew's Body* (New York: Routledge, 1991).

Calf. He values the "Golden Lucy" because he superstitiously believes that she can save him from destruction: "We so discovered with amazement, that this old wretch had only cared for the life of the pretty little creature dear to all of us, because of the influence he superstitiously hoped she might have in preserving him! Altogether it was too much for the smith or armourer, who was sitting next the old man, to bear. He took him by the throat and rolled him under the thwarts, where he lay still enough for hours afterwards" (9).

Assaulted by the armourer and threatened by the captain, loathed by the women as well as the men, Mr. Rarx is the ultimate scapegoat, a common enemy whose deviance—variously represented as sexual, economic, and spiritual—is implicitly defined as that of the racial other. Comparing the miser to the sailors and to the women passengers, Dickens identifies him as the primary threat to social order on the *Golden Mary*. After the ship's collision, the sailors "fall towards their appointed stations, like good men and true," and Mrs. Atherfield and Miss Coleshaw, "quiet and perfectly collected," set "an example" to their companions (6). But Captain Ravender finds Mr. Rarx utterly "ungovernable" (9):

> He had made a lamentation and uproar which it was dangerous for the people to hear, as there is always contagion in weakness and selfishness. His incessant cry had been that he must not be separated from the child. . . . He had even tried to wrest the child out of my arms, that he might keep her in his. "Mr. Rarx," said I to him when it came to that, "I have a loaded pistol in my pocket; and if you don't stand out of the gangway, and keep perfectly quiet, I shall shoot you through the heart, if you have got one." Says he, "You won't do murder, Captain Ravender?" "No sir," says I, "I won't murder forty-four people to humour you, but I'll shoot you to save them." (6)

A source of "contagion" to "the people," a figure whose death would ensure their salvation, Mr. Rarx is set apart from all others on the *Golden Mary* and his exclusion defines their community—as Christians who pray together, regardless of their class or gender differences (7). Mr. Rarx thus performs the same function as the savages described near the start of the Christmas Number, whose treachery and death dramatize the solidarity of the captain and mate. Introducing Steadiman, Ravender praises him as "the man who . . . struck a Malay and a Maltese dead, as they were gliding with their knives down the cabin stair aboard the barque Old England, when the captain lay ill in his cot, off Saugar Point . . . and give him his back against a bulwark, he would have done the same by half a dozen of them" (3).

As this passage suggests, the mate's allegiance to the captain is ensured by means of the threatening others against whom the English officers are defined and whose presence elides the conflicts that exist "aboard the barque Old England." For as the story of the *Bounty* reveals, English sailors and officers, like Malays and Maltese, can turn against their captain, regardless of the nationality they share. In Collins's portion of the Christmas Number, as in Dickens's own, the potential for insurrection among crew and officers goes largely unrealized. Following Dickens's lead, Collins obscures class differences and unifies Englishmen by dramatizing the deviance and death of Mr. Rarx and the successful "mining" of Mrs. Atherfield by her husband, who coins a second "Golden Lucy." In Collins's conclusion, however, the class tensions that underlie the story finally emerge, as the sailors desert Ravender, and the captain himself is stripped of his authority: a reminder that one prototype for John Steadiman is Fletcher Christian, Captain Bligh's mutinous first officer.

IV

While Dickens designs "The Wreck of the Golden Mary" to displace the problem of labor unrest in the merchant marine, he also intends it to imaginatively resolve another, and more personal, labor dispute, obscuring his status as a literary entrepreneur as well as Collins's discontent as a hired hand. As the owner of 50 percent of *Household Words*—"a *good property*" that "'goes,' in the trade phrase, admirably" (Pilgrim, 6:83)—Dickens profited from the labors of his subordinates in a way that they simply could not. But in the Christmas Number, Dickens pointedly notes that Captain Ravender, though a labor manager, is not a capitalist and does not own the *Golden Mary*. Rather, the ship belongs to the Liverpool House of Smithick and Waterby, and both Ravender and Steadiman are hired by representatives of that firm. Furthermore, while Collins objected to the job he was offered at *Household Words,* in part, because of the anonymity that reduced writers to hired hands, Dickens represents Steadiman as a unique and irreplaceable officer, and Ravender will take command of the *Golden Mary* only if he "can get John Steadiman for [his] chief mate" (2). Whereas Collins negotiated with Dickens before accepting his staff position, Steadiman accepts the captain's offer without hesitation in Dickens's narrative; the mate will "sail round the world with [Ravender] for twenty years if [he] hoist[s] the signal, and stand by [him] for ever!" (3).

Dickens was well aware that his portrait of Steadiman was a wishful construction of Collins. In describing the composition of the Christmas Number to Angela Burdett-Coutts in December 1856, for example, Dickens not only speaks of Collins as Steadiman (Pilgrim, 8:231, 234) but expresses a mixture of admiration for, and "mistrust" of, his subordinate:

> You delight me by what you say of the Golden Mary. It strikes me as the pretti-
> est Christmas No. we have had; and I think the way in which John Steadiman (to
> whom I shall give your message) has got over the great difficulty of falling into
> my idea, naturally, is very meritorious indeed. Of course he could not begin until
> I had finished; and when he read the Wreck he was so desperately afraid of the
> job, that I began to mistrust him. However, we went down to Gad's Hill and
> walked through Cobham Woods, to talk it over; and he then went at it cheer-
> fully, and came out as you see. I wish you would read a Petition to the Novel
> Writers (by him) in last week's Household Words. It strikes me as uncommonly
> droll, and shrewdly true. (Pilgrim, 8:234)

As this account of the story's production reveals, its treatment of authority and obedience is based, in part, on the collaborative relationship of Dickens and Collins and the inequities between them. Although Collins wrote as much of the story as Dickens did, his role is clearly defined as secondary and subordi-nate. While Collins's efforts are, again, "meritorious," Dickens makes it clear that the idea for the story (its originality) was his own and that Collins "could not begin" until he had completed his own section ("The Wreck"). In speak-ing of his "mistrust" of Collins, Dickens clearly means to convey an image of the younger writer intimidated by the task set before him ("desperately afraid of the job"). Yet the word also suggests Dickens's reluctance to wholly trust his subordinate. Collins may not simply be "afraid of the job," an intimidated ap-prentice; he may also resent its terms and the manner in which Dickens mini-mizes his role in the collaboration, acknowledging his authorship at *Household Words,* at best, in parentheses: "I wish you would read a Petition to the Novel Writers (by him) in last week's Household Words."

  In the account he provides to Burdett-Coutts, Dickens claims that his "mis-trust" is unfounded; Collins ultimately proves "meritorious," in large part be-cause of his willing subordination—his ability to "fall . . . into my idea," as Dickens puts it. According to Dickens, Collins went at his work "cheerfully," as contented as the common sailors aboard the *Golden Mary.* Yet Dickens con-veys his mistrust of his subordinate in the story itself: perhaps most obviously, in his choice of Bligh as a prototype for Ravender—and, by implication, of Christian for Steadiman. Although neither Dickens nor Collins explicitly refers to Bligh's mutinous first mate, his presence is palpable in a number of scenes in which Steadiman replaces Ravender at the helm or gains the authority due to the captain.

For example, Dickens describes the way in which the first mate replaces the captain in the affections of the passengers, particularly Lucy Atherfield: "I am bound to admit that John Steadiman and I were borne on her pretty little books in reverse order," Ravender concedes, "and that he was captain there, and I was mate" (3). A more literal reversal occurs on the night of the shipwreck, with disastrous results. At Steadiman's urging, Ravender goes below after eight nights on watch, leaving the mate in charge. Although Ravender warns him of an ominous change—that "the waves, as the Golden Mary parted them and shook them off, had a hollow sound in them"—the mate discounts his captain's observation: "Rely upon it, Captain Ravender, you have been without rest too long, and the novelty is only in the state of your sense of hearing" (5). But almost immediately after Steadiman assumes command in Dickens's narrative, the ship strikes an iceberg and begins to sink. Ravender later attempts to acquit his mate of wrongdoing and claims that "the circumstances were altogether without warning and out of any course that could have been guarded against" (10). Nonetheless, Dickens constructs the collision scene in such a way that readers associate the wreck with Steadiman's assumption of authority, reinforcing our sense of the captain's rightful command and superior abilities. Like the "inimitable" Charles Dickens, Ravender simply cannot be replaced.[37]

As Dickens's subordinate, and as a writer who claimed to embrace republican ideals, Collins was considerably more willing to imagine curtailing a captain's authority than Dickens was, as his 1855 story about sailing life, "The Cruise of the Tomtit," makes clear. Rather than praising common sailors for their obedience to their captain, or idealizing the authority of their officers, Collins levels these hierarchical relationships. Referring to "We Mariners of England," a *Household Words* article about labor unrest in the British merchant marine, Collins proposes a radical solution to the conflict between officers and men, imagining a "pure republic" in which the divide between management and labor is unknown.[38] On the *Tomtit,* Collins explains, no one is defined as master or servant, but everyone takes their turn as both: "No man in particular among us is master—no man in particular is servant. The man who can do at the right time, and in the best way, the thing that is most wanted, is always the hero of the situation among us. . . . Such is the perfect constitution of society at which we mariners of England have been able to arrive."[39] Naming his central characters "Jollins" and "Migott," Collins modeled "The Cruise of the

37. Trodd makes this point as well, noting that Dickens used Bligh as a prototype for Ravender to suggest "the indispensability of exceptional men with rare skills"—Dickens himself included ("Collaborating in Open Boats," 222).

38. [Wilkie Collins], "The Cruise of the Tomtit," *Household Words* 12 (22 December 1855): 495.

39. Ibid.

Tomtit" on his own experience of sailing with, and working for, Edward Pigott, editor of the *Leader,* whose democratic approach to editorial matters provided a striking contrast to that of Dickens at *Household Words.*[40]

Despite his praise for the "pure republic" on the *Tomtit,* a "perfect" society in which the roles of master and servant rotate among all men, Collins helps Dickens idealize a very different kind of social order in the 1856 Christmas Number, one in which authority and submission are valorized and vested in particular figures. While noting Steadiman's "jealousy" of Captain Ravender (11), Collins generally supports the hierarchical relationship between them and between the officers and their men. Praising Ravender's authority, Collins portrays him as a commander who always puts the interests of his subordinates before his own. Although Collins feared that Dickens would get the credit for his own writing, and objected to the "confusion of authorship" at *Household Words,* the first mate in Collins's narrative speaks of the captain as a man who continually credits his subordinates for the work he has himself performed: "Not one but had heard [the captain], over and over again, give the credit to others which was due only to himself; praising this man for patience, and thanking that man for help, when the patience and the help had really and truly . . . come only from him" (13). After Ravender falls ill and loses consciousness, Collins's first mate takes "[his] Captain's vacant place at the helm" (13) but does so regretfully, aware of his own limitations and convinced of Ravender's superior qualities: "There, worn out at last in our service, and for our sakes, lay the best and bravest man of all our company" (12).

In his narrative, Collins more fully acknowledges the threatening disorder of the men than Dickens does but describes it from an officer's point of view, as Steadiman strives to control "the people" under his charge in the surfboat, "command[ing] them to be silent" (11), "sen[ding] them to their places" (13), and plagued by fears that the men will turn on their officers. "I thought they were going mad and turning violent against me," Steadiman reports of the common sailors, before trying to "shame the men back to their proper senses" (32–33). Like Dickens, Collins defuses the threat of class unrest by turning from the "madness" of the sailors to the "delirium" of Mr. Rarx, whose deviance is even more marked in Collins's portion of the story than in Dickens's. Proving, as always, an exceptional "case," the "tough and greedy old sinner" rallies his strength in Collins's narrative, "swallow[ing] his share [of water] with a gulp that many a younger and better man in the boat might have envied," and Collins describes the animated yet perverse "maundering" that results:

40. Kirk Beetz discusses Collins's relationship to Pigott, Collins's input on the organization and content of the *Leader,* and its "'Red Republicanism'" in "Wilkie Collins and *The Leader," Victorian Periodicals Review* 15, 1 (spring 1982): 20–29.

He fancied now that he was digging a gold mine, all by himself, and going down bodily straight through the earth at the rate of thirty or forty miles an hour. "Leave me alone," says he, "leave me alone. The lower I go, the richer I get. Down I go!—down, down, down, down, till I burst out at the other end of the world in a shower of gold!" So he went on, kicking feebly with his heels from time to time against the bottom of the boat. (30)

With this image of the repugnant Mr. Rarx digging for gold "all by himself," Collins treats economic self-interest as if it were a symptom of the miser's pathology rather than a guiding principle of capitalism. Collins uses Rarx's greed as a foil for the communal efforts of the other characters as they band together during a storm, hoisting a makeshift sail and "join[ing] their voices" in the hope of being heard by a distant ship (33).

At the same time, Collins uses Mr. Rarx to sexualize the dangers facing his characters and to reconceive a class conflict as a threat to patriarchy. Developing the theme introduced by Dickens, Collins treats the miser's greed as the sign of sexual as well as economic self-interest: in effect, an unwillingness to father. Despite its images of mining and penetration ("going down bodily straight through the earth"), Mr. Rarx's fantasy of economic and sexual fulfillment, which culminates in "a shower of gold," is achieved in isolation and identifies him as a "self-abuser."[41] Conflating the miser's "solitary vice" with his interest in the prepubescent Lucy, and dramatizing his fears of drowning and engulfment at "the bottom of the shaft," Collins reveals Mr. Rarx's anxieties about female sexuality and emphasizes his failure to properly exploit the resources of mother earth:

> To hear him now . . . he was still down in his gold-mine; but was laden so heavy with his precious metal that he could not get out, and was in mortal peril of being drowned by the water rising in the bottom of the shaft. . . . He swore he saw the white frock of our poor little lost pet fluttering in the daylight, at the top of the mine, and he screamed out to her in a great fright that the gold was heavy, and the water rising fast, and that she must come down quick as lightning if she meant to be in time to help him. . . . "Quick, Golden Lucy!" screams Mr. Rarx. . . . "Quick! my darling, my beauty, quick! The gold is heavy, and the water rises fast! Come down and save me, Golden Lucy! Let all the rest of the world drown, and save me! Me! me! me! me!" (34)

Rather than answering the prayers of Mr. Rarx, Collins dramatizes his death, as he is swept away by a tremendous wave. The miser's removal marks the

---

41. For a discussion of the miser's "sexual deviance" in Victorian representations, and the relation between his greed and the "solitary vice" of masturbation, see Jeff Nunokawa, "The Miser's Two Bodies: *Silas Marner* and the Sexual Possibilities of the Commodity," *Victorian Studies* 36, 3 (spring 1993): 274.

restoration of patriarchal norms, and Steadiman ends his narrative by "tell[ing] the reader what . . . he will be glad to hear": that Mr. Atherfield, reunited with his wife, has mined a second "Golden Lucy" from her abundant stores: "Another Golden Lucy! Her hair was a shade or two darker than the hair of my poor little pet . . . but in all other respects the living child reminded me so strongly of the dead, that I quite started at the first sight of her" (36).

Despite the death of Mr. Rarx, however, and the coining of a second Golden Lucy, Collins does not bring the Christmas Number to its end as neatly as Dickens might wish. Unlike the collaborative stories for which Dickens wrote the final sections—"The Perils of Certain English Prisoners," for example, and "No Thoroughfare"—"The Wreck of the Golden Mary" ends on a discordant note. Recalling the disgruntled crews described in such articles as "Sailor's Homes Afloat," who exhibit their discontent by deserting their vessels, most of the sailors in "The Wreck of the Golden Mary" become deserters at the con- clusion of Collins's narrative, refusing to return to port. "When Rames and I proposed going back to port," Steadiman recounts, "we two, and five of our steadiest seamen, were all the officers and crew left to meet the Captain on his return from the inland country" (36). Collins blames the desertion of the sailors on the "contagion" of the miser, explaining that they "seemed bitten by old Mr. Rarx's mania for gold" (36). Yet his own depiction of their violence and agitation in the open boats suggests a class rebellion, as does the fate he reserves for Captain Ravender. While Steadiman never mutinies against his captain, Collins forces Ravender to relinquish his authority at the conclusion of the Christmas Number. Whereas Steadiman finds his services "snapped up eagerly" and is "offered any rate [he] chose to set on [them]," the captain returns to England "in the capacity of passenger only" (36). Relegated to a deck chair by Collins, Ravender learns that his authority can, indeed, be vested in another commander and that an "inimitable" leader can prove expendable after all.

In his conclusion to "The Wreck of the Golden Mary," Collins does not openly rebel against Dickens or undermine his aims, but he divests Dickens's fictional persona of authority and casts the allegiance of the captain's subordi- nates into doubt. In The Frozen Deep, the melodrama on which he and Dickens were already at work when "The Wreck of the Golden Mary" appeared, Collins more fully develops the theme of mutiny and class conflict than he does in the Christmas Number, while Dickens suppresses it in revising Collins's draft. As a work that Dickens and Collins took turns authoring and revising over a period of nearly twenty years, The Frozen Deep more clearly reveals the differences between the two writers than any other collaboration and charts the history of their working relationship.

CHAPTER 3

The Cannibal, the Nurse, and the Cook:

Variants of *The Frozen Deep*

On 3 October 1856, three days after he sent his scheme of "The Wreck of the Golden Mary" to prospective contributors, Dickens wrote to Angela Burdett-Coutts, describing the "immense excitement" created at his home, Tavistock House, when Collins arrived "with the first two acts of his play in three": "Dispatches were sent off to Brighton, to announce the fact. Charley exhibited an insane desire to copy it. There was talk of a Telegraph Message to Mr. Stanfield in Wales. It is called The Frozen Deep, and is extremely clever and interesting—very serious and very curious" (Pilgrim, 8:199). The excitement that the new play raised in the Dickens circle was understandable; Dickens's two daughters, then in Brighton, would be anxious to hear about rehearsals, since they both had roles in the melodrama, as did Charley, the eldest son. Clarkson Stanfield, the scene painter for the play, would need to know of Collins's progress. But as Dickens comically suggests in speaking of "dispatches . . . to Brighton" and "telegraph message[s] to . . . Wales"—and, later, in describing Tavistock House in a "state of siege" during rehearsals (Pilgrim, 8:242)—he perceived *The Frozen Deep* to be a source of national as well as domestic excitement. Indeed, Dickens conceived of the melodrama as a defense of the national honor; it was to safeguard the values embodied by Sir John Franklin and his lost band of Arctic explorers, national heroes in whom he had long been interested and on whose experiences the melodrama was loosely based, but who were alleged to have become cannibals in their failed struggle to survive.

Not only did these allegations sully the memory of Franklin, who had fought with Nelson at Trafalgar and governed Van Dieman's Land. More generally, they threatened social and imperial ideals. Because cannibalism was associated with the most primitive of cultures, the charges leveled against the Arctic ex-plorers called into question the moral justification of empire and blurred the boundary between the savage and the civilized. And because cannibalism was a well-established metaphor for social revolution, widely used by Victorians to represent class warfare, the allegations also subverted the image of class harmony associated with such imperial ventures as the Franklin expedition.[1]

An experienced colonial administrator and Arctic explorer, Franklin began his fourth search for the Northwest Passage in May 1845, commanding 128 sailors and officers of the Royal Navy. Sailing on the *Erebus* and the *Terror,* the members of the expedition left England with provisions for three years. Three years later, English officials had received no word from the men, last seen in July 1845, and a series of rescue parties were dispatched. Not until 1853 did one such party, led by Dr. John Rae of the Hudson's Bay Company, find evidence of Franklin's fate and earn the reward of ten thousand pounds offered by the government.

It was during his third attempt to track the lost Arctic explorers, while trav-eling in the area known as Repulse Bay, that Rae encountered a group of Eskimos who "place[d] the fate of . . . Sir John Franklin's long-lost party be-yond a doubt—a fate as terrible as the imagination can conceive."[2] When asked about having seen white men, they volunteered information about the Franklin expedition that they had gathered at second hand. These Eskimos, and others Rae met later that year, had heard about a group of approximately forty white men, seen dragging a boat and sledges near King William's Land three years be-fore. The whites had indicated to the Eskimos by signs that their ships had been destroyed by ice, and that they were traveling to a hunting ground, where they hoped to shoot deer. They appeared thin and were running short of provisions; having purchased a seal from the Eskimos, they moved on. Later in the season, near the mouth of the Great Fish River, Eskimos came upon the bodies of ap-proximately thirty white men as well as a number of graves. Some of the bod-ies were mutilated, and the Eskimos believed that they were in this condition because the whites had resorted to cannibalism; they found what they thought to be human flesh in the kettles nearby. Although none of the Eskimos whom

---

1. Lee Sterrenburg discusses cannibalism as a metaphor for social revolution as well as Dickens's rep-resentation of cannibal revolution in *A Tale of Two Cities* in "Psychoanalysis and the Iconography of Revolution," *Victorian Studies* 19 (December 1975): 241–64. James E. Marlow discusses Dickens's use of cannibalism to critique the capitalist system in "English Cannibalism: Dickens after 1859," *Studies in English Literature* 23 (autumn 1983): 647–66.

2. John Rae, M.D., "Report to the Secretary of the Admiralty," *Times* (London), 23 October 1854, 7. A version of Rae's report was published by Dickens the following year, as "Sir John Franklin and His Crew," *Household Words* 11 (3 February 1855): 12–20.

Dr. Rae met claimed to have seen the white men or their corpses, some possessed articles that belonged to members of the Franklin expedition. Rae purchased these and brought them home to England. His report, dated 29 July 1854, was published in the London *Times* on 23 October, immediately after his return.

One week later, on 1 November 1854, Dickens expressed his disbelief in Rae's report. Writing to Mrs. Richard Watson, he said that he found Rae's account "deeply interesting" but "hasty in its acceptance of the details—particularly in the statement that [the explorers] had eaten the dead bodies of their companions. Which I don't believe" (Pilgrim, 7:455–56). Later that month, Dickens wrote to Wills, asking him for a newspaper cutting of Rae's report: "It has occurred to me that I am rather strong on Voyages and Cannibalism, and might do an interesting little paper for next No. on that part of Dr. Rae's report; taking the arguments against its probabilities" (Pilgrim, 7:470). The "interesting little paper" eventually developed into a series of seven articles, of which Dickens wrote two, Morley wrote two, and Rae three. In this series, Rae defends his allegations while Dickens contests them, vindicating the explorers.[3]

Having sent two of his articles to Franklin's widow in 1854, Dickens received a memoir of the explorer from her in February 1856. The memoir was written by fellow explorer Sir John Richardson, and Dickens found Richardson's "manly friendship, and love of Franklin, one of the noblest things [he] ever knew in [his] life" (Pilgrim, 8:66). Unwilling to let the subject drop, Dickens conceived the idea of staging the nobility of the Arctic explorers at Tavistock House, where he and his friends had performed amateur theatricals on Twelfth Night since 1851, and he recruited Collins for this purpose. Collins seemed the obvious choice, since his melodrama "The Lighthouse" had been performed at Tavistock House in January 1856. "Collins and I have a mighty original notion (mine in the beginning) for another Play at Tavistock House," Dickens told Wills on 6 April. "I purpose opening on Twelfth night, the theatrical season of that great establishment" (Pilgrim, 8:81). "You . . . may be induced to take some interest in what I dare say you never saw—the growth of a play from the beginning," Dickens wrote to Burdett-Coutts on 13 May: "Mr. Collins and I have hammered out a curious idea for a new one, which he is to write, and

3. In their order of appearance, Dickens's articles are "The Lost Arctic Voyagers" (2 and 9 December 1854): 361–65 and 385–93; and Morley's are "The Lost English Sailors," *Household Words* 15 (14 February 1857): 145–47 and "Official Patriotism," *Household Words* 15 (25 April 1857): 385–90. Dr. Rae's articles are "The Lost Arctic Voyagers," *Household Words* 10 (23 December 1854): 433–37; "Dr. Rae's Report," *Household Words* 10 (30 December 1854): 457–59; and "Sir John Franklin and His Crews," *Household Words* 11 (3 February 1855): 12–20. Dickens acknowledged Rae's authorship in each of his three articles.

which we purpose, please God, to bring out on Charley's birthday" (Pilgrim, 8:118).

As Dickens conceived of it, Collins's play would dramatize the revisionist history of the Franklin expedition that he had related in *Household Words*. In his articles about the Arctic explorers, Dickens exonerated them from Rae's charges by suggesting that they were set upon and killed by Eskimos rather than by members of their own party, and Dickens's letters from 1856 reveal that he expected Collins to tell essentially the same story. While his own journal articles unified the explorers by pitting them against savage Eskimos, Collins's play would achieve the same end by defining officers and sailors against a primitive Highland woman, a character first mentioned by Dickens, who claimed credit for her creation.

But in his draft of *The Frozen Deep*, Collins does not simply deny the allegations leveled against the explorers; he examines their grounds and acknowledges their strength. Like shipwrecked men forced to the "last resource," who drew lots to determine who would be killed and consumed, Collins's explorers hold a lottery in act 2. They do so to decide who will form a search party, not who will be devoured, yet Collins acknowledges their potential for cannibalism by means of this scene. At the same time, he contrasts the privileges of the officers with the privations of the sailors, on whose labor the officers subsist.

To an extent, Collins weakens this contrast by means of Nurse Esther, the menacing Highland woman whom Dickens suggested he include in his cast. A native and a "devouring mother," she embodies the threat of racial and sexual difference and is tied to the cannibals referred to in Dr. Rae's report. Yet Collins also grants Esther the prophetic powers of second sight, representing her as a visionary of sorts, both barbarous and more perceptive than the English ladies and gentlemen who disparage her. Furthermore, he connects the nurse with John Want, the cook on the expedition; the two are disgruntled workers expected to feed their social superiors even if they themselves starve.

Dickens's letters to Collins from September 1856 register his sense that their ideas were diverging and show him trying to guide Collins in constructing the play—suggesting that Collins curtail the power of the nurse's visions, for example, and foreground the heroic manhood of the explorers (Pilgrim, 8:184–85, 186). Once Dickens had Collins's manuscript in hand, he heavily revised it, changing the language and behavior of Nurse Esther to discredit her and heightening her otherness as the barbarous "Scotch woman." He largely suppressed Collins's representations of class conflict among the explorers and rewrote the exchange between the cook and the nurse to emphasize their racial and sexual differences. As the play was performed both privately and in public theaters in 1857, it differed substantially from Collins's draft and largely supported Dickens's heroic conception of the explorers. Only by revising *The Frozen Deep* in 1866 and 1874, without Dickens's supervision, was Collins able to restore the deleted material and develop his own conception of the failed expedition that originally inspired the play, while also pointing the story in a new direction. Written four years after Dickens's death, the final version of *The Frozen Deep* is characteristic of Collins's later work. Making the female visionary his heroine, Collins uses her to address what had become, by the 1870s, his primary literary theme: the problem of gender inequities.

While accounts of Franklin and his men provided Dickens and Collins with primary source material for the melodrama, so, too, did their own collaborative relationship.[4] First written and revised in 1856, at virtually the same time as "The Wreck of the Golden Mary," *The Frozen Deep* in its earliest versions provides another self-conscious portrait of Dickens and Collins at work together as they negotiated the terms of Collins's staff position. As in the 1856 Christmas Number, the two writers use a contemporary crisis to represent their working relationship and mediate their own differences. But while "The Wreck of the Golden Mary" largely idealizes their connection, *The Frozen Deep* represents them as antagonists, at least until the final scene. Before Collins began to draft the play, he and Dickens agreed on its basic premise. Richard Wardour, to be played by Dickens, would discover that the woman he planned to marry had secretly become engaged. Wardour would join the expedition on which his rival was about to embark without knowing the man's identity. Accidentally discovering him in Frank Aldersley, to be played by Collins, Wardour would plan his revenge but ultimately prove the hero, saving Aldersley at the cost of his own life.

A study in male rivalry, *The Frozen Deep* differs from "The Wreck of the Golden Mary" in depicting the relationship between Dickens and Collins as overtly antagonistic. Yet it also redefines the grounds on which their antagonism was based. Aldersley is not Wardour's aspiring subordinate but his fellow officer, and their hostility is caused by a woman, not by economic or professional inequities. Nonetheless, Collins uses signs of class difference to portray their antagonism. In Collins's draft, Wardour discovers his rival's identity while performing the labor of a common sailor and expresses his hatred of Aldersley in the language of class resentment. In having him do so, Collins contrasts the

---

4. Sue Lonoff makes this point, treating "the denouement of *The Frozen Deep*" as "a vivid and revealing symbol of the friendship between the two writers." See "Charles Dickens and Wilkie Collins," *Nineteenth-Century Fiction* 35 (September 1980): 150. Jean Ferguson Carr approaches the play as a "forum" for Dickens's psychological "secrets" in "Dickens's Theatre of Self-Knowledge," in *Dramatic Dickens,* ed. Carol Hanbery MacKay (New York: St. Martin's Press, 1989), p. 27.

privileges of the officers with the deprivations of their men but also gives his dramatic persona the advantages usually enjoyed by Dickens's. In the collaborative works they had already authored, Dickens plays the affluent gentleman to Collins's "shabby-genteel personage" and the captain to Collins's first mate. But in his draft of *The Frozen Deep*, Collins reverses their customary positions. Although Aldersley ultimately proves to be dependent on and indebted to Wardour, who heroically nurtures him in his time of need, Collins's role had its consolations and allowed him to play the idle gentleman to Dickens's common and resentful laborer.

I

The conception of heroic self-sacrifice that Wardour ultimately embodies was largely drawn from imperial myths of Arctic exploration, often treated by Victorians as an example of British civilization at its best. Although European merchants had originally funded Arctic exploration in the hopes of finding gold as well as a commercially useful Northwest Passage, it was generally represented among Victorians as a scientific rather than an economic undertaking, the responsibility and the pride of the British Navy and the British Empire. A patriotic endeavor, it was thought to unify the social classes and suggested that their interests were one and the same.[5]

As the editor of *Household Words*, Dickens supported this idealized picture of Arctic exploration. In 1850, the journal's first year, he published R. H. Horne's "Arctic Heroes: A Fragment of Naval History." A brief dialogue between ill-fated explorers, "Arctic Heroes" is ennobled by blank verse and portrays two men trapped in "a stupendous region of icebergs and snow," who courageously face suffering and death, affirming their "endurance and resolve, which make / The power and glory of us Englishmen."[6] Morley's "Our Phantom Ship Among the Ice," published a year later, surveys the history of Arctic exploration and claims that Parry and Ross "encounter[ed] peril . . . for the gain of knowledge, for the highest kind of service that can now be rendered to the human race."[7] In Morley's "Unspotted Snow," the whiteness of the Arctic snow becomes an emblem of the moral purity of "deeds done in their clime": "The history of Arctic enterprise is stainless as the Arctic snows, clean to the core as an

5. For a discussion of Arctic exploration as a "national enterprise," see Chauncey C. Loomis, "The Arctic Sublime," in *Nature and the Victorian Imagination,* ed. U. C. Knoepflmacher and G. B. Tennyson (Berkeley: University of California Press, 1977), pp. 95–96.

6. [Richard H. Horne], "Arctic Heroes: A Fragment of Naval History," *Household Words* 1 (27 April 1850): 108.

7. [Henry Morley], "Our Phantom Ship Among the Ice," *Household Words* 3 (12 April 1851): 67.

ice mountain." Arctic exploration enables rich and poor to transcend their class differences and "help forward [their] race": "men who are elsewhere enemies and rivals hold Arctic ground . . . to be sacred to the noblest spirit of humanity," and hence no mutiny has ever "polluted" it.[8]

Having helped to idealize the Arctic explorers and their stainless history, Dickens was confronted with the sordid realities of Dr. Rae's report, which called attention to the undisciplined state of Franklin's crew members and suggested that they would have mutinied under privation. Rae's vision of the explorers cannibalizing one another conjured up frightening images of mutiny and class war. In describing the straggling band, last seen hauling their sledge over the snow, Rae distinguished between the "stout" officer in command and the thin men doing the work.[9] Such distinctions are common to myths of a cannibal revolution, in which the members of the upper class feed off their workers until the workers, in turn, cannibalize their masters.[10]

Like many of his contemporaries—for example, the Reverend Edward J. Hornby, whose angry letters to the London *Times* appeared in October and November 1854—Dickens "wished to be able to disbelieve" Rae's allegations.[11] He realized this wish by retelling, with Morley, Franklin's tale in a series of *Household Words* articles: "The Lost Arctic Voyagers" (2 December 1854); "The Lost Arctic Voyagers" (9 December 1854); and Morley's "The Lost English Sailors" (14 February 1857) and "Official Patriotism" (25 April 1857). While Morley's articles argue that the British government should fund another Arctic expedition to find the remains of the lost explorers and to search for survivors, Dickens's respond directly to Rae's report. These challenge Rae's "improbable" claim that cannibalism was practiced by the explorers, and they do so in several ways: by recounting Franklin's expedition of 1819–22, in which the men "passed through all the pangs of famine . . . yet never dreamed at the last gasp of resorting to this said 'last resource'"; by comparing Franklin and his "fine crew" to other shipwrecked men, only the most degraded of whom resorted to cannibalism (the drunken Americans on board the *Peggy*, for

8. [Henry Morley], "Unspotted Snow," *Household Words* 8 (12 November 1853): 241.

9. Rae, "Sir John Franklin and His Crews," 16.

10. Sterrenburg, "Psychoanalysis," 247.

11. Addressing his letter to Dr. Rae, and signing it with his initials ("E.J.H."), Hornby explains his objections to the report in a letter published in the London *Times* on 3 November: "My objection lay, not to your publishing your report, but only those details of it which allege that cannibalism was resorted to by the sufferers as a means of support. These details . . . rest on grounds weak and unsatisfactory; these are most painful to our feelings, and these I wished to be able to disbelieve, as I still do" (7). As Loomis notes, this wish was widely shared among the English in 1854 ("Arctic Sublime," 109). See also James E. Marlow, "The Fate of Sir John Franklin: Three Phases of Response in Victorian Periodicals," *Victorian Periodicals Review* 15 (spring 1982): 3–11.

example, or those of the *Medusa,* "the scum of all countries"); and by blaming the natives for the atrocities alleged against the British.[12]

In his letters to the *Times,* Hornby argued that Rae's case rested on "weak and unsatisfactory" grounds—on hearsay evidence that would be inadmissible in a court of law. Dickens, too, complains of the "second-hand" nature of "the Esquimaux evidence."[13] But he takes this argument a step further by attacking the character of Dr. Rae's witnesses. According to Dickens, Dr. Rae has mistaken for truth "the wild tales" and "vague babble" of "a herd of savages."[14] Although racist portraits of the savage "herd" are not unusual in Dickens's writing or in imperial literature generally, these particular representations of the Eskimos depart from those Dickens had earlier accepted. Before Dr. Rae's report appeared in October 1854, the idealized portraits of Arctic exploration published by Dickens included idealized portraits of the Eskimos. Although Dickens commonly ridicules the idea of the noble savage, he allowed Morley to make an exception in their case.[15] "Our Phantom Ship Among the Ice," for example, describes the Eskimos as "loving children of the north" who sing and dance and are "for ever happy in their lot," whether they are "hungry or full."[16] Their innocence distinguishes them from other coastal tribes in "Unspotted Snow":

While, everywhere else, intercourse with ships has demoralised . . . untutored tribes dwelling on sea coasts, the Esquimaux that see only our northern navigators have learnt no new crimes. They are a quiet amiable race; on amiable terms with visitors whose manners are invariably kind. When they see many new and attractive things lying about strange boats . . . they are not strong enough to resist always the desire to possess some of them; but a good-humoured watch is kept upon their fingers, their attempts at theft are frustrated in a pleasant way, but not resented.[17]

12. [Dickens], "Lost Arctic Voyagers," 362, 385, 388. Patrick Brantlinger discusses "the racist pattern of blaming the victim" in imperial literature. See *Rule of Darkness: British Literature and Imperialism, 1830–1914* (Ithaca, N.Y.: Cornell University Press, 1988), p. 200.

13. [Dickens], "Lost Arctic Voyagers," 361.

14. Ibid., 363, 365.

15. "I have not the least belief in the Noble Savage," Dickens writes in *Household Words,* claiming that natives are "cruel, false, thievish, murderous; addicted more or less to grease, entrails, and beastly customs" ("The Noble Savage," *Household Words* 7 [11 June 1853]: 337). On the subject of Dickens's racism, which became more virulent over the course of his career, see William Oddie, *Dickens and Carlyle: The Question of Influence* (London: Centenary Press, 1972), pp. 135–42, and "Dickens and the Indian Mutiny," *Dickensian* 68 (January 1972): 3–15; and Myron Magnet, *Dickens and the Social Order* (Philadelphia: University of Pennsylvania Press, 1985), pp. 3–4.

16. [Morley], "Our Phantom Ship Among," 70–71.

17. [Morley], "Unspotted Snow," 241.

Despite a tendency to steal, the Eskimos are "gentle and loving savages," eager to learn from their European patrons: "Teach them and they will learn, oblige them and they will be grateful."[18]

All this changes, however, with the publication of Dr. Rae's report. Those *Household Words* articles that appeared after October 1854 group the Eskimos with all other savages. The gentle "children" of Morley's "Our Phantom Ship" are bloodthirsty and depraved in Dickens's "The Lost Arctic Voyagers":

> It is impossible to form an estimate of the character of any race of savages, from their deferential behaviour to the white man while he is strong. The mistake has been made again and again; and the moment the white man has appeared in the new aspect of being weaker than the savage, the savage has changed and sprung upon him. There are pious persons who, in their practice, with a strange incon- sistency, claim for every child born to civilisation all innate depravity, and for every savage born to the woods and wilds all innate virtue. We believe every sav- age to be in his heart covetous, treacherous, and cruel; and we have yet to learn what knowledge the white man—lost, houseless, shipless, apparently forgotten by his race, plainly famine-stricken, weak, frozen, helpless, and dying—has of the gentleness of Esquimaux nature.[19]

In *Household Words,* Dickens suddenly inverts the conception of "Esquimaux nature"—not because native attacks on Europeans have been reported but be- cause Dr. Rae's report has created the need for this change. To save his im- periled ideal of Arctic exploration, Dickens sacrifices what he feels is its most expendable element, the portrait of the noble savage. Although Dr. Rae found "no reason to suspect that any violence had been offered" to the explorers by the Eskimos, Dickens tells a very different story: the explorers are not cannibals but martyrs "set upon and slain by the Esquimaux."[20]

Dr. Rae responded to Dickens's version of the Franklin story in two *Household Words* articles: "The Lost Arctic Voyagers" (23 December) and "Dr. Rae's Report" (30 December). Here, he insists on the truthfulness and the moral integrity of the Eskimos, who "show a bright example to the most civilised people." He contrasts the dutiful natives with Franklin's undisciplined crew members, whose "conduct at the very last British port they entered was not such as to make . . . them very deserving of the high eulogium passed upon them in Household Words," and who would have become insubordinate when

18. [Morley], "Our Phantom Ship Among," 71.
19. [Dickens], "Lost Arctic Voyagers," 362.
20. Rae, "Report to the Secretary of the Admiralty," 7; [Dickens], "Lost Arctic Voyagers," 362.

faced with danger.[21] In both articles, Rae makes a case for the Eskimos by comparing them favorably with Franklin's crew and, more generally, with the "lower classes in England or Scotland": "my [Eskimo] interpreter . . . speaks English fluently; and, perhaps, more correctly than one half of the lower classes in England or Scotland."[22]

In making this comparison, Dr. Rae counters Dickens's first attempt to blame savages for the ill-fate of the explorers but also anticipates his second, which depends on the barbarism of the working-class Scotswoman who replaces the Eskimos in *The Frozen Deep,* and who proves far from fluent in the English language. The idea of this "Scotch" woman was central to Dickens's conception of the melodrama, which was to be "pervade[d]" by "Scotch" themes—so he tells Wills on 6 April 1856, in the first of his letters to mention the proposed work:

> Collins and I have a mighty original notion (mine in the beginning) for another Play at Tavistock House. . . . But now a tremendous question. Is
>
> MRS. WILLS!
>
> game to do a Scotch Housekeeper, in a supposed country-house with Mary, Katey, Georgina, etc. If she can screw her courage up to saying Yes, that country house opens the piece in a singular way, and that Scotch housekeeper's part shall flow from the present pen. . . . Scotch song (new and original) of Scotch Housekeeper, would pervade the piece. (Pilgrim, 8:81)

That a Scottish housekeeper could take the place of the Eskimos in Dickens's new conception of Franklin's story is not as unlikely as it might at first seem. As Martin Green notes, the conquest of Scotland by the English in 1707 was the defining act of the British Empire.[23] In the nineteenth century, Anglo-Saxon ethnologists grouped the Scots with the Irish as racially inferior Celts, while novelists and historians often portrayed them as a savage people to be civilized by the English.[24] "The Wild Scotch," Thomas Macaulay notes, were seen as "mere savages" by the English, a view that Dickens himself promoted in *A Child's History of England* (1851–53), by describing Scotland before the 1707 Union as "a half savage country, where there was a great deal of murdering and

21. Rae, "Dr. Rae's Report," 458.

22. Rae, "Lost Arctic Voyagers," 433.

23. Martin Green, *Dreams of Adventure, Deeds of Empire* (New York: Basic Books, 1979), p. 5. As Green points out, while "most of us don't nowadays think that the United Kingdom was or is an empire," "Scots and Welsh nationalists do" (*Dreams of Adventure,* 6).

24. See L. P. Curtis Jr., *Anglo-Saxons and Celts: A Study of Anti-Irish Prejudice in Victorian England* (Bridgeport, Conn.: University of Bridgeport Conference on British Studies, 1968).

rioting continually going on."[25] *Household Words* articles compare the Scots to a host of "uncivilized" peoples—to the aboriginal "Gonds, and Bheels, and Jats" of India, for example—and the Scottish moors ("the moors where Glenfern is") to "the Moors where Othello was."[26] A "rarely . . . explored" territory that must be charted and conquered, Scotland is a domestic "Timbuctoo" inhabited by ignorant "primitives" who have no "self-control" and who "know little or nothing of English."[27]

Even more to the point, the Highlanders are explicitly compared to Eskimos by nineteenth-century writers, on the grounds that both are savage northern races. In *Waverley* (1814), Sir Walter Scott compares the entrance of the Highland rebels into the Lowlands to an invasion of "Esquimaux Indians" issuing forth "from the northern mountains of their own native country."[28] And in his *History of England* (1849–61), Macaulay suggests that an English traveler to the Highlands would "endure hardships as great as if he had sojourned among the Esquimaux or the Samoyeds."[29] This connection is made in *Household Words* as well; "The North Against the South" groups the Scot with "the man of the polar regions" as people of the North, a region that "condemn[s]" its inhabitant "to a pastoral and hunting life, and render[s] him nomadic and barbarous."[30]

Esther's status as a member of a savage northern race helps to explain her importance to *The Frozen Deep*. So, too, does her tie to mother nature. While Dickens claimed credit for the "Scotch Housekeeper," whose "part shall flow from the present pen," it is unclear whether he or Collins first thought to identify her as a former wet nurse. Nonetheless, both writers were well aware of the threatening associations of this particular female servant: a working-class woman whose indispensable services made her unusually powerful in middle-class households and whose stereotypically ravenous appetite, like her class transgressions, connects her to the alleged cannibals in Franklin's party.[31]

25. Thomas Babington Macauley, *The History of England from the Accession of James II,* 5 vols. (Philadelphia: J. B. Lippincott, 1868), 3:239; Charles Dickens, *A Child's History of England,* in *Holiday Romance and Other Writings for Children,* ed. Gillian Avery (London: J. M. Dent, 1995), p. 280.

26. [E. Townsend and Alexander Henry Abercromby Hamilton], "Indian Recruits and Indian English," *Household Words* 16 (3 October 1857): 320; [Mrs. Grenville Murray], "A Gun Among the Grouse," *Household Words* 6 (16 October 1852): 115.

27. [Thomas Noon Talfourd], "A Glimpse of the Cairngorm Mountains," *Household Words* 4 (4 October 1851): 40; [Henry Morley], "A Clouded Skye," *Household Words* 5 (17 April 1852): 99–101; [Henry Morley], "Chip: Highland Emigration," *Household Words* 5 (19 June 1852): 325.

28. Sir Walter Scott, *Waverley,* ed. Andrew Hook (1972; reprint, Harmondsworth: Penguin, 1986), p. 324.

29. Macauley, *History of England,* 3:241.

30. [John Abraham Heraud], "The North Against the South," *Household Words* 14 (6 September 1856): 191–92.

31. As Gail Turley Houston argues in her analysis of hunger and consumption in Dickens's fiction, the idealized Victorian woman had no appetite at all. "Redeemed through starvation," Dickens's heroines "exhibit a genius for self denial." More sensitive to "the alimental needs" of the working class than

II

In his letter to Wills, Dickens claims that the "mighty original notion" of *The Frozen Deep* was "[his] in the beginning." But busy with *Little Dorrit* (1855–57) and *Household Words,* he assigned the job of writing a first draft to Collins. It was to be, in Dickens's words, Collins's "summer occupation and work" (Pilgrim, 8:87). Meeting in Paris in March 1856, the two writers sketched out a rough plotline for the melodrama. Reminding Collins of his obligations in July, Dickens wrote to him about the length of time "the Play will take . . . to write" (Pilgrim, 8:161), praising one of Collins's "notion[s] for the play" and looking forward to his being "shut up . . . on pen and ink" when they next met (Pilgrim, 8:167). Back in Paris in August, the two again collaborated. Collins finished writing two-thirds of his draft by 3 October and completed it by the twenty-seventh, when Dickens read the play to Clarkson Stanfield at Tavistock House (Pilgrim, 8:214).

Collins's 1856 draft of *The Frozen Deep* consists of three acts. The first takes place in a country house in Devonshire, where four English ladies related to officers on an Arctic expedition anxiously wait for news of their loved ones, who have been gone for three years and are presumed missing or dead after a prolonged silence. Collins identifies the women as Mrs. Steventon, the wife of Lieutenant Steventon; Rose Ebsworth, the daughter of Captain Ebsworth; Lucy Crayford, the sister of Lieutenant Crayford; and Clara Burnham. Both Clara's fiancé, Frank Aldersley, and her jilted admirer, Richard Wardour, are members of the expedition. Wardour has promised to seek revenge on the man who has stolen Clara from him, but at the time of sailing he is unaware that one of his fellow explorers is his rival. The first act ends with a frightening prediction made by Esther, Clara's former nurse and surrogate mother, who claims to be endowed with second sight. She sees Aldersley "in the grasp" of Wardour and asserts that none of the explorers will ever return home.[32] The second act

---

to those of women, Dickens points to "the unnaturalness of expecting one class to starve so that another might gluttonize" but "naturalizes the expectation that women must starve for the good of the community" (*Consuming Fictions: Gender, Class, and Hunger in Dickens's Novels* [Carbondale: Southern Illinois University Press, 1994], xi, 39, 13).

32. Wilkie Collins, autograph manuscript of *The Frozen Deep*. The Pierpont Morgan Library, New York. MA 81. Act 1: p. 15; subsequent references to Collins's autograph manuscript of *The Frozen Deep* are cited parenthetically, with act numbers and page numbers from each act. Dickens heavily revised Collins's draft before it was transcribed. The fair copy (the "Prompt-Book") served as the authoritative text of the 1857 productions. Collins revised the Prompt-Book in 1866, using it as a draft for the stage production of that year. The Prompt-Book was published in 1966: see Robert Louis Brannan, ed., *Under the Management of Mr. Charles Dickens: His Production of "The Frozen Deep"* (Ithaca, N.Y.: Cornell University Press, 1966), pp. 93–160; subsequent references to the Prompt-Book are cited parenthetically in the text. In his edition, Brannan excludes Collins's revisions of 1866, since his aim is "to recover

shifts to an Arctic hut that shelters some of the explorers. Suffering from expo-
sure and starvation, they roll dice and draw lots to determine who will form a
party to search for help. The act ends with the departure of the search party,
which includes both Aldersley and Wardour. Wardour has identified Aldersley
as Clara's fiancé and joins the search party in the hopes of murdering him. The
third act is set in a cavern on the Newfoundland coast, shortly after Captain
Ebsworth and Lieutenants Crayford and Steventon have been reunited with
their female relations. With Esther and Clara, the women have traveled to
North America for that purpose. Only Aldersley and Wardour are still missing.
In the play's final minutes, Wardour enters the cave carrying Aldersley in his
arms. Emaciated and dying, Wardour has saved his rival's life at the cost of his
own and deposits him at Clara's feet, proving a martyr rather than a murderer.

Collins's draft of *The Frozen Deep,* like Dickens's articles on "The Lost Arctic
Voyagers," can be understood as a response to Dr. Rae's report; both writers
deny Rae's allegations that the starving explorers became cannibals. Unlike
Dickens, however, Collins dramatizes class conflict among the officers and crew
and entertains the possibility that they could have turned on one another.
Whereas Dickens commends the members of Franklin's "fine crew," whom he
claims maintained "a state of high discipline" in the face of starvation and
death,[33] Collins refers to them, humorously, as "mutinous rascal[s]" (MA 81,
2:2) and characterizes John Want in particular by the persistent grumbling that
amuses his superior officers. Collins opens act 2 with a comic exchange between
Want, the cook on the expedition, and Lieutenant Crayford, in a scene that
plays with Rae's allegations:

Crayford: John Want! John Want!
John Want: (*speaking from one of the bedplaces*) Give me some more sleep!
Crayford: Not a wink, you mutinous rascal! Rouse up! . . . Come here, Sir, and
  set to work on this mortar. What are you doing there?
John Want: (*Holding his chin over the fire*) Thawing my beard, sir. (*Goes back to his
  bedplace.*)
Crayford: Come here, I say! What the devil are you about now?
John Want: (*At the fire with a watch in his hand*) Thawing my watch, sir. It's been
  under my pillow all night, and the cold has stopped it. Cheerful, wholesome,
  bracing sort of climate to live in, isn't it, sir? But *I* don't grumble.
Crayford: No, we all know that. You are the only cheerful man of the ship's
  company. Look here. Are these bones pounded small enough?

---

the final script used by Dickens" in 1857 (Brannan, introduction, *Under the Management of Mr. Charles
Dickens,* 4).
  33. [Dickens], "Lost Arctic Explorers," 385–86.

John Want: (Taking the pestle and mortar) You'll excuse me, sir, but how very
    hollow your voice sounds this morning!

Crayford: Keep your remarks about my voice to yourself, and answer my
    question about the bones.

John Want: They'll take a trifle more pounding. I'll do my best with them
    today, sir, for your sake.

Crayford: What do you mean?

John Want: I don't think I shall have the honour of making much more bone
    soup for you, sir. Do you think yourself you'll last long, sir? I don't, saving
    your presence. . . . *(Bateson approaches from the inner hut.)* This man looks bad,
    too, don't he, sir? He was half an hour cutting one log of wood yesterday.
    His legs are swelling—and he loses his temper at trifles. I give *him* another
    day or two. I give the best of us a week. Most likely I shall be the last.

(MA 81, 2:1–3)

In this passage, Collins both acknowledges and defuses the threat of cannibalism among the explorers and the class antagonism it connotes. He prefaces
the exchange with an aside explaining that Want's grumbling entertains rather
than offends his superiors, "keeping up [their] spirits": "No matter how the cold
pinches, he always amuses me," the lieutenant explains (MA 81, 2:1).
Nonetheless, Want serves a serious function in the melodrama, since his grumbling comically defuses the more menacing anger of men such as Bateson, who
"loses his temper at trifles." As Want's name and his "inveterate" complaining
make clear, he is a figure for class injury and resentment, dissatisfied with his
working conditions and slow to obey his commanding officers. More particularly, Want's role as the cook associates him with the English cannibals described
by Dr. Rae, since they allegedly cooked the human flesh they consumed.
Furthermore, Want takes evident pleasure in describing the failing health of his
officers. He seems to relish the thought that they are dying and predicts that he
"shall be the last" survivor, an ominous claim under the circumstances.

    Even more to the point, Want uses his saucepan to hold and "hand . . .
round" lots drawn by the sailors in a scene that Collins bases on well-known
accounts of cannibalism among shipwrecked men (MA 81, 2:12). As the historian A. W. Brian Simpson points out, Victorians were well aware that men
driven to the "last resource" often used a lottery to determine who would be
killed, cooked, and consumed by his fellows, and Dickens himself describes
how the starving sailors on board the *Peggy,* an American sloop, "contrived to
make the lot fall on a negro whom they had on board, shot him, fried a part
of him for supper, and pickled the rest."[34] Unlike the sailors on the *Peggy,* the

34. A. W. Brian Simpson, *Cannibalism and the Common Law: The Story of the Tragic Last Voyage of the
"Mignonette" and the Strange Legal Proceedings to Which It Gave Rise* (Chicago: University of Chicago Press,

Arctic explorers in Collins's draft of *The Frozen Deep* draw lots to decide who will join a search party and set forth to find assistance for their disabled companions. As Want notes, he "has nothing to put in his saucepan but paper" (MA 81, 2:12). Nonetheless, Collins's treatment of Want and the lottery in which he participates indirectly acknowledges what Dickens more forcefully denies in his articles on Franklin—the potential for cannibalism among the English.

In Collins's draft, this potential is most fully realized by Wardour, who "hunger[s] for [the] life" of his rival (MA 81, 3:15) and whose animosity seems class driven, although both men are presumably naval officers.[35] The scene in which Wardour identifies his rival begins when he "snatches" an axe from Bateson and proceeds to "do his work for him" (MA 81, 2:17). Aldersley is leaving camp with the search party, and the sailor has been ordered to chop down the officer's wooden bedplace for firewood. Initially, Wardour believes that performing this manual labor will do him good: "that's the true Elixir of *our* life," he tells Lieutenant Crayford, "hard work that stretches the muscles and sets the blood glowing—that tires the body and rests the mind" (MA 81, 2:16). What he discovers as the scene proceeds, however, is the sense of resentment and injury created by the class division between sailors who labor and officers who "idle." "Let's do something," Wardour proposes to Crayford:

> *Wardour:* Is there no work in hand—no game to shoot, nothing to cut, nothing to carry[?] . . . (*Enter Bateson, with an axe from the inner hut*)—Here's a man with an axe. I'll do his work for him, whatever it is. (*Snatches the axe from Bateson*). . . .
> *Bateson:* (*Holding out his hand for the axe*) I beg your pardon, sir—
> *Wardour:* Nonsense! Why should you beg my pardon[?] Give me your work to do. My arm's stiff and my hands are cold. . . . Away with you—leave it to me! . . . (*Striking at the bedplace*) Down it comes—a good axe—O me! if I had been born a carpenter instead of a gentleman . . . Stop! what's here?—a name carved in the wood. C.L.A.—*Clara!* (*Throwing down the wood*) Curse the fellow and his sweetheart too!—why must she have *that* name of all the

---

1984), pp. 144–45; [Dickens], "Lost Arctic Voyagers," 386. In his article, Dickens describes five instances of shipwreck in which sailors used lots to determine who would be killed and cannibalized, or considered doing so. His point, however, is that these men lacked the moral restraint of Franklin's crew—that only the most depraved would resort to cannibalism in order to survive.

35. Collins originally listed "Lieutenant Aldersley" and "Richard Wardour" in his "Persons of the Drama." Dickens replaced "Lieutenant Aldersley" with "Frank Aldersley" to level the implied distinction between them (MA 81).

names in the world? . . . where the devil is the axe?—Work, work, work—
nothing for it but work! (*Cuts out another piece of wood*) More carving—that's
the way these young idlers employ their spare hours. . . . "F. A." Those are
his initials—Frank Aldersley—and under them here—"C. B." . . . Clara
Burnham! . . . (*His voice drops to a whisper, and he looks all round him
suspiciously.*)

(MA 81, 2:17)

This scene is one of several in which Collins underscores the class divisions
among explorers presumably united in a common, heroic cause; it resembles
the preceding scene in which the members of the search party are determined,
a process divided by social class, with officers rolling dice and men drawing lots,
and organized in strictly hierarchical order (MA 81, 2:10–12). In Wardour's
monologue, Collins dramatizes the animosity that results from these divisions,
demystifying the claim that carpenters are better off than gentlemen because
"hard work" benefits them. Eager to trade places with Bateson, Wardour learns
that labor is not an elixir but a curse and that Aldersley, the "idle" gentleman,
possesses the woman he wanted for his own. Transforming the jilted lover into
a working-class figure, and conflating his sexual jealousy with class resentment,
Collins represents the rivalry between Wardour and Aldersley as if it were a
class conflict. He reinforces this point when Wardour reappears on stage as "a
starving man" in rags, searching for Clara, and Lieutenant Steventon wonders
what a man "going through the world in those tatters" could possibly want with
a lady (MA 81, 3:11–12).

Despite Collins's analysis of class divisions and class injury among the explorers, his treatment of Wardour ultimately conveys a conservative message,
by celebrating the explorer's ability to suppress his appetite and sacrifice himself for his foe. Those few critics who have written about the melodrama argue
that this transformation reveals Wardour's strength of character and, more generally, "the power of the British hero to endure"—the ability of "the English
gentleman" to "triumph over any adversity."[36] Yet Wardour and his fellow explorers do not overcome their differences simply by drawing on their strengths.
Rather, they are united by means of the common enemy they discover in
Nurse Esther, as Collins, apparently at Dickens's prompting, includes the menacing Scotswoman in his cast. A barbarous Highlander and a former wet nurse
as well as a resentful servant, she redefines the meaning of cannibalism in the
melodrama.

36. Brannan, introduction, pp. 86–87; Fred Kaplan, *Dickens: A Biography* (New York: Avon Books,
1988), p. 359.

In Collins's draft, Mrs. Steventon provides us with our first glimpse of Esther, recalling her odd behavior at the servants' dinner table and warning Rose Ebsworth that "Nurse is likely to do the servants harm":

> *Mrs. Steventon:* Only last week she frightened them all by pretending to be in a
> kind of fit at dinner. I was sent for, and she stared at me as if I had been a
> stranger . . . and said the "power of the Sight was on her"—meaning I
> suppose the Second Sight that one reads about in books on the Highlands.
> *Rose:* I hope she is not in another fit now. Nobody seems inclined to answer
> the bell.
> (*Enter Nurse Esther*)
> *Nurse Esther:* Who rings?
> *Mrs. Steventon:* How the poor old soul stares!—No, no, nurse—we don't want
> you. Send the housemaid to take away the tray.
> *Nurse Esther:* Not want me! The day may come, mistress, when ye'll be down
> on your knees begging me to speak. Where's your husband? (*To Rose*)
> Where's your father? Where's Lucy Crayford's brother? Where's my nurse-
> child's plighted lover? Lost, all lost in the lands of ice and snow. Who sees
> them and follows them in the spirit? Who can give ye news of them when all
> earthly tidings fail? Southron lady! when ye want next to hear of your
> husband, ye'll want *me*.
>
> (MA 81, 1:11)

At dinner, Esther exercises her "power of Sight" rather than her powers of digestion, yet her claims as a visionary help to identify her as a cannibal of sorts. Something "that one reads about in books on the Highlands," Esther's second sight marks her primitivism as a member of a northern tribe, and the English ladies dismiss "her barbarous nonsense," wish her "back among her own people," and wonder why Clara "has not civilized her a little in this time" (MA 81, 1:3, 4).[37] Nonetheless, Esther uses her powers to gain ascendancy over the "Southron[ers]" who disparage her and whose "dainty flesh" seems appetizing in her eyes (MA 81, 1:12). At the same time, Esther's visions allow her to invert class and gender relations and mark her class resentment and her feminist anger. Like the subversive figure of the medium or clairvoyant, who claimed to speak for the spirits of the dead and transgressed class and gender boundaries in the process, Esther claims to "follow" the absent explorers in spirit and "give . . . news of them when . . . earthly tidings fail." Supplanting the missing

---

37. Many of the English travelogues written about Scotland in the eighteenth and nineteenth centuries treat second sight in this way; see, for example, Samuel Johnson's 1775 *Journey to the Western Islands of Scotland,* ed. J. D. Fleeman (Oxford: Oxford University Press, 1985), pp. 89–91, 211–12.

husband, father, and brother in the household, she uses her visionary knowl-edge to render the ladies subservient to her—imagining them "down on [their] knees begging [her] to speak." In a household in which the maid can be called in to perform Esther's domestic labors, the Scotswoman renders herself indis-pensable by means of her second sight: "When ye want next to hear of your husband, ye'll want *me!*"[38]

Collins develops our sense of the threat Esther poses by identifying her as a former wet nurse as well as a female visionary—a servant whose essential ser-vices and reputedly exorbitant demands made her difficult for middle-class em-ployers to control. Unlike her fellow servants, the wet nurse could not be easily disciplined or discharged. As Valerie Fildes notes, medical and childcare books often referred to the "disruptive behaviour of resident wet nurses" who "were said to demand superior food and drink, and more care and attention than their position warranted."[39] Although the wet nurse was "relatively unproductive," she demanded "a degree of comfort and a wage far higher than were enjoyed by the average servant."[40]

Collins draws on the reputation of the wet nurse as a troublesome servant in portraying Esther, but he also suggests that she challenges patriarchal authority as a maternal provider, and he uses the stereotypically insatiable appetite of this figure to identify Esther as a female cannibal. In his novel *Hide and Seek* (1854), published by Richard Bentley, Collins valorizes maternal sustenance, using it to criticize the claims and values of patriarchy. When the heroic Mrs. Peckover comes on a dying mother on the roadside, she suckles her starving infant, adopts the baby, and defends a mother's claims to her children, despite the laws deny-ing women custody rights. Years later, when she meets the grateful uncle of the infant she nursed, Mrs. Peckover refuses to accept the money he offers her; the mother's love transcends the dealings of the marketplace.[41]

But in Collins's draft of *The Frozen Deep*, Esther more closely resembles a sec-ond wet nurse who figures in his writing, one who is paid for her services and who seems to consume much more than she provides in the way of suste-nance—Mrs. Bullwinkle, the subject of an 1858 *Household Words* article. In "Mrs. Bullwinkle," Collins's narrator is a comically desperate man who finds his

38. Alex Owen discusses the Victorian medium, whose spiritual possession "circumvent[ed] rigid nineteenth-century class and gender norms" (4), in *The Darkened Room: Women, Power and Spiritualism in Late Victorian England* (Philadelphia: University of Pennsylvania Press, 1990).

39. Valerie Fildes, *Wet Nursing: A History from Antiquity to the Present* (Oxford: Basil Blackwell, 1988), p. 194.

40. Ann Roberts, "Mothers and Babies: The Wetnurse and Her Employer in Mid-Nineteenth-Century England," *Women's Studies* 3, 3 (1976): 291.

41. Wilkie Collins, *Hide and Seek*, ed. Catherine Peters (Oxford: Oxford University Press, 1993), pp. 370–71.

baby's wet nurse "much too ladylike for her station in life," but who submits to her authority and caters to her needs: "When I first met Mrs. Bullwinkle . . . I felt inclined to apologise for my wife's presumption in engaging her services. Though I checked this absurd impulse, I could not resist answering the new nurse's magnificent curtsey by expressing a polite hope that she would find her situation everything that she could wish, under my roof."[42] Conflating Mrs. Bullwinkle's appetite for upward mobility with her enormous caloric requirements as a wet nurse, Collins characterizes her as a "human cormorant" who eats her employer "out of house and home," and who undermines his success as the patriarchal provider.[43] Her eight meals a day, catalogued in detail by the horrified husband and father, bring him to the brink of financial ruin.

Like Mrs. Bullwinkle, Nurse Esther hungers to control her social superiors and is driven by both maternal and working-class appetites. At one and the same time, she is a social cannibal and a "devouring mother," a figure familiar to psychoanalytic critics. As Melanie Klein argues, the mother is perceived as cannibalistic in certain stages of development, a projection of infantile desires. When nursing infants experience oral frustration, and want to assimilate and possess their mothers, they express their feelings of cannibalistic aggression as fear of the devouring mother.[44] Such fears help to explain why Esther allegedly "harms" Clara by mothering her (MA 81, 1:11) and why Clara seems to be "wasting" away under her care, "growing paler and paler" as if she is being cannibalized by her former wet nurse (MA 81, 3:3).

Indeed, the nursing mother is often represented as a primitive figure in Victorian writing, despite the value ostensibly placed on hearth and home, and the barbarism of Nurse Esther is due to her role as the maternal provider as well as to her identity as a Highlander. In this regard, Esther recalls Goisvintha, the Gothic mother in Collins's first published novel, *Antonina; or, the Fall of Rome* (1850). Collins depicts Goisvintha as a victim of imperial brutality, her beloved children murdered by Roman soldiers. Yet her maternal instincts, thwarted by these murders, render her a "wild beast," and she rather than her more civilized brother embodies the savagery of the invading Goths.[45]

As the editor of *Household Words,* Dickens, too, promoted the connection between the maternal and the savage or "raw," by publishing articles such as "Wolf-Nurses," which identifies the nursing mother as an enemy of civiliza-

---

42. [Wilkie Collins], "Mrs. Bullwinkle," *Household Words* 17 (17 April 1858): 409.

43. Ibid., 410.

44. Melanie Klein, "Early Stages of the Oedipus Conflict," *International Journal of Psychoanalysis* 9 (1928): 167–80; see esp. 168–69.

45. Wilkie Collins, *Antonina; or, the Fall of Rome,* vol. 17 of *The Works of Wilkie Collins,* 30 vols. (New York: AMS Press, 1970), p. 225.

tion. According to this 1853 article, the wolf-nurse is found in the jungles of India, steals a child from civilization, and teaches it her bestial ways. Although male hunters ultimately defeat the wolf-nurse, the child she suckled is permanently fixed in a primitive condition, having "adopted all the habits of its foster mother": "It refused every description of food that was cooked for it, and would only eat raw flesh, which it would devour voraciously."[46] Similarly, "Scotch Coast Folk," published as Dickens and Collins collaborated on *The Frozen Deep,* represents motherhood and fatherhood as distinct stages in human evolution and contrasts the ways in which the two parents provide food for their children. Distinguishing between mother nature and fatherly nurture, an invented and hence a more highly developed form of sustenance, the article notes that the nursing mother depends on the father for her own livelihood, and it defines the natural process of nursing against the father's cultured activities of hunting and cooking:

> Salmon fishing is an admirable application of science to utility. The man who first combined a knowledge of the salmon with the contrivances of the fisher . . . was, perhaps, as well worthy of remembrance . . . as if he had won battles or spun rhymes. . . . I hear him ask himself: "How am I to put one of these splendid fish into my empty kettle? The girl who plighted with me the troth of Odin looks sunk-eyed while she suckles my boy. I promised to nourish them when beside the pillar, and I cannot do it unless I can wile the salmon into the kettle." He did it. Is there not a vast amount of observation and ingenuity combined in the practice of spearing salmon by torchlight? Was it not an application to the tenants of the water of the warfare of the sea-kings? Was not the first idea of a hook with a dragon-fly upon it a thought of genius?[47]

"Scotch Coast Folk" celebrates a turning point in human evolution—the father's leap from nature into culture by means of hunting and cooking. By inventing a way to nourish his family, the father transcends the state of nature in

46. [John Lang], "Wolf-Nurses," *Household Words* 6 (26 February 1853): 562–63. To readers familiar with *Dombey and Son* (1847–48) and the sympathetic Polly Tootles, it may seem unlikely that Dickens would disparage a wet nurse as primitive. As Paul Schacht notes, Dickens uses the natural process of breastfeeding to critique the unnatural doctrines of political economy in that novel. But as Michael Slater and others show, Dickens valorized only certain forms of womanhood, and only under certain circumstances, and had particularly hostile feelings toward his own mother. In general, Patricia Ingham argues, Dickens "disvalu[es] biological mothers" (*Dickens, Women and Language* [Toronto: University of Toronto Press, 1992], pp. 115–16). See Paul Schacht, "Dickens and the Uses of Nature," *Victorian Studies* 34 (autumn 1990): 77–102; and Michael Slater, *Dickens and Women* (London: J. M. Dent, 1983). For two discussions of Dickens's treatment of breast feeding and hand feeding in his fiction, see Virginia Phillips, "Children in Early Victorian England: Infant Feeding in Literature and Society, 1837–1857," *Tropical Pediatrics and Environmental Child Health* 24 (August 1978): 158–66; and "'Brought up by Hand': Dickens's Pip, Little Paul Dombey, and Oliver Twist," *Dickensian* 74 (1978): 144–47.

47. [John Robertson], "Scotch Coast Folk," *Household Words* 13 (5 July 1856): 587.

which the nursing mother remains fixed.[48] As anthropologists have shown, patriarchal societies consistently represent hunting and cooking as forms of mediation between nature and culture. In particular, "culinary operations" are believed to make cultural what is otherwise physiological, maternal, and raw, and to enable human beings to escape the condition of "nature and rawness" associated with childbirth, nursing, and menstruation.[49] Hence the child adopted by the wolf-nurse in *Household Words* refuses cooked food and "devours" its meat raw.

In his draft of *The Frozen Deep,* Collins treats nursing as a civilized activity but only when it is performed by men. Recounting his heroic ability to overcome temptation and save Aldersley rather than kill or abandon him, Wardour appears as a male nurse against whose "bosom" Aldersley "nestles":

> If you can't kill him, . . . the fiend whispered me, leave him when he sleeps! I set him his place to sleep in apart; but he crept between the fiend and me, and nestled his head on my bosom and slept *there*. Leave him! leave him!—the tempting voice whispered—Lay him down in the snow, and leave him. Love him, the lad's voice answered, moaning and murmuring on my bosom in his sleep—Love him, Clara, for helping me—love him for my sake! (MA 81, 3:16)

Although Clara seems pivotal here, with the promise of her love uniting Wardour with his rival, the homosocial bond between the explorers is primary. Collins conveys this impression through his image of male nursing, with Aldersley "nestled" on Wardour's breast, but also through the syntactical delay between verb ("Love him") and agent ("Clara") combined with the unexpected switch in the referent for "him"; it sounds as if Wardour were faced with the alternative of "leaving" or "loving" Aldersley, and not as if Clara were being asked to love Wardour for Aldersley's sake. Commenting on this portrait of Aldersley and Wardour—and, by implication, of Collins and Dickens—Sue Lonoff argues that it reveals "Collins's dependency" and Dickens's "need . . . to nurture, to offer himself and take vicarious comfort from the happy consequences of that offering."[50] Yet this image of male nursing reinvents the rela-

---

48. For a feminist critique of evolutionary theories based on "Man the Hunter," see Michelle Zimbalist Rosaldo and Louise Lamphere, introduction, *Women, Culture, and Society* (Stanford, Calif.: Stanford University Press, 1974), pp. 6–7.

49. Claude Lévi-Strauss, *The Raw and the Cooked,* trans. John and Doreen Weightman (New York: Harper and Row, 1969), pp. 334–38. As Sherry B. Ortner notes, although cooking is usually "woman's work," in cultures with "a tradition of *haute cuisine*—'real' cooking, as opposed to trivial ordinary domestic cooking—the high chefs are almost always men." See "Is Female to Male as Nature Is to Culture?" in *Women, Culture, and Society,* ed. Rosaldo and Lamphere, p. 80.

50. Lonoff, "Dickens and Collins," 159–60.

tionship between the two collaborators in order to idealize it, while also rendering women expendable. In a melodrama about cannibalism and the dangerous appetite of a wet nurse, the image of Aldersley "nestled" on Wardour's "bosom" suggests that mothers are unnecessary and that men do a better job of nurturing their dependents than women do.

For Dickens especially, this suggestion had much appeal, since the melodrama was performed only one year before his separation from his wife Catherine, whom he criticized for her inability to properly nurture their children, and whose Scottish background partly inspired his conception of the savage "Scotch" nurse in the play.[51] Dickens's stage directions list a number of Scottish songs to be played as Esther makes her entrances. At least one of these—"A Farewell to Lochabar"—was included in a well-known collection of Scottish airs compiled by George Thomson, Catherine's maternal grandfather, whose work Dickens knew and whose gravestone inscription he composed in 1851.[52] Collins's account of heroic male nursing, adopted by Dickens with few changes in the Prompt-Book, helped the latter make his case for Catherine's expendability while also enabling the two writers to elide their own differences and represent Collins's dependence on and subordination to Dickens as nurturing in the final minutes of the play.

III

More closely resembling the wolf-nurse described in *Household Words* than the heroic male nurse of the play's last act, Esther claims as her own a child that properly belongs to English culture and can be seen as an enemy of civilization and patriarchy. However, Collins complicates his portrait of Esther and her maternal appetite by criticizing gender norms and gender relations in the melodrama and partially justifying her claims to her "nurse-child" (MA 81, 3:3) and her attempts to overstep gender boundaries and assume male prerogatives.

51. In a statement he sent to Arthur Smith on 25 May 1858 (later referred to as the "violated letter") and that he desired to be shown "to any one who wishes to do [him] right" (Pilgrim, 8:568), Dickens justifies his separation from Catherine by criticizing her skills as a mother: "In the manly consideration toward Mrs. Dickens which I owe to my wife, I will merely remark of her that the peculiarity of her character has thrown all the children on some one else" (Pilgrim, 8:740, appendix F). For a detailed discussion of Dickens's relationship to Catherine and his unjust aspersions of her character, see Michael Slater, *Dickens and Women,* pp. 103–62.

52. Although Dickens valued Catherine's indirect link to Sir Walter Scott, describing her as "the daughter of a Writer to the Signet in Edinburgh who was the great friend and assistant of Scott" for the purposes of a biographical article in 1856 (Pilgrim, 8:131), his more casual remarks to Collins about the Hogarths and their "Scottish tongue" were derogatory: "I am dead sick of the Scottish tongue in all its moods and tenses" (Pilgrim, 7:575).

Collins begins the action of the melodrama within an exclusively female community, and he uses act 1 to consider the ties that exist among his female characters. The play opens as Mrs. Steventon and Rose Ebsworth discuss the relative merits of their female community, which Mrs. Steventon suggests is unnatural, since it lacks fathers, husbands, and brothers:

> *Mrs. Steventon:* Rose, I have been doubting lately whether it was wise of us four to shut ourselves up in this lonely old house while our natural protectors are away from us in the expedition to the Arctic Seas.
>
> *Rose:* What could we do better than wait here together till they come back[?] . . . Would it have been pleasant for you to go home, after your husband had sailed with the expedition?
>
> *Mrs. Steventon:* Home! Where they have turned their backs on me for marrying a poor man—I go home, and hear my husband despised?
>
> *Rose:* And I with no mother alive, with my father, like your husband, away with the Arctic ships, where could I have been happier than here with my dearest and oldest friend, Lucy Crayford?
>
> *Mrs. Steventon:* And Lucy certainly had no home to go to—her only near relation in the world is her brother who is serving in the expedition.
>
> *Rose:* Well, you see there are three of us, at any rate, who could have done no better than come here and make one household of it. As for the fourth, as for Clara—
>
> *Mrs. Steventon:* Clara's situation is different in one respect. It is not her father, or her brother, or her husband, who is away, but her husband that is to be. Then, again, Clara has a mother alive—
>
> *Rose:* A mother who has gone abroad, and married again—a mother who has never forgiven Clara for objecting to a foreign Stepfather!
>
> *Mrs. Steventon:* I dare say you may be right, my dear; but I cannot help doubting still whether all we women do not make each other unduly anxious by being constantly together here, and living in perfect solitude.
>
> (MA 81, 1:1–2)

In this dialogue, Mrs. Steventon and Rose describe their female community as second best, a household created not because of the primacy of relationships among women but because their "natural protectors" are away. Indeed, each of the women defines herself in relation to a man—whether husband, father, or brother—and birth mothers are notably absent from the cast, either dead or living abroad, having renounced their daughters. Mrs. Steventon proclaims her allegiance to her husband over her family of origin, and although Rose describes Lucy Crayford as her "dearest and oldest friend," she lives with her only because her father is unavailable. "I . . . have not had my father's arms round me for three long years!" she complains. "I must have my father near me, or I can never enjoy myself as I ought" (MA 81, 1:2).

In such passages, Collins rehearses the usual justifications for patriarchy, particularly the idea that women are "naturally" dependent on men rather than on other women, yet he also questions these views and suggests their inadequacies. More often than not, he reveals, men fail to protect their wives and daughters as they "ought," while the women, restricted by the rules of female propriety and separated from their mothers, find it impossible to defend themselves. Thus Clara is unable to fend off Wardour's advances or force him to explain his intentions, while her father proves unable or unwilling to defend her. Taught that she cannot play an active role in courtship, and prohibited from expressing her feelings, Clara feels powerless, while Wardour's silence proves even more powerful than his words:

> *Clara:* [Richard Wardour] never spoke of his fondness, but I could not help seeing it. I did all a girl could do to show that I was willing to be like a sister to him—and that I could be nothing else! He did not understand me, or he would not—I can't say which. . . . What could I do? He never spoke out—he seemed to treat me as if our future lives had been provided for while we were children. I could neither offend him, or make him explain himself. My situation was a very trying one, was it not, Lucy?
>
> *Lucy:* Did you never ask your father to end the difficulty for you?
>
> *Clara:* He was suffering, at that time, under the illness which afterwards caused his death, and was very unfit to agitate himself by breaking off the intercourse between his daughter and his old friend's only son.
>
> (MA 81, 1:12)

Looking ahead to Laura Fairlie in *The Woman in White* (1859–60), who feels obligated to marry Sir Percival Glyde because her father "spoke hopefully and happily of her marriage to [him] on his death-bed,"[53] Clara is, in effect, an object of exchange between men, bequeathed to her father's "old friend's only son." Less resigned to her fate than Laura Fairlie, Clara accepts the marriage proposal of another man, enraging Wardour, yet is still defined in terms of "her husband that is to be."

"I did all a girl could": with this phrase, Clara both recognizes and regrets the gender restrictions that her "brave" friend Lucy more forcefully resists by remaining "a single woman," rejecting the ideal of female resignation and patience, and proposing that she and her companions "follow the rescuing party

53. Wilkie Collins, *The Woman in White,* ed. Harvey Peter Sucksmith (1973; reprint, Oxford: Oxford University Press, 1991), p. 123.

as far as the northern shores of America" (MA 81, 1:9–10). Once in
Newfoundland, however, Lucy's brother treats her like a child, insisting that
"this is no scene for [her]!" (MA 81, 3:14). He attempts to "protect" the women
by concealing the fact that Wardour joined Aldersley on the search party, and
that those two alone are still missing: "For Heaven's sake, William, what *is* the
truth?" Lucy asks in exasperation. "I am strong enough to bear the truth.—Oh,
tell it! tell it! . . . The truth! William! tell me the truth!" (MA 81, 3:8–9).

Understood in this context, Esther seems largely justified in contesting the
claims of patriarchy and attempting to reveal the truth to the women around
her, and Collins grants much more credibility to her visionary powers than do
her companions. As a contributor to the *Leader* in the early 1850s, Collins had
already come to the defense of the clairvoyant, writing a series of six "letters"
entitled "Magnetic Evenings at Home," addressed to the skeptical G. H.
Lewes.[54] Presumably based on Collins's firsthand observations, his articles offer
readers "glimpses into the dim, dark regions of the spiritual world."[55]
Reminding us that "the incredible [is] not always impossible," Collins argues
for the truth of "the phenomena of what we term *clairvoyance*." He describes
the "second-sight" of a young Frenchwoman, "V——," whose "mind could
act and her thoughts move in the most intimate connexion with the minds and
thoughts of others," and who successfully assumed two male personae in
Collins's presence—his own and that of a friend.[56]

In his draft of *The Frozen Deep*, Esther, like "V——," "possesses . . . mysterious insight" into the minds of others.[57] Collins grants her a position analogous to narrative omniscience, conveying her "tidings" from off stage, through
a disembodied and authoritative "Voice":

> *Lucy:* What's that!
> *The Voice:* The men are lost in the land of ice and snow. In the land of ice and
> snow they shall never be found again.
> *Clara:* Nurse! nurse! What have you seen? How do you know it?—Let me go,
> Lucy—I want to ask her something.

54. In their order of appearance, these articles include: "Magnetic Evenings at Home. Letter I.—To
G. H. Lewes," *Leader* 3, 95 (17 January 1852): 63–64; "Magnetic Evenings at Home. Letter II.—To G. H.
Lewes," *Leader* 3, 99 (14 February 1852): 160–61; "Magnetic Evenings at Home. Letter III.—To G. H.
Lewes," *Leader* 3, 100 (21 February 1852): 183–84; "Magnetic Evenings at Home. Letter IV.—To
G. H. Lewes," *Leader* 3, 101 (28 February 1852): 207–8; "Magnetic Evenings at Home. Letter V.—To
G. H. Lewes," *Leader* 3, 102 (6 March 1852): 231–33; "Magnetic Evenings at Home. Letter VI.—To G. H.
Lewes," *Leader* 3, 103 (13 March 1852): 256–57; and "The Incredible Not Always Impossible. To G. H.
Lewes," *Leader* 3, 106 (3 April 1852): 328–29.
55. Collins, "Letter I," 63.
56. Collins, "Incredible," 328; "Letter I," 64; "Letter V," 232.
57. Collins, "Letter V," 232.

Lucy: No! Stop with me. Nurse! If you have any regard for your child be silent.
You agitate—you destroy her by talking in that way. . . .

Nurse Esther (mounting on the sofa to pull down the blind): If I do your bidding it's
for her sake, not for yours. Southron woman! The Second Sight is a truth.
The power of it was on me this morning, and is on me now. . . .

Clara: Nurse Esther! Speak to me, Nurse Esther. Has the Sight shown you
Frank?

Lucy: Clara! Clara!

The Voice: Has the Sight shown me Frank? Aye! and another beside him. I see
the Lamb in the grasp of the Lion—I see your bonnie bird alone with the
hawk—I see you and all around you crying Blood!

(MA 81, 1:15)

Esther ultimately proves incorrect in claiming that the explorers "shall never be
found again" and in suggesting that Wardour will prey upon Aldersley. Yet she
perceives and expresses the threat that forms the subject of the melodrama and
that her companions wish to deny. As Clara herself remarks in disgust at her
companions, "If an earthquake was shaking the house over our heads, . . . one
of you would ring for the [tea] tray and the other two would sit down to it"
(MA 81, 1:15). Rather than simply dismissing Esther's visions of the "Lion,"
Wardour, devouring the "Lamb," Collins reverses the roles of predator and
prey, suggesting that cannibalism is practiced by members of the upper classes
instead of the lower. Wardour "hungers" for Aldersley, yet Aldersley survives
by feeding off the starving Wardour: "He has given all his strength to my weakness," Aldersley explains shortly before Wardour's death (MA 81, 3:16).

In Collins's fiction, the most marginalized characters are often those who
most clearly perceive troubling social truths and bring to light certain facts that
undermine the status quo. In *The Moonstone,* Rosanna Spearman, a physically
deformed housemaid, discovers that Franklin Blake stole the missing jewel
while the gentleman himself remains oblivious to the fact, and Ezra Jennings,
an ostracized medical assistant of mixed race, deciphers the ravings of Dr. Candy
to prove that Blake committed the crime under the influence of opium. In
Armadale (1864–66), a dream-vision warns an upper-class Englishman that his
father was murdered and that his own life is in danger, but in his "intense ignorance," he dismisses it as a harmless reproduction of images perceived during
the day.[58] Only his poor friend Midwinter, a West Indian mulatto, understands
that wealthy English squires may well be objects of resentment among their social inferiors and correctly credits the dream to the powers of second sight.

58. Wilkie Collins, *Armadale,* ed. Catherine Peters (1989; reprint, Oxford: Oxford University Press,
1991), p. 143.

A Highlander, a servant, and a mother, Esther is a convenient scapegoat for the social anxieties raised by Dr. Rae's report. Nonetheless, Collins suggests that she sees through the ideals embodied in Arctic exploration, and he uses her to express the doubts raised about Franklin and his men without himself appearing to endorse them. Although Collins uses Esther to displace Rae's allegations—by identifying her own cravings as a savage Scotswoman and a former wet nurse—he proves more interested in comparing the different types of social hunger that exist among his characters than in exonerating the explorers.

Collins begins act 3 by making this comparison and placing Esther and John Want alone together on stage. Drawing attention to the comical mixture of similarities and differences between the two nourishers, he shows that the nurse and the cook have one thing in common—they are the hungriest characters in the play:

> *John Want:* (*Looking round at Nurse Esther*) There's a nice kind of fellow-servant for a cheerful man like me to keep company with! That woman is one great heap of grumbling from head to foot. If I had known, before we were all rescued, that I was to have much of her society, I think I should have preferred staying at the North Pole. . . . But never mind—it's all one to me—*I* don't grumble.
>
> *Nurse Esther:* (*Looking up, irritably*) Man! man! ye do nothing else.
>
> *John Want:* Nothing else but grumble? Is this unjoyful old woman joking? *I* grumble!!!—Who ever heard a word of complaint issue from my lips? Who ever saw a sour look on my face?
>
> *Nurse Esther:* Face? Do ye call that stickit thing on the top of your shoulders a face?—(*Aside.*) But why do I waste words on him? He's a puir weak creature!
>
> *John Want:* (*aside*) She's only a cracked old woman—it's wasting time to take any notice of her.
>
> (MA 81, 3:1)

As each accuses the other of grumbling, the nurse and the cook lose sight of their resemblance as discontented servants on whom others subsist, seeing only sexual difference in their double: to Want, Esther appears an "unjoyful" and "cracked old woman"; to Esther, Want ("Man! man!") seems "a puir weak creature," as do virtually all men. As Collins constructs the scene, its humor depends on the way in which *we* rather than *they* recognize their common ground, a connection reinforced when their social superiors enter the stage and level the same criticism at both. Having described John Want as "a croaking vagabond" who "would have grumbled in the garden of Eden," Lieutenant Steventon then turns his attention to Esther, who also "seems to have some perpetual grievance" (MA 81, 3:2–3). Like a quarrelsome Adam and Eve, the cook and the nurse have their obvious gender differences yet are "fellow servant[s]" as well, and both hunger for the fruits that their superiors alone enjoy.[59]

Of all the scenes in Collins's draft, the one that brings together John Want and Nurse Esther elicited the strongest editorial response from Dickens, who began revising Collins's manuscript in November 1856. When he came to the forty-sixth page of the draft and the line describing Esther as "only a cracked old woman—," Dickens turned it over and composed the following passage, to be inserted in John Want's aside:

> always a going on about her Second Sight. I don't believe her First Sight's much to boast of, far less mentioning a second one. Second Sight! (*with great contempt*) No woman but a Scotch woman would set any vally by a second hand eye. And like other second-hand articles, it's mostly made up of bits that she picked up here and bits that she picked up there, and then she goes and pieces 'em together, sometimes right and oftener wrong, and then forgets she did it (being but a muddle-headed female) and sets up for a Prophet! (MA 81, 3:1 verso)

Dickens's response to this scene typifies his reaction to Collins's draft as a whole. Highlighting Esther's status as "a Scotch woman" and a racial other in his additions to the manuscript, Dickens discredits her second sight, tying it to the "second-hand" information relayed by the Eskimos to Dr. Rae: her testimony, like theirs, is made up of "second-hand articles," "bits . . . picked up here and bits . . . picked up there"—and thoroughly unreliable in consequence. Associating second sight with the "second sex" and what he perceives as its false claims to primacy, Dickens elaborates on Want's misogyny, describing Esther as "a muddle-headed female" of which the "Scotch" is only the most contemptible variety.[60] Giving much more weight to Want's perspective than to Esther's in revising their exchange, Dickens severs the connection between them and forces Esther "to [the] back" of the stage (MA 81, 3:1). In effect, Dickens revises Collins's draft so as to divide the cook from the nurse and identify the Highland woman as its most menacing figure. Determined to refute Rae's allegations, Dickens brings the melodrama into line with his *Household Words* articles on Franklin by foregrounding the heroism of the explorers, obscuring their class differences, and underscoring the menacing barbarism of Esther, whom he holds accountable for the crimes alleged against the male explorers.

59. As a member of the working class, Want can only imagine earthly paradise as a place of labor: "there must have been a great deal of troublesome work with the flower-beds, in the garden of Eden!" he tells his officer (MA 81, 3:3).

60. For a discussion of Eve and "the story of woman's secondness" as told by Victorian writers, see Sandra M. Gilbert and Susan Gubar, *The Madwoman in the Attic: The Woman Writer and the Nineteenth-Century Literary Imagination* (New Haven, Conn.: Yale University Press, 1979), pp. 187–212.

Autograph manuscript, *The Frozen Deep*, page 46. The Pierpont Morgan Library, New York. MA 81.

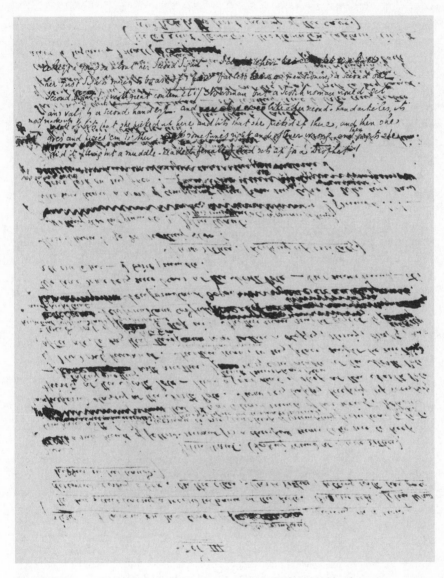

Autograph manuscript, *The Frozen Deep,* page 46 verso; Dickens's addendum to act 3, scene 1. The Pierpont Morgan Library, New York. MA 81.

IV

From the start of their correspondence about *The Frozen Deep,* Dickens seemed most anxious about Collins's representation of Esther. Writing to him on 12 September, Dickens commends his decision to endow her with second sight, "*an admirable idea*" (Pilgrim, 8:184) but expresses some reservations about this idea as well. "It is so very strong," he remarks, that it may create an "anti-climax," detracting from the "relief and joy" produced by Wardour's heroism (Pilgrim, 8:184). Collins and Dickens concur that the play's "suspended interest" hinges on our suspicions of Wardour. But Dickens suggests that these suspicions should be conveyed through psychological rather than visionary means, and by Lieutenant Crayford: "An honest bluff man previously admiring . . . me—conceiving the terrible suspicion—watching its growth in his own mind—and gradually falling from me in the very generosity and manhood of his nature—would be engaging in itself . . . and would greatly strengthen the suspended interest aforesaid" (Pilgrim, 8:184–85). Emphasizing the fallacy and aggression of Esther's "blood-red Second Sight" (Pilgrim, 8:217), Dickens reminds Collins on 13 September that her predictions about Wardour are "right to a certain extent, and absolutely wrong as to the Marrow" (Pilgrim, 8:186).

As he drafted the second act of the play, Collins adopted Dickens's suggestions about Crayford, and the state of his manuscript suggests that he responded to Dickens's comments about Esther by going back to what he had already written and inserting some passages in which characters complain of the bad influence of the "superstitious" nurse.[61] But Dickens did not find these changes extensive enough. Thus when Collins delivered his manuscript of acts 1 and 2 in early October, Dickens heavily revised it. Minimizing the extent and importance of his revisions in a letter of 9 October, Dickens tells Collins that his changes are "mostly verbal," and serve to "bring the Play closer together" (Pilgrim, 8:203). Yet his "verbal" changes alter the meaning of the play and involve virtually every line spoken by Nurse Esther, transforming the insightful, if menacing, character into one that is more clearly primitive and utterly unreliable.

---

61. In discussing Clara's condition, for example, Mrs. Steventon originally tells Lucy that she "ought to remember that [Clara] was always nervous and fanciful from a child." Revising the passage, Collins has Mrs. Steventon add "and you ought to make allowances for the influence of that superstitious old nurse over her" (MA 81, 1:6). A number of other emendations serve this end. Rose initially offers Clara her company: "Clara, if you want somebody to read to you tonight, send for me." But Collins transforms this offer into a warning: "If you want somebody to keep you company tonight, don't send for Nurse Esther—send for me" (MA 81, 1:7–8).

In Collins's draft, Esther generally speaks correct English and sounds as well educated as the upper-class characters. Her way of speaking gives credibility to her visions, which underscore the willful blindness of those she serves. When Rose Ebsworth dismisses the nurse's warnings that the explorers are endangered, explaining that English ladies "don't believe in the Second Sight," Esther's response leads the women to "start and look at each other" (MA 81, 1:12), and forces them to acknowledge and discuss their anxieties about the missing men, despite their wish to "keep silent on the subject" (MA 81, 1:12):

> *Nurse Esther:* Not believe in the Sight! Look at me. Not believe, my deary,
>   when I stand here before you, with the power of the Sight strong on me
>   now—strong on me ever since the morning dawn[?] Can you look me in the
>   face, with those bright black eyes of yours, and feel no shuddering at the
>   roots of your hair, no creeping of your dainty flesh? Do you know what day
>   this *is*? Do you know what day this *was* three years ago?
> *(Rose and Mrs. Steventon start and look at each other)*
> *Mrs. Steventon:* The anniversary, Rose, of the farewell party that was given
>   before the expedition sailed! I remembered it when I lay awake last night.
> *Rose:* And I, when I woke this morning.
>
> (MA 81, 1:12)

After some consultation with Dickens, apparently, Collins returned to this exchange charged with the task of weakening Esther's credibility. He replaced the responses of Rose and Mrs. Steventon, which lend force to Esther's claims, with a passage in which the nurse exhibits a penchant for superstition, quickly uncrossing knives that foretell of bloodshed, she believes. Yet it is left to Dickens to make such changes wholesale, discrediting Esther's premonitions of conflict among the explorers and diminishing her effect on the other characters in the melodrama. He does so by developing her identity as the barbarous racial other and by eliding the original source of conflict alleged against the explorers—the class divisions that lead the people to cannibalize their masters in Victorian representations of social revolution.

Having revised the previous exchange between Esther and the English ladies as it appears in Collins's manuscript, Dickens transcribed it into the Prompt-Book in the following way:

> *Nurse Esther:* Don't believe in the Second Sight? Look at me! No believe my
>   deary, when I stand here afore you wi' the power o' th' Sight coming strong
>   on me the noo'—coming aye stronger and aye stronger sin' the purple morn,
>   but no' at its height yet! Can you look me in the face with they bright black
>   een o' yours and no feel a shuddering at the roots o' your hair, no feel a

creeping ower your dainty flesh? No, no, no; ye know me too weel, Missy. . . . (*Becoming dreamy*) It's aye cooming on me, it's aye cooming! I ha' warned ye I shall speak o' the lost men who are wandering ower the Icy North.

Mrs. Steventon: (*To Rose*) Can't you persuade her to be quiet? (*Coming to work-table . . . Mrs. S. and Rose wind off a skein of silk, during the remainder of their dialogue at Rose's work-table.*)

(Prompt-Book, 105)

In rewriting this passage, Dickens minimizes the importance of class differences, in part through his new stage directions; like their servants, the ladies have work to do. Dickens provides Mrs. Steventon and Rose with "two little Work Tables with baskets of work on them," repeatedly has them "take their work" in hand, and alters the action so that Mrs. Stevenson joins the housemaid in arranging and watering the flowers (Prompt-Book, 101–2). In Collins's manuscript Rose "rises and rings the bell; then returns to her place" (MA 81, 1:11); in Dickens's transcription, she "rises and rings the bell; then takes her work at her table" (Prompt-Book, 103). In effect, Dickens eliminates the distinction between labor and leisure on which Collins originally structured the scene. Similarly, in revising act 2, Dickens represents the captain and officers as much less remote from the men than they appear in Collins's draft. He shows the men and their officers simultaneously casting lots and rolling dice to see who will join the search party rather than retaining Collins's organization of the action according to class and rank (MA 81, 2:9–10; Prompt-Book, 126–29). He deletes a number of commands issued by the officers, which "the men obey" (MA 81, 2:12), as well as a confrontation between Lieutenant Crayford and the unruly sailors: "Order there! order while the officers cast the dice" (MA 81, 2:10).

Dickens elides the class divisions that organize certain scenes in Collins's draft, but, more obviously, he heightens our sense of the racial differences between Esther and her fellow characters. He makes her speak in broken English ("they bright black een" rather than "those bright black eyes," for example) and represents her premonitions as a sign of her Highland primitivism. While Collins argued for the credibility of clairvoyance in the *Leader,* Dickens exposed the "hoax" of spiritualism in *Household Words.*[62] In revising Collins's draft, he

62. These articles include [Henry Morley], "The Ghost of the Cock Lane Ghost," *Household Words* 6 (20 November 1852): 217–23; Dickens's "The Spirit Business," *Household Words* 7 (7 May 1853): 217–20; his "Stores for the First of April," *Household Words* 15 (7 March 1857): 217–22; and his "Well-Authenticated Rappings," *Household Words* 17 (20 February 1858): 217–20. Writing to Wills on 12 July 1860, Dickens objects to the conclusion of Eliza Lynn Linton's "Modern Magic," published in *All the Year Round* on 28 July, which grants too much credibility to spiritualism in his view: "You will find it said that after deduction for imposition, lies, and so forth, there remains a 'large residuum' of something

discredits Esther's prophecies as well, connecting them to the evidence the Eskimos provided to Dr. Rae, which he dismisses as savage "chatter" and "babble" in "The Lost Arctic Explorers"; her knowledge, like theirs, is unreliable, inadmissible, and "second hand." No longer "starting" at Esther's remarks, Mrs. Steventon is simply disdainful: "Can't you persuade [Esther] to be quiet?" she asks Rose.

Dickens uses the cannibals portrayed in Defoe's *Robinson Crusoe* (1719) as prototypes for the Highland seer, reinforcing our sense that Esther's visionary claims are barbarous, and that she is the man-eater in the play, not the explorers. In the prologue he wrote for the melodrama, Dickens refers to the "savage footprint" in Defoe's novel, which "terrify'd [Crusoe] to the last degree,"[63] and which he contrasts with "the footprints of heroic men, / Making a garden of the desert wide / Where Parry conquer'd and Franklin died" (Prompt-Book, 97). Defining Defoe's cannibals against heroic explorers, Dickens prepares the audience for the entrance of Nurse Esther, whose attempts to speak English are as fragmentary and imperfect as those of Friday, the savage whom Crusoe saves and educates. Such phrases as "no believe," "no feel," and "no believe me" in Esther's speech echo Friday's "no kill," "no angry," and "no send Friday away."[64] At the same time, Dickens makes Esther's prophesying appear as self-serving and false as that of the savage spiritual leaders in Defoe's novel, whose heathen "priestcraft" allows them to control and exploit their ignorant followers.[65] Placing Esther on stage during a private conversation between Clara and Lucy, Dickens discredits her prophetic visions, revealing that they are based on information she gathers by eavesdropping, in an attempt to impress and control the women she serves. Representing her as a foreign spy rather than a prophet, Dickens strips her visions of their omniscient quality, changing "The Voice" to "Nurse Esther" in the script and eliminating her role as the medium of a higher, spiritual power.

In his draft, Collins includes both male and female savages in his cast. While the English ladies find Esther "barbarous," Clara fears Wardour's "savage nature" (MA 81, 1:13), which provides an implicit critique of patriarchal strength and privilege. Wardour physically assaults Clara, considers her his property, and continually disparages her sex. "The only hopeless wretchedness in this world is the wretchedness that women cause," he tells Crayford: "Say the word

---

to be accounted for. I think this wants qualifying. At all events I would take out 'large,' and let her know it" (Pilgrim, 9:271).

63. Daniel Defoe, *Robinson Crusoe,* ed. Angus Ross (1965; reprint, Harmondsworth: Penguin, 1985), p. 162.

64. Ibid., pp. 220, 227.

65. Ibid., p. 219.

Woman, and you have said enough—you have explained all" (MA 81, 2:14–15). But in Dickens's revision, savagery seems a strictly female trait. Wardour treats Clara civilly, and neither she nor her female companions appear unhappy with a woman's lot. Dickens deletes those passages in which Clara and Lucy criticize the gender restrictions placed on them, as well as the one in which Clara describes Wardour's "savage nature" and the way he "caught [her] round the waist and kissed [her]" against her will (MA 81, 1:12–13), tempering the adjectives used to describe the explorer: from "surly" and "mad" to "moody," and from "rough" to "abrupt" (MA 81, 1:13, 2:18). In Collins's manuscript, Wardour describes himself as a "fiend," laughs demonically ("Ha! ha! ha!"), and "exults" in violence (MA 81, 2:18, 20), but in Dickens's revised portrait, he does none of these things. Not only Wardour but Want appears less savage in the Prompt-Book, since Dickens omits the cook's ominous prediction that he "shall be the last" survivor. Instead, Dickens has Want imagine a more palatable end for himself and his companions than that of cannibalism: "If we don't all die a natural death of frost, we should be buried alive here on the frozen deep" (MA 81, 2:2).

V

First staged as an amateur theatrical at Tavistock House in January 1857, *The Frozen Deep* was publicly performed later that year to benefit the family of Douglas Jerrold, who had died in June. In London's Gallery of Illustration, it was produced before Queen Victoria and her guests on 4 July and before public audiences on 11 and 25 July, and 8 August. On 21 and 22 August, the play was performed in the Free Trade Hall, Manchester, with professional actresses playing the roles initially assigned to Dickens's two daughters and his sister-in-law, and Collins's brother Charles included in the cast.[66]

In the years following the 1857 productions, both Dickens and Collins returned to the melodrama, with Dickens adapting some of its elements in *A Tale of Two Cities* (1859) and Collins twice revising *The Frozen Deep* itself. "I first conceived the main idea of this story," Dickens writes in his preface to *A Tale of Two Cities,* "when I was acting, with my children and friends, in Mr. Wilkie Collins's drama of The Frozen Deep."[67] Representing class warfare among

66. These actresses were Ellen and Maria Ternan and their mother; they were recommended to Dickens by Alfred Wigan. *The Frozen Deep* was thus the means by which Dickens met his future mistress. See Claire Tomalin, *The Invisible Woman: The Story of Nelly Ternan and Charles Dickens* (New York: Knopf, 1991).

67. Charles Dickens, *A Tale of Two Cities,* ed. George Woodcock (1970; reprint, Harmondsworth: Penguin, 1980), p. 29.

French revolutionaries and aristocrats rather than British explorers, Dickens re-casts Wardour's heroic self-sacrifice in that of Sydney Carton, who dies on the guillotine in place of Charles Darnay; like Wardour, Carton saves the life of his romantic rival for the sake of the woman they both love. As he had in the 1857 Prompt-Book, Dickens defines male restraint and self-sacrifice against the ex-cesses of the female cannibal, with Madame Defarge performing much the same function as Nurse Esther. Once again, the threatening hunger of unruly and savage women overshadows that of an insurgent working class.

Among the French revolutionaries, Dickens asserts, "the men were terri-ble . . . but, the women were a sight to chill the boldest," "urging one another, and themselves, to madness with the wildest cries and actions"—when, for ex-ample, the wealthy contractor Foulon is killed by the mob:

> Villain Foulon taken, my sister. Old Foulon taken, my mother. Miscreant Foulon taken, my daughter. . . . Foulon who told the starving people they might eat grass. Foulon who told my old father that he might eat grass, when I had no bread to give him. Foulon who told my baby it might suck grass, when these breasts were dry with want. . . . Hear me, my dead baby and my withered father: I swear on my knees, on these stones, to avenge you on Foulon! Husbands, and brothers, and young men, Give us the blood of Foulon, Give us the head of Foulon, Give us the heart of Foulon, Give us the body and soul of Foulon, Rend Foulon to pieces, and dig him into the ground, that grass may grow from him. With these cries, numbers of the women, lashed into blind frenzy, whirled about, striking and tearing at their own friends until they dropped into a passionate swoon, and were only saved by the men belonging to them from being trampled under foot.[68]

As Dickens represents the revolutionary "frenzy" of French daughters, wives, and mothers, the domestic ties and affections that presumably elevate women above men instead reduce them to the level of bloodthirsty savages. Associated with the "rawness" of the maternal, yet thwarted in their attempts to suckle their babies because their "breasts [are] dry with want," they urge their more civilized male relations to avenge their wrongs. Cannibal-like, they demand the blood and heart of their enemy. The leader among these hungry "sisters," Madame Defarge lacks the restraint of her husband, whom she dominates and circumvents, and Dickens uses her and her fellow "Furies" to transform the class injury and resentment that fuels social revolution into feminist hunger and a damning assertion of women's rights: "We can kill as well as the men," Madame Defarge proclaims.[69]

68. Ibid., p. 252.
69. Ibid., pp. 252, 245.

As we have seen, Dickens cites "Mr. Wilkie Collins's drama of The Frozen Deep" as a source for his 1859 novel, acknowledging Collins's influence on his own work. A number of critics have taken their cue from Dickens's preface, identifying his "debt" to Collins in *A Tale of Two Cities*—most obviously, in the "theme . . . of regeneration through self-sacrifice."[70] However, as it was performed by Dickens and his friends, *The Frozen Deep* was hardly Collins's own drama, and *A Tale of Two Cities* more closely resembles Dickens's 1857 Prompt-Book than it does Collins's original draft—not only in its celebration of male self-sacrifice but also in its use of the threatening primitivism of women. Rather than revealing Dickens's debt to Collins, *A Tale of Two Cities* suggests their growing divergence: whereas Dickens develops the figure of hungry Nurse Esther in Madame Defarge and the French "Furies," Collins omits the female primitive from his later versions of *The Frozen Deep*.

Collins decided to revive *The Frozen Deep* in 1866, having been approached by theater manager Horace Wigan, who wished to produce it at the Royal Olympic in London. Collins accepted his proposal and began revising the melodrama, writing to Dickens to see if the original stage scenery was still viable, which it was not.[71] Opening on 27 October, the revised play received some favorable reviews but was not a popular success and ran for only six weeks, failing to pay its own costs.

Returning to the play in 1866 as a single author, without Dickens's views to consider, Collins cuts Esther from its cast while granting her subversive powers to Clara Burnham. Understood in relation to the ten-year history of *The Frozen Deep* and its revisions at Dickens's hands, this change can be seen to "correct" Dickens's disparaging portrait of the savage seer: as an attempt to grant credibility to the female visionary, now an Englishwoman rather than a Highlander. Whereas Esther incorrectly predicts that Wardour will murder Aldersley, Clara is saved from such errors. She knows the ships have been wrecked by ice, that Wardour has identified Aldersley as his rival, and that the two men are alone together "in the frozen desert," but she has not yet envisioned the end of their conflict.[72] As Lucy explains, Clara "firmly believes, if

70. Henry J. W. Milley, "Wilkie Collins and 'A Tale of Two Cities,'" *Modern Language Review* 34 (1939): 531. As Harland S. Nelson notes, critics also credit Collins with the tight plot construction of Dickens's 1859 novel, a view that Nelson himself contests. See "Dickens' Plots: 'The Ways of Providence' or the Influence of Collins?" *Victorian Newsletter* 19 (1961): 11–14.

71. Responding to Collins's inquiry on 4 October 1866, Dickens explains that while the original scenery of the melodrama is "carefully preserved" at the warehouse of Chapman and Hall, it had been "cut down into small panels" to decorate Tavistock House, and "would put the Olympic Painter into chains, instead of helping him" (Pilgrim, 11:251). Although Dickens attended a dress rehearsal at the Olympic in October, he did not record his reaction to the play.

72. Wilkie Collins, *The Frozen Deep: A Drama. In Three Acts* (London: C. Whiting, 1866), p. 13; subsequent references to *The Frozen Deep: A Drama* are cited parenthetically in the text.

the trances could be renewed, that . . . she would know for certain whether [Frank] is a dead or a living man" (35). Clara's visions of Wardour and Aldersley, received in a "Trance" in Devonshire, are fully corroborated by the accounts that Crayford and Wardour provide in the third act and by Collins's staging in the first. Appearing on an iceberg at the back of the stage, gun in hand, Wardour stands behind the "recumbent" figure of Aldersley, as Clara delivers the following speech: "Frank—Frank—Frank, rise on the iceberg and defend yourself. Richard Wardour knows the truth. Richard Wardour has sworn to have your life. [rays of red light "from the aurora borealis" spread from behind the iceberg] The crimson stain. The crimson stain. It floods the dreary sky. It reddens the dreadful ice" (14). Because Wardour only discovers that Aldersley is his rival in act 2, after Clara's speech has been delivered, the structure of the play confirms that she is prophetic, as does Lieutenant Crayford, who "starts" when she describes her vision of the missing men: "Dream or vision, it showed her the truth! . . . I myself questioned our comrades when they came back to us. The last they saw of Frank and Wardour, those two were afloat on a drifting iceberg—and the northern lights were aflame in the dreary sky" (38–39). As if Crayford's secondhand evidence were not convincing enough, Collins provides us with Wardour's account as well: "I stood on the floating iceberg, looking down on [Aldersley] at my feet! And the Tempter crimsoned the sky with blood" (44).

As in Collins's 1856 draft, Crayford wishes to "protect" women by keeping them "in ignorance" (34), and both he and Lieutenant Steventon lie to Clara about Wardour's supposed death. But with a "resolute self-possession" new to her character (37), she rejects their explanations, cross examining the other officers and violating gender boundaries in her search for truth. Clara's behavior undermines stereotypes of female weakness, as does the failure of medical "science" to diagnose her condition, despite the attempt of a "great physician from London" to do so (7–8).

Collins makes the fallacies of gender construction and the medical knowledge of women the central theme of his final, narrative version of *The Frozen Deep,* written for his 1873–74 American reading tour and expanded and published as a short novel by Richard Bentley in 1874. In this version of the story, Clara is "viewed simply as a case . . . by no means unfamiliar to medical practice," and her visionary powers explained as a "disorder . . . of the brain and the nervous system" or as a "hysterical malady."[73] But Clara's visions prove truthful, not delusional, and Collins accounts for and justifies her transgressive behavior by

73. Wilkie Collins, *The Frozen Deep,* in *The Frozen Deep and Other Stories,* 2 vols. (London: Richard Bentley and Son, 1874), 1:19–20; subsequent references to *The Frozen Deep* (1874) are cited parenthetically in the text.

underscoring the restrictions placed on her by virtue of her sex. "What right have you to control my actions?" she asks Wardour when he appears to claim her hand (52). Referring to both the Amazons and to Atalanta, the Greek maiden who tried to outrun her suitors in the hope of remaining single, Collins suggests that women need alternatives to marriage, although it is routinely "prescribed" for them: "Her marriage would make a healthy and a happy woman of her," Clara's doctor asserts (165).

Collins is primarily concerned with gender inequities in his final version of *The Frozen Deep,* yet vestiges of its topical origins remain: Rae's charge that cannibalism was practiced among Franklin and his men. Removing the figure of the devouring wet nurse from the story, Collins focuses on forms of hunger among the Arctic explorers, including their appetite for women: Aldersley "feasts his eyes on [Clara's] lovely downcast face" (41) and "drink[s] a last draught of her beauty" (45). At the same time, Want and Wardour "hunger" for the lives of their privileged male companions (216), and Collins develops the theme of class injury by describing the "voracious" Wardour (205) as a "figure of . . . want" who begs from the well-fed officers, "his eyes glar[ing] like the eyes of a wild animal . . . at the well-spread table" (203). In the 1856 draft, "Wardour looks fixedly at the food in his hand . . . and puts away the bread and meat quickly in an old bag slung over his shoulder," saving it for Aldersley (MA 81, 3:11). But in the 1874 narrative, Wardour's hunger cannot be suppressed: "with lean, long-nailed hands that looked like claws," the "starving creature" seizes the food he has come to beg, which he "devoured voraciously" (204–5). Conversely, the officers eventually lose their appetite for Want's grumbling and the pleasure he takes in their ill-health; Lieutenant Crayford "seems to have lost his former relish for the humour of John Want," the narrator notes (177).

As Collins often does in his fiction, he qualifies his social critique in the 1874 narrative, partially reinscribing the norms he sets out to question. Thus the "resolute" Clara turns to Lieutenant Crayford for protection when Wardour reappears, rejecting Lucy's offer of assistance: "'I'm frightened, dreadfully frightened!' she said to him, faintly. '*You* keep with me—a woman is no protection'" (201). Clara is happily reunited with Aldersley at the end of the story, as if to confirm the doctor's prescription of marriage for her well-being, and the transgressive power of her second sight and her vision of Wardour's menace are countered by the conventional Christian lesson delivered by Lucy, who wishes "to raise her to the better and nobler belief in the mercy of God" (185). Indeed, Aldersley is saved by a Christlike Wardour, described by Lieutenant Crayford as a "martyr" who "has died in the moment of victory. . . . Not one of us here but may live to envy *his* glorious death" (214, 220).

Crayford's orthodoxy reminds us that Collins often contains the more subversive elements of his writing, as Tamar Heller notes. Yet the textual history of *The Frozen Deep* reveals the extent to which Collins's radicalism was also contained by Dickens. Because Collins drafted the play, Dickens heavily revised it, and Collins alone returned to and altered the work in 1866 and 1874, *The Frozen Deep* provides an unusually striking example of the counterpoint between the two writers. In particular, the changing representations of Nurse Esther illustrate their disagreement over the merits of English nationalism and the significance of racial differences. Though it often takes more subtle forms, their division on these issues underlies the two stories they coauthored for *Household Words* in 1857 in response to the Indian Mutiny, each writer contributing his own chapters—"The Lazy Tour of Two Idle Apprentices" and "The Perils of Certain English Prisoners."

CHAPTER 4

Class Consciousness and the Indian Mutiny:

The Collaborative Fiction of 1857

Toward the end of November 1857, three months after his last performance as Richard Wardour in *The Frozen Deep,* Dickens wrote to Angela Burdett-Coutts describing the Christmas Number he and Collins had just finished writing for *Household Words:* "It is all one story this time, of which I have written the greater part (Mr. Collins has written one chapter), and which I have planned with great care in the hope of commemorating, without any vulgar catchpenny connexion or application, some of the best qualities of the English character that have been shewn in India" (Pilgrim, 8:482–83). In speaking of the "best qualities" shown by the English in India, Dickens refers to their "heroic" resistance against the native sepoys, who had begun to mutiny in May of that year. The sepoys had political and economic grievances, but the immediate cause of their revolt was religious. The British had introduced Enfield rifles into the army, and the sepoys had to bite off the ends of the greased cartridges before they were loaded. Suspecting that the cartridges were greased with cow and pig fat, and hence sacrilegious to Hindus and Muslims, the sepoys concluded that the British were forcing them to commit sacrilege and rebelled. Some murdered their officers as well as English women and children.[1] Every day, accounts of Indian atrocities and examples of British martyrdom were reported in the British press: the sale of Englishwomen to Indians in the

---

1. For discussions of the Indian Mutiny from different vantage points, see Wayne G. Broehl Jr., *Crisis of the Raj: The Revolt of 1857 through British Lieutenants' Eyes* (Hanover, N.H.: University Press of New England, 1986); Pratul Chandra Gupta, *Nana Sahib and the Rising at Cawnpore* (Oxford: Clarendon Press, 1963); Christopher Hibbert, *The Great Mutiny: India 1857* (New York: Penguin, 1980); Thomas Metcalf, *The Aftermath of Revolt: India, 1857–1870* (Princeton, N.J.: Princeton University Press, 1964); and Vinayak Savarkar, *The Indian War of Independence, 1857* (Bombay: Phoenix Press, 1947).

streets of Cawnpore, for example.[2] Predictably enough, these accounts elicited calls for repression and retribution. "No episode in British imperial history raised public excitement to a higher pitch than the Indian Mutiny," Brantlinger observes.[3]

Dickens shared in this so-called "excitement." Like many of his contemporaries in 1857, he called for the extermination of the Indian race. His genocidal response to the mutiny is recorded in a letter written to Burdett-Coutts on 4 October 1857. But as this letter makes clear, Dickens's racism was generated by domestic as well as imperial anxieties, since class tensions in England, not only racial hostilities in India, were brought to the fore by the mutiny:

> When I see people writing letters in the Times day after day, about this class and that class not joining the Army and having no interest in arms—and when I think how we all know that we have suffered a system to go on, which has blighted generous ambition, and put reward out of the common man's reach—and how our gentry have disarmed our Peasantry—I become Demoniacal.
>
> And I wish I were Commander in Chief in India. The first thing I would do to strike that Oriental race with amazement (not in the least regarding them as if they lived in the Strand, London, or at Camden Town), should be to proclaim to them, in their language, that I considered my holding that appointment by the leave of God, to mean that I should do my utmost to exterminate the Race upon whom the stain of the late cruelties rested; and that I begged them to do me the favor to observe that I was there for that purpose and no other, and was proceeding, with all convenient dispatch and merciful swiftness of execution, to blot it out of mankind and raze it off the face of the Earth. (Pilgrim, 8:459)

Dickens addresses what appear to be two separate concerns in this letter—the disinterest of working-class men in joining the army and the need to punish the sepoys for their "cruelties." Yet these two concerns are inseparable in his thinking. Not only did racial conflict in India expose class differences in England; the image of the treacherous sepoy enabled Dickens to imaginatively resolve those very differences. In the summer and fall of 1857, the London *Times* had printed letters complaining of the reluctance of working-class men to join the fight against the sepoys as well as letters justifying their reluctance and calling for easier promotion from the ranks. If one out of three commissions went to noncommissioned officers or privates, a writer argued on 2 October, the

2. *Examiner* (5 September 1857); quoted by William Oddie, "Dickens and the Indian Mutiny," *Dickensian* 68 (January 1972): 4.

3. Patrick Brantlinger, *Rule of Darkness: British Literature and Imperialism, 1830–1914* (Ithaca, N.Y.: Cornell University Press, 1988), p. 199.

"prospect of promotion would be added to the motive from righteous indignation at atrocities greater than any which are known to have been perpetrated
since the world began."[4] Addressing this problem in his letter to Burdett-
Coutts, Dickens justifies the resentment of "the common man" and his reti-
cence to fight the sepoys, since the army system reinforces class differences by
"blight[ing] . . . ambition" and "put[ting] reward out of . . . reach." He then
goes on to attack the Indian mutineers in a way that resolves these differences—
by defining the otherness of the "Oriental" against the sameness of all
Englishmen, regardless of their class: the Indians are "not in the least" to be
viewed "as if they lived in the Strand, London, or at Camden Town."
Conveying his sense of English solidarity rhetorically, Dickens puts himself in
the shoes of the common man and wishes for a promotion himself ("I wish I
were Commander in Chief").

Like Dickens, Collins was interested in the relationship between class identity and nationalism, and understood that representations of racial difference
often serve a unifying and nationalistic end. From nearly the start of his literary
career, he considered the tension between class and national allegiances and its
consequences for imperialism. Drawing on a number of historical sources in
Antonina; or, the Fall of Rome, Collins attributes Rome's fall to class divisions at
the heart of the ancient empire. Rather than joining the fight against the invading barbarians, the discontented character Probus, angered by the political
and economic abuses of the aristocrats ruling his own country, welcomes them
to Rome:

> Goths! . . . Is there one among us to whom this report of their advance upon
> Rome does not speak of hope rather than of dread? Have we a chance of rising
> from the degradation forced on us by our superiors until this den of heartless
> triflers and shameless cowards is swept from the very earth that it pollutes? . . . Do

4. *Times* (London), 2 October 1857, 4. Shortly before the mutiny, Dickens himself published an article criticizing the "snail-like" pace of "promotion from the ranks" during the Crimean War and contrasting the English army system with the French system of "promotion by merit": "Once in the ranks,
always in the ranks, is the maxim in the English army; and the man who accepts the shilling from the
recruiting-sergeant . . . bids adieu to all hope of rising in the military profession." See [Reeves],
"Promotion, French and English," *Household Words* 15 (24 January 1857): 91. Similarly, "Why We Can't
Get Recruits" argues that no "educated man of the English working classes" will join the army because
he "hope[s] to better himself" (*All the Year Round* 14 [9 December 1865]: 464). Dickens continued to
publish articles on the English army system, criticizing the priority given to "money" over "merit." See,
for example, "Money or Merit?" *All the Year Round* 3 (21 April 1860): 30–32; and "Pay For Your
Places," *All the Year Round* 4 (27 October 1860): 67–69. Brian Bond discusses the Indian Mutiny and
the problem of army recruitment in the 1850s, as well as the reforms to which the crisis gave rise, in
"Prelude to the Cardwell Reforms, 1856–68," *Journal of the Royal United Service Institution* 106 (1961):
229–36, and "Recruiting the Victorian Army, 1870–92," *Victorian Studies* 5 (June 1962): 331–38.

you wonder now that . . . I say to the Goths—with thousands who suffer the same tribulation that I now undergo—"Enter our gates! Level our palaces to the ground! Confound, if you will, in one common slaughter, we that are victims with those that are tyrants!"[5]

Although Collins's novel is set in antiquity, its recurring refrain—"in Ancient Rome, as in Modern London"—makes it a warning parable for those governing the British Empire in the 1850s.[6] Indeed, Collins's image of citizens failing to defend "their" empire from barbarians because they feel "exile[d]" from their own "country's privileges" recurs in Dickens's letter to Burdett-Coutts as well as those written to the *Times* in 1857.[7] Without the promise of promotion from the ranks, the common man in Victorian England, like Collins's ancient Probus, will never feel the "righteous indignation" necessary to fight the sepoys and may identify with the mutinous barbarians instead.

The problem of the army system and the disaffection of the common man inform the two stories conceived by Dickens and coauthored by Collins in 1857—"The Lazy Tour of Two Idle Apprentices," serialized in *Household Words* in October, and "The Perils of Certain English Prisoners," published in December as the Christmas Number. While "The Perils" has been identified as Dickens's story about the Indian Mutiny, "The Lazy Tour" has not. Yet Dickens responds to the mutiny in both works, although in a rather surprising way: by seeking to repair class relations. In fact, the class divisions revealed by recruitment efforts in England during the mutiny prove to be a more pressing concern for Dickens than race relations themselves, and he uses racial conflict as one of several ways in which to overcome the class differences and class resentment that were exposed to view by events in India. In "The Lazy Tour," Dickens elides class differences by imagining an England in which all labor is suspended, in which "all degrees of men, from peers to paupers," are members of an idle class.[8] In "The Perils," he displaces the class resentment of English privates with racism, transforming their socially subversive feelings of class injury into a socially quiescent hatred of natives.

In his own contributions to these stories, Collins both complies with and resists Dickens's aims; his response marks the political differences between the

5. Wilkie Collins, *Antonina; or, the Fall of Rome*, vol. 17 of *The Works of Wilkie Collins*, 30 vols. (New York: AMS Press, 1970), pp. 81–82.

6. Ibid., p. 481.

7. Ibid., p. 80.

8. Charles Dickens and Wilkie Collins, "The Lazy Tour of Two Idle Apprentices," in *The Lazy Tour of Two Idle Apprentices and Other Stories* (London: Chapman and Hall, 1890), p. 89; subsequent references to "The Lazy Tour" are cited parenthetically in the text.

two writers as well as the changing terms of their relationship. Since the publication of Nuel Pharr Davis's *Life of Wilkie Collins,* critics have noted that Collins's response to the mutiny differed markedly from Dickens's and that the virulent racism that characterizes Dickens's remarks about Hindus—"low, treacherous, murderous, tigerous villains . . . who would rend you to pieces at half an hour's notice" (Pilgrim, 8:473)—is notably absent from Collins's writing, or expressed by figures we are meant to distrust. In "A Sermon for Sepoys," published in *Household Words* in 1858, Collins points to "the excellent moral lessons" provided by "Oriental literature" and advocates the moral reform of Indians rather than their extermination.[9] Less anxious to elide class differences than Dickens, Collins has no *need* for the virulent racism that Dickens expresses. As his portrait of Probus in *Antonina* suggests, Collins is willing to imagine— and justify—an alliance between the members of an imperial underclass and those of a subject race, and he does so in the works that follow the Indian Mutiny as well as in those that precede it.

In the 1857 stories, Collins more clearly stakes out his own position and questions that of Dickens than he had in such works as "The Seven Poor Travellers" and "The Wreck of the Golden Mary." He was encouraged to do so by his growing professional success and by his increasingly important role as Dickens's companion and confidante. In 1857, Dickens's marital unhappiness and his romantic pursuit of the young actress Ellen Ternan left him in a state of "restlessness" (Pilgrim, 8:423), and he often sought the companionship and support of the younger writer, whose own unconventional relationship with Caroline Graves dates from that year: "Any mad proposal you please, will find a wildly insane response in. Yours Ever," Dickens concludes his letter of 11 May 1857 (Pilgrim, 8:323). "On Wednesday Sir—on Wednesday, if the mind can devise any thing sufficiently in the style of Sybarite Rome in the days of its culminating voluptuousness," Dickens tells Collins on 22 May, "I am your man" (Pilgrim, 8:330). A staff member rewarded for his "devot[ion]" and "great service" to *Household Words* with an annual pay raise of fifty pounds (Pilgrim, 8:440, 457), Collins remained well aware of the value placed on his "submission" to Dickens, but he was also newly conscious of Dickens's vulnerability to public opinion and of his own crucial importance to his famous friend.

Thus when Catherine Peters describes Collins in 1857 as "a willing instrument and extension of Dickens" (*King,* 168), her portrait is incomplete. In "The Lazy Tour" and "The Perils," Collins proves considerably less compliant than Peters suggests and challenges as well as supports Dickens's strategies and aims. Writing as Thomas Idle in "The Lazy Tour," Collins accepts a role that ob-

9. [Wilkie Collins], "A Sermon for Sepoys," *Household Words* 17 (27 February 1858): 244.

scures his subordination to Dickens at *Household Words,* playing the part of a fellow apprentice whose obscurity is due to a disinclination for work, not to the suppression of his name in publications. But while embracing the idleness that Dickens ascribes to his fictional persona, Collins also identifies it as a mark of Idle's gentility and develops its meaning as a class privilege in his interpolated tale. Using the 1857 mutiny to ally the apprentices, whatever their differences may be, Dickens refers to India as a place "which Idle and Goodchild did not [like]" (6). By contrast, Collins parodies the rhetoric intended to unify Englishmen against threatening others, comically deriding the "smouldering treachery" of "equine nature" (102) rather than that of the "Oriental race."

In his chapter of "The Perils," similarly, Collins deflates the elevated tone of Dickens's narrative, debunking the martyrdom allegedly suffered by the English at Indian hands. Dickens seeks to "commemorat[e] . . . the best qualities of the English character shewn in India," but Collins takes a more equivocal position. He treats the rebel leader as a mirror image of "dandies . . . in London," reminding his readers that the mutiny was caused, in part, by the excesses of English officers who abused their Indian subordinates.[10] Allying the English privates and sailors with the natives alongside whom they labor, Collins suggests that working-class Englishmen may have more in common with mutinous sepoys than Dickens allows. In a story about mutiny, Collins exhibits his own penchant for insubordination, although his resistance to Dickens often takes subtle and compromised forms.

I

Drawing the names of their protagonists from William Hogarth's sequence of engravings entitled *Industry and Idleness* (1747) in "The Lazy Tour of Two Idle Apprentices," Dickens and Collins describe the adventures of Francis Goodchild and Thomas Idle as they travel into the north of England in September 1857, with Dickens writing from Goodchild's perspective and Collins from that of Idle. In the opening section, Dickens explains that the apprentices, "exhausted by the long, hot summer, and the long, hot work it had brought with it," have run away from their employer—whom he identifies as "lady . . . Literature"—in the hopes of "making a perfectly idle trip, in any direction" (3). In the first chapter, Dickens recounts their departure from London

10. Charles Dickens and Wilkie Collins, "The Perils of Certain English Prisoners," in *The Lazy Tour of Two Idle Apprentices and Other Stories,* p. 269; subsequent references to "The Perils" are cited parenthetically in the text.

and their stay in Carlisle and Heske, while Collins describes their ascent of Carrock Fell, on which Idle sprains his ankle. In the second chapter, Dickens brings the apprentices to Wigton and then to an unnamed Cumberland town, where they meet Dr. Speddie and his assistant Mr. Lorn. Taking up the narrative, Collins writes an interpolated tale related by Dr. Speddie, in which a poor young man pronounced dead one afternoon returns to life that evening. In chapter 3, Dickens describes the apprentices' arrival in Allonby, while Collins recounts the disasters caused by Idle's attempts at industry. Dickens concludes the chapter by taking the characters from Allonby to an intermediate railway station, and on to Lancaster. Chapter 4, written solely by Dickens and set in Lancaster, is largely taken up with an interpolated tale narrated by a ghost who describes forcing his young bride to die by the power of his will and murdering her male defender, and who confesses to being hanged for his crimes in the previous century. In the final chapter, Dickens describes the apprentices as they travel through Leeds to Doncaster, arriving during race week for the running of the St. Leger, while Collins explains Idle's dislike of "equine nature."[11]

As Dickens's letters from September 1857 make clear, the plotline of "The Lazy Tour" generally follows the itinerary of the two writers as they made their way from London to Doncaster, composing weekly installments of the story as they went from place to place, and each of the chapters selectively describes events they experienced on their travels. Collins badly sprained his ankle on Carrock Fell, for example, and Dickens went to the St. Leger in Doncaster, although the fact that he accompanied Ellen Ternan to the races goes unmentioned in the story.[12]

Dickens first refers to the story that became "The Lazy Tour" in a letter written to Collins on 29 August 1857, soon after his last performance in *The Frozen Deep:*

11. Generally speaking, critics agree on how to divide the literary labors of Dickens and Collins in "The Lazy Tour." Using the 1890 Chapman and Hall edition of the story, Nuel Pharr Davis attributes its authorship as follows: chapter 1, Dickens, pp. 1–11, Collins, pp. 11–19; chapter 2, Dickens, pp. 20–28, Collins, pp. 28–49; chapter 3, Dickens, pp. 50–55, Collins, pp. 55–65; chapter 4, Dickens, pp. 66–86; chapter 5, Dickens, pp. 87–96, Collins, pp. 97–103, Dickens, pp. 103–4. Davis mistakenly attributes a portion of chapter 3 to Collins (the description of the railway station, which Dickens authored [see Pilgrim, 8:454]), but otherwise his attributions agree with my own. Frederic G. Kitton is less accurate in his analysis of "The Lazy Tour"; citing Forster, he mistakenly attributes all of chapter 5 to Collins. Yet as the Pilgrim editors explain, Forster purposely misattributed chapter 5 to Collins to "avert . . . attention from the revealing passages" that describe Goodchild's infatuation with a young woman modeled on Ellen Ternan (Pilgrim, 8:448 n. 1). See Davis, *The Life of Wilkie Collins* (Urbana: University of Illinois Press, 1956), p. 326 n. 24; and Kitton, *The Minor Writings of Charles Dickens* (London: Elliot Stock, 1900), p. 134.

12. Claire Tomalin discusses Dickens's meetings with Ellen Ternan in Doncaster, noting that Dickens chose it as his destination because he knew that the Ternans were scheduled to perform there. See *The Invisible Woman: The Story of Nelly Ternan and Charles Dickens* (New York: Knopf, 1991), pp. 102–5.

Partly in the grim despair and restlessness of this subsidence from excitement, and partly for the sake of Household Words, I want to cast about whether you and I can go anywhere—take any tour—see any thing—whereon we could write something together. Have you any idea, tending to any place in the world? Will you rattle your head and see if there is any pebble in it which we could wander away and play at Marbles with? We want something for Household Words, and I want to escape from myself. (Pilgrim, 8:423)

Citing this letter, critics and biographers discuss Dickens's need to "escape from [him]self" in the fall of 1857—or, rather, his desire to escape from his wife Catherine—arguing that his growing sense of marital unhappiness and his interest in Ellen Ternan lay "behind his ostensibly 'lazy tour' with Collins."[13] Wishing for a separation from Catherine, but fearing "it is impossible" (Pilgrim, 8:434), Dickens planned a trip that would bring him to Doncaster when Ellen and her family members were scheduled to perform at the Theatre Royal, traveling with Collins, whom he knew would not find his extramarital interests at all offensive. Indeed, Dickens refers to Collins's own aversion to matrimony in his portion of chapter 3—when he describes Idle's desire to "eat Bride-cake without the trouble of being married" (64–65)—and both writers complain of the caprices and difficulties of women in their interpolated tales.

But if Dickens's tour enabled him to escape from the confinement of his marriage, the story itself is escapist in another sense. Deborah Thomas notes that "The Lazy Tour" can be read as "a kind of creative game" that Dickens and Collins played together, a work that expresses a "holiday *jeux d'esprit*."[14] Yet this holiday spirit serves a serious social end. Representing his characters as the members of an all-inclusive idle class, a nation gone on holiday, Dickens solves the problem of resentment in the rank and file.

The social anxieties that underlie "The Lazy Tour" are suggested by the context in which the story first appeared as well as by its own treatment of class relations. Its first installment in *Household Words* was immediately followed by "Indian Recruits and Indian English," an article describing the "lesson written in fire and blood" by the treacherous sepoys, "a horde of blood-thirsty enemies," but that begins by acknowledging the scarcity of army volunteers back home: "In Europe, the task of recruiting-sergeant is anything but a sinecure. In

13. Deborah A. Thomas, *Dickens and the Short Story* (Philadelphia: University of Pennsylvania Press, 1982), p. 113. Like Thomas, Harry Stone reads "The Lazy Tour" as an "intensely and avowedly autobiographic" work that registers "Dickens' troubled flight away from self." See *Dickens and the Invisible World: Fairy Tales, Fantasy, and Novel-Making* (Bloomington: Indiana University Press, 1979), pp. 288, 291.

14. D. Thomas, *Dickens and the Short Story,* pp. 80–81.

fact, scarcely any nation relies on any other than forced conscription to replenish its armies. England alone seems able to furnish an adequate number of volunteers, and even in England, the demand is often much beyond the supply."[15]

In Dickens's opening section of "The Lazy Tour," as in this *Household Words* article, the recruiting-sergeant makes his appearance, in a scene reminding us that volunteers are scarce. "Through all the . . . bargains and blessings" offered during market morning in Carlisle, Dickens observes, "the recruiting-sergeant watchfully elbowed his way, a thread of War in the peaceful skein. Likewise on the walls were printed hints that the Oxford Blues might not be indisposed to hear of a few fine active young men; and that whereas the standard of that distinguished corps is full six feet, 'growing lads of five feet eleven' need not absolutely despair of being accepted" (8). To Dickens's original readers, his passing references to the recruiting sergeant, on the one hand, and to the Oxford Blues (or Royal Horse Guards), on the other, would have brought to mind the problem of the army system as he describes it to Burdett-Coutts. Directed by the commander in chief of the army and headed by aging aristocrats who had last fought at Waterloo, the Horse Guards were notoriously elitist and anachronistic in the 1850s. "The spirit of persistence in old blunders is certainly not national, but is of the Horse Guards, local, and only of the old school military," an article later published by Dickens explained.[16] Because commissions in the Horse Guards were among the most expensive, the regiment made the class divisions in the army and the elitism of its officers particularly apparent. Whereas a commission in the infantry cost £450 in 1821, the purchase price for a commission in the Horse Guards was £1,200.[17] By the time "The Lazy Tour" was published, the elitism of cavalry officers had become a familiar subject of political cartoons, which represented them as "wasp-waisted" dandies.[18] Although the "hints" printed on Carlisle's market walls in "The Lazy Tour" suggest that those "few . . . fine men" who wish to join the Horse Guards "need not absolutely despair of being accepted," Dickens's readers understood that the common man, pursued by the recruiting-sergeant, had little interest in joining the ranks.

15. [E. Townsend and Alexander Henry Abercromby Hamilton], "Indian Recruits and Indian English," *Household Words* 16 (3 October 1857): 320, 319.

16. "Tape at the Horse Guards," *All the Year Round* 6 (6 March 1862): 568. "Soldier's Law," similarly, speaks of the "brute inert opposition [to reform] on the part of the ancient generals at the Horse Guards" (*All the Year Round* 16 [28 July 1866]: 55), as does "The Horse Guards Rampant" ([Henry Morley], *Household Words* 8 [31 December 1853]: 428–31). "At the horse guards," the military historian Correlli Barnett notes, "old men . . . stultified progress" (*Britain and Her Army, 1509–1970* [New York: William Morrow, 1970], p. 282).

17. Edward M. Spiers, *The Army and Society, 1815–1914* (London: Longman, 1980), p. 11.

18. Jerome J. McGann, *The Beauty of Inflections: Literary Investigations in Historical Method and Theory* (Oxford: Clarendon Press, 1988), p. 195.

Having alluded to the class tensions underlying his story, Dickens goes on to relieve them—not by advocating reform in the army system but by eliding class distinctions. Transforming industry into idleness and work into play, Dickens represents Englishmen as members of a leisure class, whether they are high or low born, wealthy or impoverished. For example, "the working young men" of Carlyle idle about town with "their hands in their pockets" and "nothing else to do" (7). The fishermen in Allonby "never fish," but "g[e]t their living entirely by looking at the ocean" (53). Although the appearance of workers in Wigton is "partly of a mining, partly of a ploughing, partly of a stable charac-ter," they do not labor in mines, fields, or stables. Instead they "look . . . at nothing—very hard": "Their backs are slouched, and their legs are curved with much standing about. Their pockets are loose and dog's-eared, on account of their hands being always in them" (23).

In "The Lazy Tour," such idleness is not a symptom of economic depression or unemployment but a feature of an idyll in which men earn their keep with-out labor and in which objects themselves deny their use value. Thus in the drawing room of the inn at Heske, as Dickens describes it, the furniture and dishes pass themselves off as purely ornamental, as "nick-nack[s]" rather than tools. "The copper tea-kettle . . . took his station on a stand of his own at the greatest possible distance from the fire-place, and said: 'By your leave, not a kit-tle, but a bijou.' The Staffordshire-ware butter-dish . . . got upon a little round occasional table in a window, with a worked top, and announced itself . . . as an aid to polite conversation, a graceful trifle in china to be chatted over by callers, as they airily trifled away the visiting moments of a butterfly existence" (10). In Dickens's portions of "The Lazy Tour," virtually everyone shares this "butterfly existence." The apprentices travel "deep in the manufacturing bosom of Yorkshire" but see no signs of factory life, and they soon arrive at Doncaster during race week to find "all work but race-work at a stand-still; all men at a stand-still" (89). It is September, and harvest time, but the crops are "still un-reaped" (8): "No labourers [are] working in the fields" (91) because the busi-ness of play engages "all degrees of men, from peers to paupers" (89).

This suspension of labor is all the more striking when "The Lazy Tour" is compared to the story that Nuel Pharr Davis identifies as its literary source—Collins's "A Journey in Search of Nothing," published in *Household Words* on 5 September 1857.[19] In this story, Collins's narrator is a professional author whose "weary right hand ache[s] . . . with driving the ceaseless pen."[20] Told that he has "been working too hard" by his doctor, who orders him to "do

19. Davis, *Life of Wilkie Collins*, p. 204.
20. Wilkie Collins, "A Journey in Search of Nothing," *Household Words* 16 (5 September 1857): 217–23; *My Miscellanies*, vol. 20 of *The Works of Wilkie Collins*, p. 26.

nothing" as a cure, he travels to retired country villages but discovers that he cannot escape from labor.[21] Each town to which he travels, no matter how remote or leisurely it appears, reminds him of the "necessities of work."[22] Observing "the sons of labor" in these villages, "cadaverous savages, drinking gloomily from brown mugs," he contrasts romantic depictions of such figures with "modern reality," debunking the pastoral idealizations of workers in the poetry of Keats and the paintings of Claude and Poussin: "Where are the pipe and tabor that I have seen in so many pictures; where are the simple songs that I have read about in so many poems?"[23]

In "A Journey in Search of Nothing," Collins restores the realities of labor to the poetry and paintings of the romantics, but in "The Lazy Tour" Dickens asks him to do the reverse—to imagine the English as members of a nationalized leisure class. Dickens's escape from material realities takes its most personal form in his representation of himself and Collins as Goodchild and Idle—"misguided young men" who have run away from their "employer," "a highly meritorious lady (named Literature), of fair credit and repute" (3). As the conductor of *Household Words,* Dickens and not "lady . . . Literature" was Collins's employer, and the two writers set off for Cumberland, in part, because copy was needed for the journal. But Dickens identifies Goodchild and Idle as fellow apprentices on vacation, obscuring the authority he wields in their working relationship as well as the labor they performed during their tour. In his letters from Doncaster, Dickens speaks of "fall[ing] to work for HW," and recounts the daily routine that he and Collins followed in order to produce the necessary amount of copy (Pilgrim, 8:448). "Collins is sticking a little with his story," Dickens told Wills on 17 September, "but I hope will come through it tomorrow" (Pilgrim, 8:448). Such difficulties are eliminated in "The Lazy Tour," however, in which the vacationing apprentices produce only "lazy sheets" from "lazy notes" (70).

If any work is accomplished on the tour, Dickens claims, it is performed by Goodchild, who has no real idea of idleness. "You *can't* play," Idle complains to Goodchild in Dickens's narrative: "You make work of everything" (66). Whereas "Goodchild was laboriously idle," Dickens explains, and "had no better idea of idleness than that it was useless industry," Idle "was an idler of the unmixed Irish or Neapolitan type; a passive idler, a born-and-bred idler, a consistent idler, who practices what he would have preached if he had not been too idle to preach" (4). Justifying the inequities between himself and his staff

21. Ibid., pp. 24–25.
22. Ibid., p. 46.
23. Ibid., pp. 39, 29–30.

member and the discrepancies in their recognition and rewards, Dickens models Goodchild on the "industrious apprentice" of Hogarth's series and Collins's Idle on his foil, while also suggesting that *true* idleness—the "born-and-bred" variety—is not English but "Irish or Neapolitan."

Whereas Dickens attributes idleness, in its purest form, to racial others, Collins identifies it as English—and upper class. Like his aristocratic taste for "sedan-chair[s]" (100), the idleness embraced by Collins's Idle is the sign of a specific class identity. In Collins's narrative, Idle lies on the sofa, crippled by his exertions on Carrock Fell, and wistfully remembers "that the current of his life had hitherto oozed along in one smooth stream of laziness, occasionally troubled on the surface by a slight passing ripple of industry" (56). Resolving "never to be industrious again" (60), he recounts the "disasters" that resulted from his "activity and industry" in the past, efforts that he made at public school, on the cricket field, and in the legal profession: places that define his class identity. Idle's industry results in disaster, Collins suggests, because it violates what he facetiously describes as "the great do-nothing principle" of English gentlemen (59). Playing the part of Idle, Collins undoubtedly enjoyed imagining himself as a "do-nothing" gentleman defined against a hopelessly industrious Dickens. While enjoying this fantasy, however, Collins also used it to a subversive end: to illustrate class privilege in a story designed to obscure class differences.

Collins more fully develops the social meaning of idleness in the interpolated tale he contributed to chapter 2 of "The Lazy Tour," a short story later anthologized in *The Queen of Hearts* (1859) as "The Dead Hand." Narrated by Dr. Speddie, who is called in to treat Idle's sprained ankle, the tale recounts the experiences of an impoverished man pronounced dead in an inn one afternoon but brought back to life that night by the doctor, in the presence of the young man occupying the same double-bedded chamber as the "corpse." Compared to Collins's melodrama *The Red Vial* (1858), in which a body in a morgue is revitalized, "The Dead Hand" is generally disparaged as an exercise in the macabre or as a way in which Collins "padded out" his contribution to *Household Words*.[24] But in portraying the privileged figure who discovers signs of life in his roommate—a wealthy gentleman of leisure named (appropriately) Arthur Holliday—Collins reworks the central theme of "The Lazy Tour," undermining the social idyll constructed in the larger story.

Like the workers in Carlyle and the fishermen in Allonby, whom Dickens describes in his portions of "The Lazy Tour," Collins's Arthur Holliday has no need to work for a living. Unlike the leisure of Dickens's idle figures, however, Holliday's idleness marks his class privilege. The son of a wealthy manufacturer,

---

24. Kenneth Robinson, *Wilkie Collins: A Biography* (New York: Macmillan, 1952), p. 116.

he is "comfortably conscious of his own well-filled pockets" (31). Sauntering into Doncaster during race week without having troubled to reserve a room, he is amused by "the novelty of being turned away into the street, like a penniless vagabond" (29). But instead of endorsing Arthur's "holiday" spirits, Collins attributes them to the callous complacency of the leisure class and contrasts them with the bitterness of the poor man brought back to life only to perform whatever work "will put bread into [his] mouth" (42).

The interpolated tale that Dickens contributed to "The Lazy Tour" also calls attention to the sufferings of those who labor but does so in a safely distanced way, by criticizing the slave trade of Lancaster merchants in the previous century.[25] Having inherited the wealth of his dead bride, the ghostly narrator of Dickens's tale invests it in the "dark trade" at "Twelve Hundred Per Cent" (80). But like the slave merchants to whom Dickens refers when he first describes Lancaster, the narrator fails to benefit from profits derived from "wretched slaves":

> Mr. Goodchild concedes Lancaster to be a pleasant place. A place . . . possessing staid old houses richly fitted with old Honduras mahogany, which has grown so dark with time that it seems to have got something of a retrospective mirror-quality into itself, and to show the visitor, in the depth of its grain, through all its polish, the hue of the wretched slaves who groaned long ago under old Lancaster merchants. (65)

In this passage, Dickens assumes the role of a social critic who exposes hidden wrongs—the past sufferings of the "wretched slaves" whose labor brought wealth to Lancaster but whose exploitation is largely invisible and forgotten. However, Dickens obscures as much as he exposes here: perhaps most notably, the industrial "slavery" of the Lancashire operatives who are themselves hidden from view in "The Lazy Tour," yet compared to slaves of African descent by Victorian social reformers.[26] In *The Pickwick Papers*, published twenty years earlier, Dickens himself complains that the people of Muggleton condemn slavery

25. A story in which an older man forces his young wife to die by the power of his will, Dickens's interpolated tale usually interests critics because of its disturbing autobiographical elements and the way it conflates hostility toward an "encumbering wife" with the desire to shape and control a young woman named "Ellen" in the narrative (D. Thomas, *Dickens and the Short Story*, p. 113). See Stone, *Dickens and the Invisible World*, pp. 288–94; and Michael Slater, *Dickens and Women* (London: J. M. Dent, 1983), pp. 142–43.

26. For a discussion of this analogy as it was developed by chartists and abolitionists in the 1830s, see Betty Fladeland, "'Our Cause being One and the Same': Abolitionists and Chartism," in *Slavery and British Society, 1776–1846*, ed. James Walvin (Baton Rouge: Louisiana State University Press, 1982), pp. 69–99.

abroad while condoning its practice in the English mills; they have presented "no fewer than one thousand four hundred and twenty petitions against the continuance of Negro slavery abroad, and an equal number against any interference with the factory system at home."[27] But in "The Lazy Tour," Dickens avoids such analogies; the factory workers themselves never appear in the story, and the Lancaster slave merchants of the eighteenth century are compared not to the mill owners of Dickens's own day but to the mythical Eastern oppressors who figure in *The Arabian Nights* and whose "money turned to leaves" (65).

Furthermore, Dickens's "retrospective" look at the slaves who "groaned long ago" under Lancaster merchants implies that England's history of racial exploitation is just that: a thing of the past. Referring to "Uncle Tom" and "Miss Eva" in "The Lazy Tour" (9), Dickens reminds his readers that slavery is practiced by Americans in 1857, not by the English, whose role is to liberate rather than enslave. As one *Household Words* article asserts, "It is England's proudest boast that wherever her flag is unfurled, wherever her supremacy is established, there she carries the blessings of liberal institutions: she conquers but to set free. The same justice which is provided for the proudest son of Albion, is sent forth across the waters to attend on the meanest swarthy subject of Her Majesty, in distant India."[28]

In 1857, such claims about the "blessings" of English liberalism and the freedom bestowed through conquest were challenged on two fronts: by common men unwilling to join the army and by sepoys in open revolt. In "The Lazy Tour," Dickens responds to this crisis by evading it, imagining working men as gentlemen of leisure and referring to India only briefly, to dismiss the subject: "There was a lecture on India for those who liked it," he notes, "which Idle and Goodchild did not" (6). While Collins does not defend the sepoys in his portions of "The Lazy Tour," he proves less evasive in his treatment of the mutiny than Dickens does and suggests that the exploitation of the "subject races" by the English is hardly a thing of the past.

Writing at a time when calls for retribution against the sepoys were commonplace, Collins parodies the rhetoric used to describe them in his final section of the story, which represents the comic musings of Idle on the "treachery" of "equine nature." Idle's stereotype of the horse echoes that of the mutinous Indian, satirizing the racist hysteria that reduced the sepoys to ungrateful and dangerous beasts:

27. Charles Dickens, *The Pickwick Papers,* ed. Robert L. Patten (1972; reprint, Harmondsworth: Penguin, 1981), p. 161.

28. [John Capper], "Law in the East," *Household Words* 5 (26 June 1852): 347.

I prefer coming at once to my last charge against the horse, which is the most serious of all, because it affects his moral character. I accuse him boldly, in his capacity of servant to man, of slyness and treachery. I brand him publicly, no matter
how mild he may look about the eyes, or how sleek he may be about the coat, as
a systematic betrayer, whenever he can get the chance, of the confidence reposed
in him. . . . When he had made quite sure of my friendly confidence . . . the
smouldering treachery and ingratitude of the equine nature blazed out in an in-
stant. . . . What would be said of a Man who had requited my kindness in that
way? (99, 102)

Informing this passage is the standard British explanation of the mutiny, which
reduced a religious and political movement to yet another example of the innate treachery of "that Oriental race." A number of the articles that Dickens
published on the subject of the mutiny explain it in this way: "Hindoo Law,"
for instance, describes the "savage cruelty" of the seemingly "mild" Hindus,
which has broken out "like a long-smouldering flame," and Dickens himself
defines "the Oriental character" for Emile de la Rue as "low, treacherous, murderous, tigerous" in a letter of 23 October 1857 (Pilgrim, 8:473).[29]

Using this language in his account of "equine nature" to describe a pony that
fell while carrying Idle and a horse that shied, Collins makes it sound grossly
overblown and suggests its failure to explain the sepoys' behavior. His comic
account of the "revolt" of various animal species "overtaxed" by humankind
suggests, too, that the sepoys have reason to rebel; "the cow that kicks down
the milk-pail," for example, "may think herself taxed too heavily to contribute
to the dilution of human tea and the greasing of human bread" (102). Even
more pointedly, Collins repeatedly speaks of Idle's fears of "losing caste" at public school (56–57), referring to what those sympathetic to the sepoys understood to be the immediate cause of their revolt—not the innate treachery of
their race but their fear that the British were forcing them to commit sacrilege.
"You will soon lose your caste altogether," a low-caste Hindu allegedly told
the first sepoy mutineer; "the Europeans are going to make you bite cartridges
soaked in cow and pork fat."[30]

Collins's parody of mutiny rhetoric in "The Lazy Tour," and his suggestion
that the English as well as the Hindus have a "caste" system, look ahead to his
treatment of the sepoy revolt in "The Perils of Certain English Prisoners"—
and, later, in *The Moonstone* as well. While Dickens uses the image of the
treacherous sepoy to elide class differences in "The Perils," Collins puts English

29. [Henry Richard Fox Bourne], "Hindoo Law," *Household Words* 18 (25 September 1858): 337.
See also Brantlinger, *Rule of Darkness*, pp. 202–3.
30. Hibbert, *Great Mutiny*, p. 63.

privates and sailors in the position usually occupied by those subject to colonial rule, acknowledging the social inequities obscured by his collaborator.

II

While "The Lazy Tour" was running in *Household Words,* Dickens began to conduct research for the upcoming Christmas Number, which Collins agreed to coauthor. On 18 October, Dickens wrote to Morley, whose articles often focused on South and Central America. Explaining that he "particularly want[s] a little piece of information, with a view to the construction of something for Household Words," Dickens asks him to "consider and reply to the following question":

> Whether, at any time within a hundred years or so, we were in such amicable re-lations with South America as would have rendered it reasonably *possible* for us to have made, either a public treaty, or a private bargain, with a South American Government, empowering a little English Colony . . . to work a Silver-Mine (on purchase of the right). And whether, in that suppositious case, it is reasonably *pos-sible* that our English Government at home would have sent out a small force, of a few Marines or so, for that little Colony's protection; or (which is the same thing), would have drafted them off from the nearest English Military Station.
>
> Or, can you suggest, from your remembrance, any more probable set of cir-cumstances, in which a few English people—gentlemen, ladies and children—and a few English soldiers, would find themselves alone in a strange wild place and li-able to hostile attack?
>
> I wish to avoid India itself; but I want to shadow out in what I do, the bravery of our ladies in India. (Pilgrim, 8:468–69)

Morley responded by sending Dickens Carl Scherzer's *Travels in the Free States of Central America: Nicaragua, Honduras, and San Salvador* (1857). Forwarding the book to Collins on 22 October, Dickens referred him to specific passages on silver mining, told him that they must "come to some conclusion, right or wrong," about their story, and scheduled a meeting with him for the next af-ternoon (Pilgrim, 8:470).

Although Dickens tells Collins that the material he has received "compli-cates" his plans for the story (Pilgrim, 8:470), his conception of its plot and aims, as described to Morley, is largely realized in the finished work, which he and Collins completed by the end of November. Consisting of three chap-ters—the first and third by Dickens and the second by Collins—"The Perils" brings together English gentlefolk and English soldiers in "a strange wild place."

Narrated by Gill Davis, a private in the Royal Marines, it describes an attack on a "very small English colony" in Central America; the colony is an island off the coast of Honduras, where the silver taken from a mine on the mainland is temporarily stored. The British governor of Belize, acting on orders from home, sends twenty-four marines stationed in his settlement to "Silver-Store" to protect it against a "cruel gang of pirates." Along with a crew of sailors, they arrive there on the *Christopher Columbus,* a sloop that brings supplies to the island once a year, and then transports the annual accumulation of silver to Jamaica for sale and distribution "all over the world" (240). After a large party of marines and sailors is lured out to sea, the pirates raid the island for the silver, attacking English women and children as well as soldiers and male civilians, and killing some of them. These mutineers are a heterogeneous band and include "Malays, . . . Dutch, Maltese, Greeks, Sambos, Negroes, and Convict Englishmen from the West India Islands . . . some Portuguese, too, and a few Spaniards" (264). They are aided by a character named Christian George King, a composite of a black "sambo" and an American Indian, who betrays his English benefactors and is ultimately killed by them in reprisal. In the first chapter, Dickens depicts the leisurely life on the island before the attack and ends with the victory of the pirates over the colonists and their defenders, who are transported to the mainland. In the second, Collins recounts the difficult six-day march of the English through the forest, where they are imprisoned in a crumbling Indian ruin but eventually escape. In the third, Dickens describes their moonlit journey on rafts down a dangerous river and their eventual victory over their captors.

Dickens sets "The Perils" in Central America in 1744 rather than India in 1857, but many of its characters and events have obvious mutiny prototypes, and its earliest reviewers read it in the way that Dickens hoped they would—as a patriotic story "commemorating . . . some of the best qualities of the English character . . . shewn in India" (Pilgrim, 8:482–83). The reviewer in the London *Times* of 24 December, for example, felt that Dickens had captured "the salient traits so recently displayed by his countrymen and countrywomen":

> Their intrepidity and self-confidence, their habit of grumbling at each other without occasion and of helping each other ungrudgingly when occasion arises, the promptitude with which they accommodate themselves to any emergency and the practical ability with which they surmount every embarrassment . . . in short, the spirit of mutual reliance, of reciprocal service and sacrifice, which they have exhibited in fact Mr. Dickens has striven to reproduce in fiction.[31]

31. *Times* (London), 24 December 1857, 4.

Recent critical approaches to "The Perils" call the reputed heroism and sacrifice of the English colonists into question, but they too emphasize the story's connection to the Indian Mutiny. The treacherous "sambo" Christian George King, critics point out, is based on Nana Sahib, an Indian leader responsible for massacres at Cawnpore, and the bureaucratic bumbler Commissioner Pordage on "Clemency Canning," the lenient lieutenant governor of India in 1857.[32]

In their readings of "The Perils," critics emphasize Dickens's concern with imperial affairs. Brantlinger notes that Dickens "was deeply disturbed by the news from India," and Oddie argues that the mutiny made such "a deep . . . impression" on him that it inspired *A Tale of Two Cities* as well as "The Perils."[33] In Oddie's view, the representation of class revolution in *A Tale of Two Cities* is informed by the sepoy rebellion: "Behind the fevered intensity of Dickens's evocations of French atrocities must lie also his feelings about the massacre of English victims in India."[34] Yet it is equally true that Dickens's fear of class conflict informs his treatment of the mutiny—that his representation of native insurrection in "The Perils" both disguises and resolves the anxieties about class relations that underlie his portions of the story. His two chapters are characterized by a series of displacements that enable the narrator, an illiterate private in the Royal Marines, to abandon his feelings of class hatred and to recognize his *real* enemies—his racial "inferiors" rather than his social superiors.

When Gill Davis first arrives at the English colony, Dickens characterizes him as a man consumed by feelings of class consciousness and animosity toward his social superiors. A "foundling child" starved and beaten by his father and neglected by the parish beadle, Davis resents the "idle class" living on the island and criticizes what he sees as the unjust separation of capital and labor:

I had had a hard life, and the life of the English on the Island seemed too easy and too gay to please me. "Here you are," I thought to myself, "good scholars and good livers; able to read what you like, able to write what you like, able to eat and drink what you like, and spend what you like, and do what you like; and much *you* care for a poor, ignorant Private in the Royal Marines! Yet it's hard,

32. Oddie, "Dickens and the Indian Mutiny," 7–9. In the most recent study of "The Perils" to date, Laura Peters examines Dickens's debt to press coverage of the mutiny in the *Illustrated London News*, considers the ways in which he "stoke[s] the fires of empire" (126) in his portions of the story, and discusses his "imperial role" as editor of *Household Words*. See "'Double-dyed Traitors and Infernal Villains': *Illustrated London News, Household Words,* Charles Dickens and the Indian Rebellion," in *Negotiating India in the Nineteenth-Century Media,* ed. David Finkelstein and Douglas M. Peers (New York: St. Martin's Press, 2000), pp. 110–34.

33. Brantlinger, *Rule of Darkness*, p. 206; Oddie, "Dickens and the Indian Mutiny," 15.

34. Oddie, "Dickens and the Indian Mutiny," 15.

too, I think, that you should have all the halfpence, and I all the kicks; you all the smooth, and I all the rough; you all the oil, and I all the vinegar." (241)

As his portrait of the dissatisfied private reveals, Dickens writes "The Perils" with the topical issue of the unjust army system in mind; he begins the story by presenting a common man who feels that the system has cheated him and put reward out of his reach. Davis is conscious of his merits and feels that they go unrecognized and unrewarded. He asserts that *he*, the private, deserves to be officer rather than such "delicate" gentlemen as Lieutenant Linderwood and Captain Maryon: "I thought I was much fitter for the work than they were, and that if all of us had our deserts, I should be both of them rolled into one" (241).

Furthermore, Dickens repeatedly distinguishes between the commissioned and the noncommissioned officers, revealing the inequities between them, and implicitly criticizing the elitism of the army system. Unlike Lieutenant Linderwood and Captain Maryon, Corporal Charker and Serjeant Drooce have risen from the ranks. But even as officers who have demonstrated their merit, they remain subordinates. When it is believed that the pirates are hiding on the mainland, Drooce and Charker are excluded from the pursuit by their commissioned superiors and left to supervise the presumably compliant native population on the island: "Because it was considered that the friendly sambos would only want to be commanded in case of any danger (though none at all was apprehended there), the officers were in favour of leaving the two noncommissioned officers, Drooce and Charker. It was a heavy disappointment to them" (253).[35]

In spite of such inequities and disappointments, however, these characters do not act on their feelings of resentment in Dickens's chapters and claim their "deserts." Instead, their class consciousness is assaulted—first by the nationalism of Miss Maryon, the sister of Captain Maryon, and then by the "mutiny" itself. Miss Maryon appeals to the Englishness of Davis and Charker, implicitly asking them to put aside their sense of class consciousness in the name of national brotherhood and sisterhood. Defining herself as "an English soldier's daughter" rather than as a "lady," Miss Maryon suggests that she and they have a common genealogy. Offering to show the "English soldiers how their countrymen and countrywomen fared, so far away from England" (242), she takes them on a tour of the living quarters in the colony.

Shortly after Miss Maryon identifies private Davis and Corporal Charker as Englishmen rather than as members of the working class, the pirate attack oc-

35. As the writer of "Why We Can't Get Recruits" notes, officers "have an intense dislike to any scheme which narrows the gulf between the commissioned and non-commissioned ranks" (466).

curs. The most striking and curious feature of this attack is that it more closely resembles a class revolt than it does the Indian Mutiny. In "The Perils," Dickens uses the treacherous Christian George King and the band of pirates to represent the Indian mutineers. Like the allegedly merciless sepoys, they lay siege to the English fort and commit atrocities, killing English women and children. Yet the pirate band is made up of Europeans as well as the members of "subject races," and their motives as well as their origins set them apart from the mutinous sepoys as Dickens elsewhere describes them. In *Household Words,* the mutiny is generally attributed to the "tigerish" and "treacherous" nature of the Oriental, but Dickens's pirates act for economic reasons, attacking the colonists because they want the silver in their possession. Like a proletarian mob— Dickens describes them as the "scum of all nations" (317)—they seize the capital of the colony, a treasure produced by a labor force that is never identified or described in Dickens's narrative. In effect, the pirates take the place of this absent labor force, their attack substituting for the mutiny threatened by Davis and his sense of class injury.

As the colonists and privates defend themselves against the pirates in chapter 1, the distinctions among them dissolve. Dickens unites Davis with his officers—in part, by underscoring their common manhood as they protect the treasure of the island, which includes the sexual resources of the Englishwomen as well as the mineral resources of the colony, as Dickens's full title reveals: "The Perils of Certain English Prisoners, and Their Treasure in Women, Children, Silver, and Jewels." Like other works of mutiny fiction, Dickens's narrative represents the mutineers as rapists and Englishmen as chivalric defenders of an imperiled female virtue.[36] "I want you to make me a promise," Miss Maryon tells Davis: "That if we are defeated, and you are absolutely sure of my being taken, you will kill me." "I shall not be alive to do it, Miss," Davis replies. "I shall have died in your defence before it comes to that" (260).

As this image of the chivalric English private suggests, Dickens unites Davis with his superiors by obscuring their class differences as well as highlighting their common manhood. During the siege, the lower-class private demonstrates his nobility while the gentlefolk demonstrate their ability to labor. In "The Lazy Tour," Dickens elides class differences by representing the English as members of a nationalized idle class, but in "The Perils" he does so by identifying them all as workers. The English ladies and gentlemen whom Davis had disdained for

---

36. For a detailed analysis of "the colonial rape narrative" generated by the Indian Mutiny, and the political functions it served, see Nancy L. Paxton, "Mobilizing Chivalry: Rape in British Novels About the Indian Uprising of 1857," *Victorian Studies* 36, 1 (fall 1992): 5–30.

their delicacy prove to be determined and effective laborers rather than members of the idle class:

> What I noticed with the greatest pleasure was, the determined eyes with which those men of the Mine that I had thought fine gentlemen, came round me with what arms they had: to the full as cool and resolute as I could be, for my life—ay, and for my soul, too, into the bargain! . . . Steady and busy behind where I stood . . . beautiful and delicate young women fell to handling the guns, hammering the flints, looking to the locks, and quietly directing others to pass up powder and bullets from hand to hand, as unflinching as the best of tried soldiers. (259, 261)

While class distinctions are weakened during the attack, racial differences are strengthened and defined by Dickens in their threefold character: Christian George King, Dickens tells us, is "no more a Christian than he [is] a King or a George" (241). In aiding the pirates, the ostensibly faithful native proves to be not only un-Christian, un-aristocratic, and un-English—he is subhuman as well. While the pirate attack illuminates the nobility of the private and the energy and endurance of English gentlefolk, it also exposes the bestiality of the native. At the outset of the story, the English colonists accept Christian George King as one of their own. Miss Maryon tells Davis that King is "very much attached" to the colonists and "would die" for them (243), and he cries "in English fashion" when the ship springs a leak (245). But in the third chapter, Dickens unmasks him as an ungrateful and vicious animal, when he is shot in the jungle:

> Some lithe but heavy creature sprang into the air, and fell forward, head down, over the muddy bank.
> "What is it?" cries Captain Maryon from his boat. . . .
> "It is a Traitor and a Spy," said Captain Carton. . . . "And I think the other name of the animal is Christian George King!" (324)

Throughout "The Perils," Davis is troubled by his sense of being other than the gentlefolk around him, and he repeatedly tells Miss Maryon that "England is nothing to [him]": "England is not much to me, Miss, except as a name" (315). But just as Dickens displaces Davis's mutinous feelings onto the pirates, so he displaces his otherness onto Christian George King. In exposing the native as a false Englishman, Dickens identifies the private as a true one, a point underscored when King is shot through the combined efforts of Davis and his superior, Captain Carton; although the captain pulls the trigger, the private loads the gun. Appealing to the racial hatred generated by the Indian Mutiny and demonstrating the need to "exterminate" the treacherous "animals," Dickens unifies the English characters in his chapters of the story and thus solves the problem of class resentment in the rank and file. At the expense of the native, he compensates the common man, who has been alienated by a system that promotes class differences and puts reward out of his reach.

Collins offers the common man a different sort of compensation in his portion of "The Perils," however, and proposes a more radical solution to the problem of class conflict than Dickens does. In his chapter of the story, Collins reworks the allegiances established by Dickens in the opening section, highlighting class differences among the English characters, associating the privates and sailors with native laborers, and criticizing imperial practices instead of defending them.

In their discussions of "The Perils," Collins's critics and biographers contrast the high seriousness of Dickens's chapters with the facetiousness of his own, noting that the younger writer did not share Dickens's racist view of the mutiny. Nuel Pharr Davis argues that Collins makes "a burlesque out of Dickens' philippic against the sepoys," and Nicolas Rance reiterates the point: "Collins was unable to rise to the hysterical pitch of the editor of *Household Words*. The cool and sardonic tone of the part of the narrative by Collins is not conducive to identifying with the prisoners in their plight."[37] In chapter 1, Dickens presents the pirate captain as a sadistic figure who threatens to sexually violate the Englishwomen and who takes pleasure in mutilating his prisoners. By contrast, Collins compares his "flourish with his sword" to "the sort that a stage-player would give at the head of a mock army" (279) and portrays the English prisoners struggling to suppress their laughter as "the Don" plays his guitar "in a languishing attitude . . . with his nose conceitedly turned up in the air" (231). "As for the seamen," Collins writes, "no stranger who looked at their jolly brown faces would ever have imagined that they were prisoners, and in peril of their lives" (277).

Unlike Dickens, Collins approaches the mutiny and the imprisonment of the English as a comic rather than a tragic subject, and he reworks Dickens's opening chapter in other ways as well, redefining prototypes and dramatizing the plight of native laborers. While identifying the pirate captain as a Portuguese ruffian, Dickens models him on the stereotype of the sadistic sepoy; he speaks in broken English and "laugh[s] in a cool way" as he commits violent acts, hitting Davis crosswise with his cutlass "as if [the private] was the bough of a tree

37. Davis, *Life of Wilkie Collins*, pp. 207–8; Nicholas Rance, *Wilkie Collins and Other Sensation Novelists: Walking the Moral Hospital* (Rutherford, N.J.: Fairleigh Dickinson University Press, 1991), p. 131.

that he played with: first on the face, and then across the chest and the wounded arm" (267). Collins, too, depicts the pirate captain in racially charged terms—as "lean, wiry, brown" and "cat-like" (269, 271). But he also describes him speaking English "as if it was natural" to him (270) and dressing in "the finest-made clothes," like one of "the dandies in the Mall in London" (269). Portrayed by Collins as a "gentleman-buccanier," he parades among his camp followers in stiffened coat-skirts and lace cravat, recalling the arrogant English officers notorious for their extravagant living and their inhumanity toward their Indian servants. Abusing the natives, the pirate captain in Collins's chapter speaks of "Indian beasts" whose "dirty hides shall suffer" for burning his food (304), and he uses the back of a "nigger" under his command as a writing desk, complaining of the man's stench, and covering his nose with "a fine cambric handkerchief" scented and edged with lace (270–71).[38] A parodic mirror image of dandified English officers, Collins's pirate leader conflates their abuses with the lawlessness attributed to the sepoys. At times, Collins uses racist language in his narrative—when he refers to the "black bullock bodies" of the "Sambos" (270), for example. But he also declines to make martyrs of the English colonists and instead suggests that their wrongdoing was partly responsible for the mutiny.

Furthermore, Collins questions the celebrated unity of the English by developing the tie between the "Sambos" and Indians on the one hand, and the English privates and sailors on the other. Thus Collins puts Davis in much the same position as the "nigger" used by the pirate captain as a writing desk, as Miss Maryon "place[s a] paper on [his] breast, sign[s] it, and hand[s] it back to the Pirate Captain" (274). Facing forward rather than backward, Davis seems less dehumanized than the native, yet the connection between them is clear. It is reinforced during the march through Honduras, when the pirates eat meat from a store of provisions they have brought from the English colony, but Davis and his companions eat beans and tortillas, "shar[ing] the miserable starvation diet . . . with the Indians and the Sambos" (281). Instead of considering the natives their enemies, as they do in Dickens's chapters, the English prisoners see them as allies. "Dread the Pirate Captain, Davis, for the slightest caprice of his may ruin all our hopes," Collins's Miss Maryon proclaims, "but never dread the Indians" (302).

---

38. Hibbert briefly discusses the physical and verbal abuse of Indian servants by the English in *The Great Mutiny*, pp. 30–31. In using the term "nigger" to describe his native subordinates, Collins's pirate captain resembles the young officers criticized in the *Illustrated London News* in August 1857 and held accountable for the mutiny. Ignorant and arrogant, these officers referred to "proud and sensitive high-caste Brahmins as 'niggers' with whom it was degrading to associate" (quoted by L. Peters, "'Double-dyed Traitors,'" 113).

Indeed, the working-class Englishmen and the Central American Indians prove to have much in common in Collins's chapter. Despite their racial differences, both groups constitute a labor force that the pirate captain hopes to command and exploit in restoring the ruined Mayan palace he claims as his headquarters. As Davis and his companions prepare to enter the forest, the private is surprised to see "a large bundle of new axes," which he assumes the natives will use to cut through overgrown forest paths. But when the group arrives at the edge of the woods, the Indians use their machetes instead, and the sight of the axes, as yet unused, begins to "weigh . . . heavily" on Davis's mind (286). We soon learn that Davis has good cause for his anxieties, since the captain has only kept the soldiers alive because he wants "[their] arms to work for [him]," chopping down a forest of trees and making planks "to roof the Palace again, and to lay new floors over the rubbish of stones" (295). By having the English privates perform the manual labor assigned to "Negroes" and "Caribs" in the colonies of Central America,[39] Collins points to the regressive social ends of empire building. Whereas the resentful Probus welcomes the Goths to the gates of Rome in *Antonina*, hoping they will "level our palaces to the ground," Collins's English privates are forced to restore a dilapidated palace and, in the process, to rebuild the ruins of an ancient empire.

Collins brings us from the flourishing English colony of Silver-Store to the ruins of the Mayan empire; in so doing, he raises pressing questions about imperial decline and fall. In Collins's chapter, Davis finds himself in a "mysterious ruined city" built "by a lost race of people" (288), a place that Collins models on the ancient Mayan ruin of Copan, first explored by an Englishman in 1839:[40]

> A wilderness of ruins spread out before me, overrun by a forest of trees. In every direction . . . a frightful confusion of idols, pillars, blocks of stone, heavy walls, and flights of steps, met my eye; some, whole and upright; others, broken and scattered on the ground; and all, whatever their condition, overgrown and clasped about by roots, branches, and curling vines. . . . High in the midst of this desolation . . . was the dismal ruin which was called the Palace; and this was the Prison in the Woods which was to be the place of our captivity. (289)

Among Victorians, the discovery and excavation of the ruins of ancient empires, whether Egyptian, Greek, Roman, or Mayan, brought the stability of

39. E. G. Squier, *The States of Central America; Their Geography, Topography, Climate, Population, Resources, Productions, Commerce, Political Organization, Aborigines, Etc., Etc.* (New York: Harper and Brothers, 1858), p. 199.

40. As a source for his descriptions, Collins probably relied on the well-known account of the Mayan ruins provided by John Lloyd Stephens in *Incidents of Travel in Central America*, a work first published in 1841. Stephens visited Copan in the company of the English artist Frederick Catherwood in 1839.

their own to mind and suggested that no empire is invulnerable. "Comparisons have often been drawn between the Roman and the British empires," one article in *All the Year Round* notes, "and the question asked: Will Britain lose its strength and fade away, as Rome faded?"[41] This question seemed especially troubling in 1857, when the hitherto faithful sepoys revealed their allegedly treacherous nature. Rather than holding unruly natives responsible for imperial decline, however, Collins suggests that social inequities among the colonizers themselves may bring about an empire's fall. He conveys this point by staging scenes in which English privates and sailors are forced to labor like Indians and plot their own rebellion among the "dismal ruin[s]" of a once-powerful empire.

Whereas Dickens resolves the problem of class resentment in the rank and file by pitting privates against natives, Collins, in a scene that mirrors the pirate raid but casts the thieves as heroes, represents English workers seizing the goods they have produced. Davis and his companions are industrious in felling trees but only because they mean to profit from their own labor. As the sailor Short explains, they can use the timber for their own purposes, to build rafts and escape captivity:

> When we began to use the axes, greatly to my astonishment, [Short] buckled to at his work like a man who had his whole heart in it; chuckling to himself at every chop. . . . "What are we cutting down these here trees for?" says he.
>
> "Roofs and floors for the Pirate Captain's castle," says I.
>
> "*Rafts for ourselves!*" says he, with another tremendous chop at the tree, which brought it to the ground—the first that had fallen. . . . "Pass the word on in a whisper to the nearest of our men to work with a will; and say, with a wink of your eye, there's a good reason for it." (296–97)

In Dickens's two chapters, Davis is angered by the separation of capital from labor but learns to see such distinctions as insignificant. Having defined those who "have all the half-pence" against those who have "all the kicks" (241) in the first chapter, he declines to accept the "purse of money" he is offered by his superiors in the third. By the time Mr. Fisher, one of the English mine owners, tells Davis that he "heartily wish[es] all the silver on our old Island was yours" (314), Davis no longer wants to possess it, and the wealth of Silver-Store is not redistributed when the treasure hoard is finally recovered at the end of the story. In Collins's narrative, by contrast, the English soldiers and sailors seize what they produce, even though the dandified pirate captain claims to own it all.

41. "Touching Englishmen's Lives," *All the Year Round* 15 (30 June 1866): 582.

The subversive implications of their act of seizure in Collins's chapter are wholly muted by Dickens in the third, which rewards Davis for his bravery but does so by putting him in his proper place. Having proved his nobility, the private is rewarded, though not with a share of the silver he has helped to protect nor with a promotion to the rank of sergeant; instead, he is transformed into a subservient vassal, who pledges himself to his lady, Miss Maryon, in chivalric fashion:

> "I think it would break my heart to accept of money. But if you could condescend to give to a man so ignorant and common as myself, any little thing you have worn—such as a bit of ribbon—"
>
> She took a ring from her finger, and put it in my hand. And she rested her hand in mine, while she said these words:
>
> "The brave gentlemen of old—but not one of them was braver, or had a nobler nature than you—took such gifts from ladies, and did all their good actions for the givers' sakes. If you will do yours for mine, I shall think with pride that I continue to have some share in the life of a gallant and generous man." (325)

Despite the reference to Davis's "noble . . . nature," Dickens's narrative valorizes his feudal subordination and conforms to the dual pattern of imperial literature as Brantlinger describes it, justifying both aristocratic and imperial rule.[42] At the end of "The Perils," Dickens places the common man in a state of utter dependence on his social superiors. After his return to England, Davis becomes the object of their charity, living on the estate of Admiral Carton and his wife, the former Miss Maryon. Although Dickens initially contrasts the noble private with the bestial native, he brings them into an analogous relationship with the English ruling class. Offering a socially regressive solution to the problem of the army system and the class divisions it promotes, Dickens places the private in the position reserved for the faithful native at the beginning of the story; the difference between the two is that Davis deserves the charity of the gentlefolk while Christian George King does not.

In proving his nobility, Davis paradoxically learns to accept his state of dependence and see himself as an "ignorant and common" man: "It may be imagined what sort of an officer of marines I should have made, without the power of reading a written order," he says in Dickens's narrative, thinking back on his earlier social presumption. "And as to any knowledge how to command the

---

42. Brantlinger discusses the "regressive" patterns of imperial literature throughout *Rule of Darkness*, but see pp. 35–39 in particular. See also Abdul R. JanMohamed's analysis of "racial romance," which serves "to justify the social function of the dominant class and to idealize its acts of protection and responsibility" (72), in "The Economy of Manichean Allegory: The Function of Racial Difference in Colonialist Literature," *Critical Inquiry* 12, 1 (autumn 1985): 59–87.

sloop—Lord! I should have sunk her in a quarter of an hour!" (241–42). While Captain Carton is promoted and becomes "Admiral Sir George Carton, Baronet," Davis is not. Yet Dickens makes it clear that the private has not been unfairly overlooked. Davis is not promoted because he, like the native, has inherent limitations, and not because he is oppressed by the system: "I was recommended for promotion, and everything was done to reward me that could be done; but my total want of all learning stood in my way. . . . I could not conquer any learning, though I tried" (326). In Collins's chapter, Davis watches as a native, forced to his knees, serves as a desk upon which the pirate captain writes, and then provides a similar service for Miss Maryon; "knowing how to write" (271) thus appears a class privilege and illiteracy a mark of class injury. But in Dickens's portions of "The Perils," illiteracy is innate, and Davis cannot learn, although he is given the chance. Unable to read or write, he needs Lady Carton's help to tell his story. As she puts his oral account of the pirate attack into writing, Dickens inscribes the regressive social ideal of "The Perils" into its narrative form.

At the conclusion of "The Perils," Davis appears wholly dependent on the former Miss Maryon for support and expression, yet she, too, has been put in her proper place. Dickens's treatment of Miss Maryon demonstrates that imperial fiction, like chivalric romance, idealizes the subordination of women while seeming to dramatize their strength. Resembling the mutiny novels discussed by Nancy L. Paxton, which "mobilize" chivalry to conservative social ends, Dickens's narrative naturalizes Victorian gender norms as well as imperial relations, countering "demands for women's greater political and social equality."[43] Although Dickens claims that his story will "shadow out . . . the bravery of our ladies in India" (Pilgrim, 8:469), their bravery, as he represents it, consists largely of endurance. Miss Maryon "handl[es] the guns, hammer[s] the flints, [and] look[s] to the locks" during the siege (261), but her primary function is maternal in Dickens's narrative: "Miss Maryon had been from the first with all the children, soothing them, and dressing them . . . and making them believe that it was a game of play, so that some of them were now even laughing" (259). Rather than taking up arms herself, she gives Davis "the strength of half a dozen men" through her dependence, encouragement, and praise of the "brave soldier" (260).

Dickens justifies Miss Maryon's dependence by illustrating the dangers of letting her think for herself. He holds her womanly misperception of the natives partly responsible for the imperial crisis at hand and in so doing models her on

43. Paxton, "Mobilizing Chivalry," 6.

the English ladies of whom he complained to Emile de la Rue in October 1857; these women "know nothing of the Hindoo character" yet unwisely "rush[ed] after" visiting "Indian Princes" three years before: "Again and again, I have said to Ladies, spirited enough and handsome enough and clever enough to have known better[,] . . . 'what on earth do you see in those men to go mad about? You know faces, when they are not brown; you know common expressions when they are not under turbans; Look at the dogs—low, treacherous, murderous, tigerous villains who despise you while you pay court to them, and who would rend you to pieces at half an hour's notice'" (Pilgrim, 8:472–73). Like these ladies, Miss Maryon "pay[s] court" to "treacherous" natives in Dickens's portion of "The Perils," much to Davis's surprise:

> "Under your favor, and with your leave, ma'am," said I, "are [the Sambos] trustworthy?"
> "Perfectly! We are all very kind to them, and they are very grateful to us."
> "Indeed, ma'am? Now—Christian George King?—"
> "Very much attached to us all. Would die for us."
> She was, as in my uneducated way I have observed very beautiful women almost always to be, so composed, that her composure gave great weight to what she said, and I believed it. (243)

When it comes to natives, Dickens suggests, the knowledge of "uneducated" Englishmen exceeds that of Englishwomen, however well born.

In his collaborations with Collins, stereotypes of women and their failings sometimes serve Dickens well, providing common ground for the two writers—when they joke about the female contributors to *Household Words*, for example, or jointly illustrate the dangers of female emancipation in "The Wreck of the Golden Mary." But increasingly, gender issues became a source of contention for the two writers, as the history of *The Frozen Deep* makes clear, and their portraits of Miss Maryon, like those of Nurse Esther, diverge. Without minimizing the class privileges enjoyed by Miss Maryon, Collins suggests that gender norms unduly restrict her. Like Davis, she demands her own fair share—not of wealth or property but of "work" and "risk": "It is time that the women, for whom you have suffered and ventured so much, should take their share," she tells the private in Collins's narrative (302). Unlike the ill-judging woman who fails to see the natives for what they are in Dickens's first chapter, Collins's Miss Maryon carefully observes the pirate guards and their routine, discovering the means of drugging their food and making possible the prisoners' escape. "I have resolved that no hands but mine shall be charged with the work of kneading [the poison] into the dough," she asserts (302).

In such passages, Collins gives new meaning to women's work, using Miss Maryon to subvert the gender norms that his characters generally accept but that Davis comes to question:

> "How can a woman help us?" says Short, breaking in on me.
> "A woman with a clear head and a high courage and a patient resolution—all of which Miss Maryon has got, above all the world—may do more to help us, in our present strait, than any man of our company," says I. (298–99)

Courageous and resolved as well as patient—perhaps more effective "than any man"—Collins's Miss Maryon looks back to Lucy Crayford in his draft of *The Frozen Deep* and ahead to Marian Halcombe in *The Woman in White*. But she also anticipates the mountaineering heroine who figures in the next and final work that Collins and Dickens coauthored, "No Thoroughfare," in which the dangers of female autonomy and strength again prove a subject of debate between the two writers.

CHAPTER 5

"No Thoroughfare":

The Problem of Illegitimacy

In the summer of 1861, as he was working on his novel *No Name,* Collins found himself at a pivotal point in his career. Writing to his friend Charles Ward, Collins promises "news that will astonish you." He goes on to explain that he has decided—"with Dickens's full approval"—to resign from the staff of *All the Year Round,* since a much more lucrative offer has come his way: "Smith & Elder have signed agreements to give me *Five Thousand Pounds,* for the copyright of a new work, to follow the story I am now beginning. . . . No living novelist (except Dickens) has had such an offer as this for *one* book. If I only live to earn the money, I have a chance at last of putting something by against a rainy day, or a turn in the public caprice, or any other literary misfortune."[1] "Prepare yourself for an immense surprise," Collins tells his mother before regaling her with this "literary business": "Smith & Elder have *bought* me away from All The Year Round under circumstances which *in Dickens's opinion* amply justify me in leaving. . . . Five thousand pounds, for nine months or, at most, a year's work—nobody but Dickens has made as much. . . . If I live & keep my brains in good working order, I shall have got to the top of the tree, after all, before forty."[2]

In the ten years between the publication of "The Perils of Certain English Prisoners" and "No Thoroughfare," Collins came into his own. After the remarkable success of *The Woman in White,* rival publishers bid against each other

1. Autograph letter signed (ALS) to Charles Ward, 22 August 1861. The Pierpont Morgan Library, New York. MA 3151.27. *The Letters of Wilkie Collins,* ed. William Baker and William M. Clarke, 2 vols. (London: Macmillan, 1999), 1:200.
2. ALS to Harriet Collins, 31 July 1861. The Pierpont Morgan Library, New York. MA 3150.61. *The Letters of Wilkie Collins,* 1:197–98.

for his works, and the market value of his copyright rose as high as five thousand pounds. At the end of 1857, Collins was Dickens's staff member and valued subordinate, a modestly successful writer with four novels to his name, the most recent (*The Dead Secret*) serialized in *Household Words*. By 1867, he had written *No Name* and *Armadale* as well as *The Woman in White*, and was a famous novelist in his own right, publishing *Armadale* with Smith & Elder in the monthly *Cornhill* rather than with Dickens in *All the Year Round*. The change in Collins's stature is captured in an illustration of the "committee of concoction" at *All the Year Round*, an 1861 plate from the *Queen* (see frontispiece). Purporting to show "Jupiter and his satellites" at work on "Tom Tiddler's Ground," in an article parodying Collins's sensation fiction, it depicts Collins captivating the group with "Something Horrid" and suggests that he rather than Dickens is the center of attraction.

In August 1860, Collins wrote to Dickens, accepting "the renewal of [his] engagement with 'All the Year Round'" for two years, and outlining the conditions of his contract: he accepted a weekly salary of seven guineas in addition to "renumeration equivalent to one eighth share of the whole annual profits of All The Year Round—paid . . . at the time when the profits are regularly divided between the partners." While not actually making Collins a partner with himself and Wills, Dickens acknowledged the rising status of the younger writer by tying his salary to the profits of the journal. In return, Collins agreed to write a serial novel of about the same length as *The Woman in White*—the work that became *No Name*—with "five unoccupied months" to prepare it before its publication began, retaining the copyright, and also to contribute articles to the journal when not working on the serial. "I am not to write . . . for any other periodical," Collins concedes, and will "assist . . . in any joint periodical production of which I may feel myself able to undertake a share" (Pilgrim, 9:568, appendix E).

Between 1858 and 1861, these "joint periodical production[s]" included four Christmas Numbers, although none were authored solely by Collins and Dickens. In 1858, Collins worked with Dickens on the frame narrative of "A House to Let" and contributed the chapter entitled "Trottle's Report." The next year, Dickens included Collins's "The Ghost in the Cupboard Room" in "The Haunted House," and in 1860, Collins collaborated with Dickens on two chapters of "A Message from the Sea" while also contributing "The Seafaring Man" to it. Finally, he wrote "Picking Up Waifs at Sea" for "Tom Tiddler's Ground" in 1861. After 1861, when he resigned from Dickens's staff, Collins declined to contribute to the Christmas Numbers. "I am really quite concerned that you should have bothered your sufficiently-occupied mind about the Xmas No.," Dickens tells Collins in October 1862, referring to "Somebody's

Luggage": "Of course it seems very strange and bare to me not to have you in it; but I never seriously contemplated . . . your being able to do any thing for it" (Pilgrim, 10:137).

As Collins's letters from the summer of 1861 suggest, Dickens remained his model of success, the writer against whom he measures himself and evaluates his offers: "no living novelist (except Dickens) has had such an offer"; "nobody but Dickens has made as much." Collins continues to value Dickens's opinion and approval, assuring his mother and Ward that Dickens supports his decision to leave *All the Year Round* for Smith & Elder. But Collins also emphasizes how easily his departure from the journal could be misconstrued and repeatedly imagines rumors of a falling out between himself and Dickens circulating in the London papers: "Keep all this *a profound secret* from everybody," Collins tells his mother, "for fear of false reports about me and 'All The Year Round' getting into the papers."[3] "*Keep* all these changes and future projects *a profound secret from everybody,*" he warns Ward. "Otherwise, misrepresentations of my withdrawal from All The Year Round might get about."[4]

Collins's "withdrawal" from Dickens's journal resulted, most obviously, from the rising market value of his fiction, since he was "bought . . . away" by Smith & Elder. As Catherine Peters explains, "Wilkie was now worth more to *All the Year Round* . . . than the magazine connection, with its relatively modest salary, was worth to him" (*King,* 237). Yet the ground for Collins's departure from Dickens's staff was laid, in part, by the differences in opinion and aim that inform their collaborations to that point, and by Collins's growing reluctance to accept the role of "right hand" man in fictions casting Dickens as the authority figure: "Trottle (whom I always call my right hand) has been in my service two and thirty years," Dickens's narrator explains in "A House to Let," introducing Collins's fictional persona. "He is the best of creatures, and the most respectable of men; but, opinionated."[5]

Despite his agreement to "assist" in "joint periodical production[s]" as a member of Dickens's staff, Collins proved an "opinionated" subordinate and pursued his own interests in the Christmas Numbers to which he contributed between 1858 and 1861. At a time when Dickens was trying to give greater cohesion to these stories, Collins's narratives often have little to do with Dickens's central themes and reflect, instead, his own continuing concern with class and

3. ALS to Harriet Collins, 7 August 1861. The Pierpont Morgan Library, New York. MA 3150.62. *The Letters of Wilkie Collins,* 1:199.
4. ALS to Charles Ward, 22 August 1861. The Pierpont Morgan Library, New York. MA 3151.27. *The Letters of Wilkie Collins,* 1:200.
5. Charles Dickens, "A House to Let" ("Over the Way"), in *Christmas Stories,* ed. Ruth Glancy (London: J. M. Dent, 1996), p. 259.

gender inequities, and with imperial wrongdoing. For example, Dickens planned the 1859 number, "The Haunted House," to refute spiritualism—more specifically, to answer William Howitt, who had criticized him for publishing a series of skeptical articles in *All the Year Round*. But with his own interest in spiritualism and the transgressive figure of the medium, Collins had little reason to refute Howitt. Treating spiritualism as a sham in his portions of the Christmas Number, Dickens argues that houses are only haunted by "our own imaginations and remembrances," and he is particularly critical of women's claims to spiritual power, deriding what he terms their "powers of catalepsy" as well as "Woman's rights, Woman's wrongs, and everything that is Woman's with a capital W."[6] Rather than following Dickens's lead, however, and disparaging spiritualism and the women it empowered, Collins returns to the subject of empire in his portion of "The Haunted House," describing an English sailor "haunted" by his early experiences in South America. The articles that Dickens published on South America commonly distinguish the high moral motives of British "liberators" from the greed of the Spanish.[7] But Collins questions this distinction in "The Ghost of the Cupboard Room." His narrator, Nat Beaver, is one of those Englishmen who aided Simon Bolivar in his revolutionary struggle against Spanish rule, yet only by selling gunpowder to the rebels, in a commercial venture intended to turn a profit. Collins sends the Englishman to South America on board a ship facetiously named the *Good Intent*—"a queer name enough, you will tell me," his narrator concedes.[8]

Collins's noncompliance with Dickens's aims becomes a theme of the 1860 Christmas Number, "A Message from the Sea," in which Collins writes as the "seafaring man," the shipwrecked Hugh Raybrock. In a story that depended, in Dickens's view, on the pretense of oral narration, Collins started to draft a written tale, in a narrative mode reminiscent of *The Woman in White*. "Wilkie brought the beginning of his part of the Xmas No. to dinner yesterday," Dickens told Georgina Hogarth on 14 November. "I hope it will be good. But is it not a most extraordinary thing that it began: 'I have undertaken to take pen in hand, to set down in writing—&c. &c—' like the W in W narratives? Of course, I at once pointed out the necessity of cancelling that, 'off,' as

---

6. Charles Dickens, "The Haunted House" ("The Ghost in the Corner Room"), in *Christmas Stories*, ed. Glancy, pp. 339, 318, 324.

7. See, for example, "How to Make Money," *All the Year Round* 2 (3 December 1859): 125–28, which criticizes the Spanish slave trade, an enterprise with which "we Englishmen, thank Heaven, have nothing to do" (125).

8. Wilkie Collins, "The Ghost in the Cupboard Room," republished as "Blow Up with the Brig! A Sailor's Story," in *The Woman in White (Part Two) and Short Stories*, vol. 2 of *The Works of Wilkie Collins*, 30 vols. (New York: AMS Press, 1970), p. 544.

Carlyle would say 'for evermore from the face of this teeming earth'" (Pilgrim, 9:339). Although Dickens pokes fun at Collins's narrative formula here, and vaunts his own editorial powers, he is clearly troubled by the growing autonomy of his staff member, which resulted, in part, from the immense success of "the W in W."

Appropriately, the problem of controlling a "fraternity" of storytellers is dramatized in "The Club-Night," the chapter of "A Message from the Sea" that introduces and contains the interpolated tales of Dickens's contributors. In a passage that Deborah Thomas ascribes to Dickens but that Collins may have originally drafted, the members of a storytelling club try to speak all at once or refuse to speak at all, ignoring the authority of their chairman, and Collins's seafaring man proves particularly uncooperative:

> He had, after some pressing, begun a story of adventure and shipwreck: at an interesting point of which he suddenly broke off, and positively refused to finish. . . . The question raised on these premises, appeared to be, whether the seafaring man was not in a state of contumacy and contempt, and ought not to be formally voted and declared in that condition. This deliberation involved the difficulty . . . that it might make no sort of difference to the seafaring man whether he was so voted and declared, or not.[9]

We eventually learn that Collins's fictional persona has good reason to withhold his tale, since it involves the allegation that his father's legacy is stolen money. Nonetheless, the representation of Raybrock's refusal to produce his story, and of his probable indifference to being excluded from the "club" of

9. "A Message from the Sea," *All the Year Round,* Extra Christmas Number (13 December 1860): 11. Although Dickens told Wills on 3 November that he and Collins had "arranged and parcelled out the Xmas No." (Pilgrim, 9:336), there is some uncertainty over the attributions in "A Message from the Sea." According to Deborah Thomas, who relies on the list of authors in *The Christmas Numbers of All the Year Round,* published by Dickens from the original stereotype plates in 1868, Dickens wrote the first chapter ("The Village"), collaborated with Collins on the second ("The Money"), introduced and linked together the interpolated tales in the third ("The Club-Night"), and collaborated with Collins on the fifth ("The Restitution"), while Collins authored the fourth ("The Seafaring Man"). She lists the other contributors as Charles Collins, Harriet Parr, Henry F. Chorley, and Amelia B. Edwards (*Dickens and the Short Story* [Philadelphia: University of Pennsylvania Press, 1982], pp. 147–48). But Frederic G. Kitton, relying on a marked office set of *All the Year Round,* substitutes Robert Buchanan for Chorley, and claims that Dickens was the sole author of chapters 2 and 5, while Collins contributed to chapters 1 and 3 (*The Minor Writings of Charles Dickens* [London: Elliot Stock, 1900], p. 163). Harry Stone discusses these discrepancies and identifies Dickens's probable contributions in "Dickens Rediscovered: Some Lost Writings Retrieved," in *Dickens Centennial Essays,* ed. Ada Nisbet and Blake Nevius (Berkeley: University of California Press, 1971), pp. 205–26. Stone finds it "likely . . . that Collins wrote an initial draft of the introduction [to "The Club-Night"] and that Dickens subsequently went over the draft, rewrote it heavily, and added important sections" (210).

storytellers in the Christmas Number, registers the collaborators' shared sense of Collins's independence as a writer and anticipates his status as a free agent in the literary marketplace.

As he had in "The Haunted House," Collins writes at cross purposes with Dickens in "Tom Tiddler's Ground," contributing a story that seems strangely out of keeping with Dickens's designs for the work. Dickens based the 1861 Christmas Number on his encounter with James Lucas, a wealthy recluse from Hertfordshire whom he had met in June, and intended the story to show "the dependence of mankind upon one another—and on the wholesome influences of the gregarious habits of humanity."[10] In his own sections of "Tom Tiddler's Ground," Dickens illustrates the hermit's "reversal" of our "social nature," showing how "unnatural solitude" leads people to "brood and be suspicious" and to imagine that they are "full of wrongs and injuries."[11] Dickens finds an antidote to this diseased state of mind in the "wholesome sympathy" that develops between a gentleman traveler and a poor tinker in his narrative, despite their class differences.[12] In "Picking Up Waifs at Sea," however, Collins dissolves such camaraderie, writing a comic tale about the arbitrary and unjust nature of class identity, and the "wrongs and injuries" of the lowborn. Describing the circumstances under which the identities of two babies born at sea are confused, he outlines the different fates that await them because of the class positions of the parents to whom they are randomly assigned: the infant given to the steerage passengers "fails in the world," "a man of the lower order," while the one sent home with the genteel couple inherits a fortune and "prospers."[13] Dickens described Collins's story to Robert Lytton as "exceedingly droll" (Pilgrim, 9:548), but he was no doubt aware that it did little to celebrate the "wholesome influence" of social interactions.

Dickens's letters to Collins remained affectionate throughout the 1860s, although they were written less and less often, and Dickens clearly regretted Collins's withdrawal from *All the Year Round*: "I am very sorry that we part company (though only in a literary sense)," Dickens writes in January 1862, "but I hope we shall work together again, one day" (Pilgrim, 10:5). Despite his desire to "work together," however, the suggestions he and Collins made to

10. Percy Fitzgerald, "Charles Dickens in the Editor's Chair," *Gentleman's Magazine* 250 (1881): 731; quoted by Glancy, ed., *Christmas Stories,* p. 417. Fitzgerald quotes from the letter Dickens sent to prospective contributors to the 1861 Christmas Number, explaining its central theme.

11. Charles Dickens, "Tom Tiddler's Ground" ("Picking Up Soot and Cinders"), in *Christmas Stories,* ed. Glancy, pp. 419, 429, 443, 445.

12. Ibid., p. 445.

13. Wilkie Collins, "Picking Up Waifs at Sea," republished as "The Fatal Cradle: Otherwise, the Heart-Rending Story of Mr. Heavysides," in *The Woman in White (Part Two) and Short Stories,* pp. 509–10.

one another about their works in progress were usually declined—sometimes rebuffed. "'Could it have been done at all, in the way I suggest, to advantage?' is your question," Dickens writes in October 1859, after Collins advised him to draw the connection between Dr. Manette and Darnay earlier in *A Tale of Two Cities*. "I don't see the way, and I never have seen the way, is my answer. I cannot imagine it that way, without imagining the reader wearied, and the expectation wire-drawn":

> I do not positively say that the point you put, might not have been done in your manner; but . . . it would have been overdone in that manner—too elaborately trapped, baited, and prepared. . . . I think the business of Art is to lay all that ground carefully, but with the care that conceals itself—to shew, by a backward light, what everything has been working to—but only to SUGGEST, until the fulfilment comes. (Pilgrim, 9:127–28)

"The child notion enchants me," Dickens tells Collins on 31 October 1861, accepting his idea for the character Kitty Kimmeens in what became "Tom Tiddler's Ground." "I think Our Hidden Selves a very good title," Dickens goes on to say, "but I also think a better can come of it. . . . Now I quite discern where your notion tends, I will try if I can find a better" (Pilgrim, 9:490). In October 1862, a few months after Collins rejected the twenty-six titles Dickens proposed for *No Name* (Pilgrim, 10:21), Dickens explains to Collins "the difficulty of carrying out [his] suggestion [for 'Somebody's Luggage']": "—it would destroy a good deal of the effect of the end" (Pilgrim, 10:137).

In his letters to Collins, Dickens repeatedly speaks of the "strange dash of pride" he takes in the "hard work" of the younger writer and praises the "power and force" of Collins's fiction (Pilgrim, 10:128). Yet he consistently criticizes Collins's narrative technique, urging him to "conceal" more and "only to suggest." "The great pains you take express themselves a trifle too much," Dickens remarks after reading a portion of *The Woman in White*, "and you know that I always contest your disposition to give an audience credit for nothing—which necessarily involves the forcing of points on their attention—and which I have always observed them to resent when they find it out" (Pilgrim, 9:194). In similar terms, Dickens complains to Georgina Hogarth that "the creaking of the wheels is so very loud" in *No Name* that he has felt compelled to give Collins "a little advice on that head" (Pilgrim, 10:22).

In asserting that Collins's novels are too "loud," Dickens not only objects to the "creaking" of their narrative "wheels" but also to their outspoken social commentaries. His sense that Collins is "forcing . . . points" on the attention of readers anticipates Swinburne's claim that the social "mission" of such novels as *Man and Wife* (1870) brings them "nigh perdition."[14] Thus Dickens, in January 1862, advises Collins to "mitigate the severity" of *No Name* by giving the novel "some touches of comicality" and urges him to make his heroine a more conventional figure: less "business-like" and manly in responding to the news of her illegitimacy and disinheritance (Pilgrim, 10:20).[15] Dickens undoubtedly found Collins at his "loudest" when representing such subversive female characters. Commenting on the dramatic adaptation of *Armadale* in 1866, particularly the portrait of Lydia Gwilt, Dickens warns Collins against the "difficult[y] and danger" of placing a scheming and sexualized heroine on stage (Pilgrim, 11:221), and he praises the opening section of *The Moonstone* the following year, in part, because it seemed to lack such transgressive female figures, with "nothing belonging to disguised women or the like" (Pilgrim, 11:385).[16]

In 1867, the controversy surrounding Charles Reade's novel *Griffith Gaunt* (1866) heightened the contrast between Dickens, reluctant to offend readers on sexual matters, and Collins, more than willing to do so. Because of its frank depiction of sexual intercourse and bigamy, *Griffith Gaunt* caused a stir in England and America, and Reade found himself accused of morally corrupting his readers. In turn, Reade attacked his critics, suing the *Round Table,* a New York weekly, and the *London Review* for libel.[17] Collins wrote to Dickens in the midst of this legal controversy, hoping he would testify in Reade's behalf. Asking Collins to "say everything that is brotherly in Art from me to Reade," Dickens took a copy of *Griffith Gaunt* with him on a tour to Scotland and promised to write to Collins of his decision as soon as he had "got through the story" (Pilgrim, 11:313).

Despite his "brotherly" feelings, Dickens was not necessarily Reade's ally. Earlier in the 1860s, Reade had tested—and overstepped—Dickens's political limits as the conductor of a journal aimed at the middle class. Having serialized

14. A. C. Swinburne, "Wilkie Collins," *Fortnightly Review* (1 November 1889); *Wilkie Collins: The Critical Heritage,* ed. Norman Page (London: Routledge & Kegan Paul, 1974), p. 262.

15. As William Baker notes in discussing Collins's manuscript, he may have amended *No Name* somewhat in response to Dickens's advice but "was not prepared to do all that Dickens wanted" and maintained his "authorial independence." See "Wilkie Collins, Dickens, and *No Name*," *Dickens Studies Newsletter* 11 (June 1980): 52.

16. Whereas Dickens disliked Collins's "disguised" and transgressive heroines, Collins disliked Dickens's idealized and angelic ones. Commenting on *Oliver Twist* in the margins of Forster's *Life of Dickens,* Collins singles out the prostitute Nancy for praise, "the finest thing he ever did": "He never afterwards saw all the sides of a woman's character" ("Wilkie Collins About Charles Dickens. [From a Marked Copy of Forster's 'Dickens']," *Pall Mall Gazette* [20 January 1890]: 3).

17. For a discussion of this controversy and, more generally, Dickens's relation to Reade, see Walter C. Phillips, *Dickens, Reade, and Collins* (New York: Columbia University Press, 1919); and Winifred Hughes, *The Maniac in the Cellar: Sensation Novels of the 1860s* (Princeton, N.J.: Princeton University Press, 1980).

Reade's novel *Very Hard Cash* in 1863, Dickens felt compelled to publish a disclaimer immediately following the final installment of Reade's work, explaining that while "the statements and opinions of this Journal generally, are, of course, to be received as the statements and opinions of its Conductor . . . this is not so, in the case of a work of fiction first published in these pages as a serial story, with the name of an eminent writer attached to it": "I do not consider myself at liberty to exercise that control over his text which I claim as to other contributions."[18] Disturbed by Reade's sensational treatment of lunatic asylums and his use of well-known psychiatric reformers (Drs. John Conolly and Alexander Sutherland) as prototypes for the villainous Dr. Wycherley, Dickens refuses to accept any credit for *Very Hard Cash.* "Mr. Reade . . . damages a good cause," Dickens tells Dr. T. H. Tuke, Conolly's son-in-law (Pilgrim, 10:315), and he complains to Wills that, because he knows Conolly and Sutherland, he finds his position as Reade's publisher "perfectly shocking" (Pilgrim, 10:318). "Reade is rather dropping us," Dickens informs Collins in April 1863 (Pilgrim, 10:237), equally bothered by the effect of *Very Hard Cash* on the circulation of *All the Year Round.* With the conservative reaction against sensation fiction gaining momentum, Reade's novel "lost readers in droves," perhaps as many as three thousand.[19] And it made Dickens even more wary of publishing potentially offensive material than he already was.

Considering Dickens's experience with *Very Hard Cash,* his reaction to *Griffith Gaunt* is not surprising. When he had finished reading the novel, his "brotherly" feelings for Reade were tempered by his sense that certain scenes were "extremely coarse and disagreeable." Writing to Collins on 20 February 1867, he explains that, as "the Editor of a periodical of large circulation," he could not possibly defend the novel in court and would not have permitted certain passages to be published:

> If I had read to me in court those passages about Gaunt's going up to his wife's bed drunk and that last child's being conceived, and was asked whether, as Editor, I would have passed those passages . . . I should be obliged to reply No. . . . Asked if I should have passed the passage where Kate and Mercy have the illegitimate child upon their laps and look over its little points together? I should be again obliged to reply No. (Pilgrim, 11:318)

From Dickens's standpoint, these particular scenes would require censorship not only because of their explicit treatment of sexuality but also because of their

18. Charles Dickens, "Note," *All the Year Round* 10 (26 December 1863): 419.

19. John Sutherland, introduction and note on the text, *Armadale* (Harmondsworth: Penguin, 1995), pp. xxiii, xxx. See also Sutherland's "Dickens, Reade, and *Hard Cash*," *Dickensian* 81, 1 (spring 1985): 5–12.

radical social implications. Dickens is not simply offended by the "coarseness" of the scenes in which Gaunt consummates his bigamous marriage and in which Kate and Mercy examine the features of Mercy's illegitimate child, but by their use of sex and illegitimacy to represent women's wrongs and challenge the double standard. In the 1850s, members of Parliament repeatedly discussed the problem of illegitimacy in the context of marriage law reform, generally representing it as a threat to patrilineal succession, with a wife's adultery resulting in the birth of "spurious heirs." When the Matrimonial Causes Act was passed in 1857, the different conditions under which men and women were permitted to divorce reflected the dangers associated with female sexual transgression; a husband could sue for divorce on the grounds of his wife's adultery, but a wife could divorce her husband only if his adultery was compounded by incest, bigamy, or cruelty.[20] As Lord Cranworth, the Lord Chancellor, argued in defending this legal discrepancy, a wife's adultery "might be the means of palming spurious offspring upon the husband, while the adultery of the husband could have no such effect with regard to the wife."[21]

In *Bleak House,* Dickens largely supports this argument, representing the illegitimacy of Esther Summerson as Lady Dedlock's badge of "shame."[22] Lady Dedlock marries Sir Leicester long after her affair with Captain Hawdon, believes her illegitimate daughter is dead, and makes no attempt to "palm" Esther upon her unwitting husband, yet Dickens treats him as the injured party, magnanimous in the "full forgiveness" he wishes to offer his wife once he "knows his wrongs."[23] By contrast, Reade criminalizes a husband's adultery in *Griffith Gaunt,* making him a bigamist whose sexual transgressions "wrong" two women: "They looked [the child] all over, discussed his every feature learnedly, . . . and, comprehending at last that to have been both of them wronged by one man was a bond of sympathy, not hate, the two wives of Griffith Gaunt laid his child across their two laps, and wept over him together."[24] Unlike Esther Summerson, the illegitimate child in Reade's novel indicts a wayward father rather than a wayward mother and creates a bond be-

20. See Mary Lyndon Shanley, *Feminism, Marriage, and the Law in Victorian England* (Princeton, N.J.: Princeton University Press, 1989), pp. 39–44.

21. Quoted by Lynda Nead, *Myths of Sexuality: Representations of Women in Victorian Britain* (Oxford: Basil Blackwell, 1988), p. 53.

22. Charles Dickens, *Bleak House,* ed. Norman Page (1971; reprint, Harmondsworth: Penguin, 1985), p. 815.

23. Ibid., pp. 820, 815. In her discussion of *Bleak House,* Laurie Langbauer argues that Dickens uses the figure of the sexually transgressive woman to displace his own resistance to structures of power and to distance himself from the genre of romance, to which he is himself transgressively drawn. See *Women and Romance: The Consolations of Gender in the English Novel* (Ithaca, N.Y.: Cornell University Press, 1990), pp. 127–56.

24. Charles Reade, *Griffith Gaunt; or, Jealousy* (Boston: James R. Osgood, 1875), p. 207.

tween women of different social classes. In what is perhaps his most daring passage, Reade depicts their relationship as a marriage of sorts, both women "kiss[ing] one another again and again," as Mary tells Kate "we are both one flesh and blood."[25]

In making illegitimacy his subject in *No Name,* Collins takes a position much closer to Reade's than to Dickens's. "Mr. Vanstone's daughters are Nobody's Children," his heroine Magdalen learns, not simply because they are born out of wedlock but because they are female.[26] As Virginia Blain argues, Magdalen's illegitimacy "serves . . . as an evocative and subversive metaphor for the position of all women as non-persons in a patriarchal and patrilineal society."[27] Whether or not their parents were married when they were born, Englishwomen cannot claim their own possessions after marriage, and thus Magdalen's landlady, like her illegitimate lodger, has no property rights or legal identity under common law, and is "rob[bed] . . . of her little earnings, as usual," by her husband.[28]

"Oh, if I could be a man," Magdalen wishes toward the end of the novel.[29] In Blain's view, Collins enters into "a literary debate with Dickens" by creating a heroine who voices such wishes, "invit[ing] . . . comparison" between Magdalen and Esther Summerson. "Unlike Esther," Blain notes, Magdalen "refuses to take upon herself any guilt for her position," rejecting the shame and powerlessness associated with illegitimacy.[30] Whether or not we accept Blain's judgment that "Collins comes much closer to a true sympathy with the plight of women . . . than Dickens," Dickens clearly conceived of illegitimacy in a more conservative sense than Collins did.[31] Inspired, in part, by their disagreement over Reade, Dickens returned to the theme of illegitimacy in "No Thoroughfare," collaborating with Collins on a story about illegitimate sons, their fallen mothers, and London's Foundling Hospital. A story about male partnership and its dissolution as well, "No Thoroughfare" also reflects on the relationship between Collins and Dickens, although less clearly and much less affirmatively than the earlier collaborations did, with both writers using the foundling theme to consider the meaning of literary legitimacy and the process by which it is conferred.[32]

25. Ibid., p. 208.

26. Wilkie Collins, *No Name,* ed. Virginia Blain (1986; reprint, Oxford: Oxford University Press, 1991), p. 98.

27. Virginia Blain, introduction, *No Name,* p. xix.

28. Collins, *No Name,* p. 518.

29. Ibid., p. 533.

30. Blain, introduction, p. xx.

31. Ibid., p. xix.

32. Although some critics have discussed the 1867 Christmas Number and its dramatic adaptation in passing, only one full-length article has been devoted to them, Jerome Bump's "Parody and the Dickens-Collins Collaboration in *No Thoroughfare,*" *Library Chronicle of the University of Texas at Austin* (1986):

I

In January 1866, Dickens wrote to Collins to see "if, in the remote dark coming ages[,] . . . [he] would care to come back to the old quarters . . . for Idle Apprentices and such-like wanderings," telling him "that Wills with Carte blanche . . . await[s]" him (Pilgrim, 11:135). Dickens repeated his offer on 1 May 1867, asking if Collins would like to coauthor the upcoming Christmas Number of *All the Year Round:*

> Would you like to do the next Xmas No. with me? We two alone, each taking half? Of course I assume that the money question is satisfactorily disposed of between you and Wills. Equally, of course, I suppose our two names to be appended to the performance.
>
> I put this to you, I need hardly say, before having in any way approached the subject in my own mind as to contrivance, character, story, or anything else. (Pilgrim, 11:360)

The terms Dickens now offered were considerably more generous than they had been in 1856, when he first negotiated Collins's contract. As Collins told his mother ten days later, "They leave *me* to ask my terms at All The Year Round": "Forty eight of my written pages will fill half the Christmas number—and these, at the Smith & Elder rate, are worth £400."[33] Dickens no longer expected his collaborator to publish his work anonymously, assuring Collins that both their names will "be appended" to the Christmas Number, and represented himself as open to suggestion about all elements of the story.

Although Dickens claimed precedence by writing the "Overture" to the Christmas Number, and although Collins's terms were not fully met, with Wills paying only £300 for his half of the story, Collins accepted Dickens's proposal and made one of his own in return, offering to write the serial that became *The*

38–53. Bump's remarks on collaboration are provocative, but his reading is based on the fallacy (derived from bibliographer Richard Herne Shepherd) that Dickens wrote portions of the play. Shepherd wrongly assumed that, because Dickens wrote the "Overture" to the story, he must have written the "Prologue" to the drama as well. Thus what Bump takes to be Dickens's "self-parody" (45) in the dramatic adaptation is actually Collins's reworking of Dickens's portions of the Christmas Number. "The Drama was entirely written by me," Collins told Chapman on 11 May 1873 (quoted by Kitton, *Minor Writings*, p. 173); and in an essay about Charles Fechter, he explains that "Dickens took his departure for the United States, leaving the destinies of the unwritten play safe, as he kindly said, in my hands." See Collins, "Wilkie Collins's Recollections of Charles Fechter," in *Charles Albert Fechter*, ed. Kate Field (1882; reprint, New York: Benjamin Blom, 1969), p. 163.

33. ALS to Harriet Collins, 11 May 1867. The Pierpont Morgan Library, New York. MA 3150.101. *The Letters of Wilkie Collins,* 2:285.

Moonstone. Busy with the first three numbers of that novel, which he read to Dickens on 30 June, Collins discussed "No Thoroughfare" with his coauthor in June and July but did not suspend his work on *The Moonstone* until late August, when Dickens told him that the "Overture" was done (Pilgrim, 11:413). Throughout September and the first half of October, they wrote their respective portions of "No Thoroughfare," occasionally meeting at Dickens's home, Gad's Hill, or at the office of *All the Year Round* to discuss particulars and exchange manuscripts. Before Dickens left for America on 9 November, they agreed that Collins would adapt the story for the stage, which he did in November and December. Collins was to send Dickens his manuscript of the play "Act by Act," as he wrote it (Pilgrim, 11:492). A popular success, "No Thoroughfare" appeared as a Christmas Number on 12 December and opened at the Adelphi Theatre two weeks later, with Charles Fechter cast in the starring role.

In its narrative form, "No Thoroughfare" is divided into an "Overture" and four acts and subdivided into chapters, and it poses a particular challenge to critics wishing to distinguish Dickens's contributions to the collaborative works from those of Collins. It is clear that Dickens wrote the "Overture" and act 3 of the Christmas Number and that Collins wrote act 2.[34] But both contributed to acts 1 and 4, and Collins flatly refused to identify his own portions of them when asked to do so by Frederic Chapman in 1873, so that they could be omitted from forthcoming editions of Dickens's works. However, a partial manuscript of "No Thoroughfare" held by the Pierpont Morgan Library reveals Collins's contribution to the coauthored acts. Written solely in Collins's hand, this manuscript consists of "The Housekeeper Speaks" and the first portion of "Exit Wilding," two chapters from act 1; "The Clock-Lock" and "Obenreizer's Victory," two chapters from act 4; and preliminary drafts and sketches for the Christmas Number. The manuscript also indicates, through various notes and directives from Collins to the printers, that Dickens authored the remaining portions of acts 1 and 4.

"No Thoroughfare" tells the story of Walter Wilding, raised in the London Foundling Hospital and reclaimed at age twelve by his presumed birth mother. Set in and around the foundling in 1835 and 1847, the "Overture" ends with the reunion of mother and son. Act 1 opens in London in 1861, soon after the death of Wilding's mother, who has established him in the wine trade. Ailing and confused, Wilding welcomes George Vendale as a partner in his business,

---

34. "We can arrange *to start you for a long run, beginning immediately after Wilding's death*," Dickens tells Collins on 10 September, as he brings act 1 to an end, explaining that he will work on "the Alpine ascent and adventures" while Collins writes act 2 (Pilgrim, 11:423).

which he hopes to run along "patriarchal" lines, living with his employees as if they "all form[ed] a kind of family."[35] Having hired a former foundling nurse, Sally Goldstraw, as his housekeeper, Wilding learns that his adoptive mother had mistaken him for her *real* child, an infant adopted and taken to live in Switzerland shortly before his own arrival at the institution. Wilding vows to find "the true Walter Wilding" (152), whom he feels he has deprived of an inheritance and a mother's love. Wilding's partner as well as his lawyer, Mr. Bintrey, agree to help him in his search.

Act 1 introduces three Swiss characters: Jules Obenreizer, an agent of a Swiss wine firm in Neuchâtel with which Wilding and Vendale do business; his niece and ward Marguerite; and her companion Madame Dor. Vendale knows Obenreizer and his ward, having met them on his Swiss tours; enamored with Marguerite, he calls on these characters in Soho Square, where Obenreizer's antipathy to him becomes clear. The act ends with the death of Wilding, disappointed in his hopes of finding the man whose place he has usurped.

Act 2 develops the relations among Obenreizer, Vendale, and Marguerite, as Vendale declares his love for Marguerite but is told by an angry Obenreizer that he cannot marry her until he earns three thousand pounds a year. Determined to do so, Vendale is dismayed to learn that a five-hundred-pound payment to the firm that employs Obenreizer was never received. The Swiss merchants tell Vendale that someone in their pay is embezzling funds and ask him to send them his forged receipt. Vendale chooses to deliver it himself, and Obenreizer offers to accompany him. We soon learn that Obenreizer is the embezzler; he vows to prevent discovery by stealing the forged document and murdering Vendale, if necessary. At the end of the act, despite Marguerite's repeated warnings that her guardian poses a threat to him, Vendale sets off for the Alps with Obenreizer as guide.

Set in Switzerland, act 3 depicts their perilous journey through the Alps in February, their experience in a violent storm, and Obenreizer's attempt to rob and murder Vendale. Unable to obtain the forged receipt in the lowlands, Obenreizer drugs and attacks Vendale on the Simplon Pass, leaving him for dead in a frozen ravine. But he is rescued by two Swiss guides and Marguerite; she has secretly followed Vendale and Obenreizer from England, accompanied by Joey Ladle, Vendale's cellarman. Months later, in the final act, Obenreizer is accused of his crimes by Bintrey, Vendale, and Marguerite in the town of Brieg and forced to sign a document relinquishing control of his ward. By steal-

---

35. Charles Dickens, "The Curtain Rises," "No Thoroughfare," in *The Lazy Tour of Two Idle Apprentices and Other Stories* (London: Chapman and Hall, 1890), pp. 118, 117; subsequent references to "No Thoroughfare" are cited parenthetically in the text.

ing the documents of a Swiss notary, Maître Voigt, Obenreizer has learned that Vendale is the real Walter Wilding and reveals his identity in the hope that Marguerite will refuse to marry "a bastard, brought up by public charity" (229). But the revelation only heightens her devotion to the Englishman, who inherits Wilding's fortune. The story ends with the marriage of Marguerite and Vendale and with the announcement of Obenreizer's death in an avalanche.

In proposing that he and Collins collaborate again after a hiatus of several years, Dickens imagines a return to "Idle Apprentices and such-like wanderings" (Pilgrim, 11:135), but "No Thoroughfare" demonstrates that such a return was impossible. Rather than representing fellow apprentices on holiday together, or a captain and mate drawn together by the perils of shipwreck and social disorder, "No Thoroughfare" depicts a male partnership, but one that dissolves almost as soon as it forms and that gives way to working relationships characterized by subordination and resentment. Although neither Dickens nor Collins is assigned a specific persona in the story, fictional versions of their relationship include the short-lived partnership of Wilding and Vendale, fellow apprentices in years past, engaged in a business that resembles an "art" (138); the inequitable tie between Vendale and the cellarman Joey Ladle, a resentful employee reminiscent of John Want; and the hostile connection between Vendale and Obenreizer, who serves as the English gentleman's peasant guide through the Alps and whose hatred conflates class resentment with native treachery. The strategies that enabled the collaborators to mediate their differences in years past have lost their power in "No Thoroughfare," as representations of female autonomy and native revolt fail to unify the coauthors or their fictional counterparts. Writing at cross-purposes, Collins and Dickens tell very different tales about the position of women and the relationship between the English and the foreign, a disjunction particularly apparent in their treatment of "lost" women and the London Foundling Hospital.

In using the foundling as the setting for his "Overture," Dickens covered what was familiar ground. His interest in that institution dated from the late 1830s, when he and his wife lived on nearby Doughty Street and attended services at its chapel. Although Dickens gave up their pew when they moved to Devonshire Terrace, he returned on occasion to enjoy the "manly, Christian sermon[s]" given there (Pilgrim, 7:335). Dickens refers to the London Foundling in *Sketches by Boz* (1836) and *Barnaby Rudge* (1841); and, in *Little Dorrit*, he describes it at some length when Mr. and Mrs. Meagles take Tattycoram, "one of [its] little children," "to be a little maid to Pet."[36] In 1853, Dickens and Wills

---

36. Charles Dickens, *Little Dorrit,* ed. John Holloway (1967; reprint, Harmondsworth: Penguin, 1982), p. 56.

coauthored an article on the foundling for *Household Words* that demonstrates Dickens's thorough knowledge of the aims, history, and procedures of the institution.

In "Received, a Blank Child," Dickens traces the changes in the admission procedures and policies of the foundling since its opening in 1741. As he explains, its governors initially accepted infants without asking about their origins, simply requiring that each baby pass a medical examination and be given a token of some sort by which it could later be identified and reclaimed. These procedures were soon altered, however, since many more infants were brought to the foundling than could be received there. Thus the governors decided to hold lotteries for admission. In the 1750s, parliamentary funds were provided, compelling the hospital to accept all babies brought to its doors. The increased infant mortality rate that resulted put an end to the policy after less than four years. By 1801, the foundling had instituted the admission procedures still in use in Dickens's day—a system of maternal petitioning in which each mother filled out a petition form providing information that was reviewed and investigated:

> The child must have been the first-born, and preference is given to cases in which some promise of marriage has been made to the mother, or some other deception practiced upon her. She must never have lived with the father. The object of these restrictions . . . is as much to effect the restoration of the mother to society, as to provide for her child.[37]

As Dickens's account of the foundling makes clear, the policies governing admission in the 1800s initiated a new control over the women who brought their infants there. These policies reflected a new interest in policing female sexuality and discriminating between women who could and could not be morally reformed.[38] As historian Françoise Barret-Ducrocq points out, because the foundling would only receive infants conceived under specific circumstances—the first born of seduced and deserted women—the self-representations provided by the petitioners were those of women "betrayed" and "dishonoured" by men.[39] In effect, women were *required* to tell stories of

37. Charles Dickens and W. H. Wills, "Received, a Blank Child," *Household Words* 7 (19 March 1853): 49–53; *Charles Dickens' Uncollected Writings from "Household Words," 1850–1859,* ed. Harry Stone, 2 vols. (Bloomington: Indiana University Press, 1968), 2:460.

38. As Ruth K. McClure notes, the requirements established in 1801 marked a change "in the spirit of English benevolence," and "emphasized prevention and rehabilitation instead of simple relief of human misery" (252). See *Coram's Children: The London Foundling Hospital in the Eighteenth Century* (New Haven, Conn.: Yale University Press, 1981).

39. Françoise Barret-Ducrocq, *Love in the Time of Victoria: Sexuality and Desire among Working-Class Men and Women in Nineteenth-Century London,* trans. John Howe (Harmondsworth: Penguin, 1991), pp. 43–45.

their victimization to have their infants admitted. The foundling, Barret-Ducrocq observes, "granted help only to those it believed to be victims of male cynicism and sexual immorality," and "did everything in its power . . . to enable the mother effectively to 'rebuild her life,' remarry, and perhaps one day take her bastard child back."[40]

The foundling and its procedures figure prominently in Dickens's "Overture," which he sets "near the postern gate of the Hospital" (107). However, Dickens intentionally *mis*represents these procedures to identify a mother's claim to her children as transgressive. Dickens begins his story by referring to the change in policy instituted in 1801 but alters what he knew to be one of the main hopes of its governors—that mother and child would eventually be reunited: "Time was, when the Foundlings were received without question in a cradle at the gate. Time is, when inquiries are made respecting them, and they are taken as by favour from the mothers who relinquish all natural knowledge of them and claim to them for evermore" (107). Although the governors of the foundling investigated the circumstances in which the infants of petitioners were conceived, they also encouraged mothers to reclaim their children, required them to leave a token with their babies for this very purpose, and provided each with a receipt to "carefully ke[e]p . . . in case the child should be claimed."[41] But the mother Dickens portrays in the "Overture" must break the rules of the foundling to learn the identity of her child and attempts to bribe a nurse, Sally Goldstraw, for this purpose. Asked to "listen to [her] prayer" (109), Sally rejects her "present" of two guineas and then refers her to "the Good Father of All" to whom all prayers should be "put up" (109). Yet when appealed to as a woman who "aspire[s] to become a proud mother," Sally divulges the forbidden knowledge:

> "What are the names they have given my poor baby? I ask no more than that . . . . What have they called him?"
>
> Down upon her knees in the foul mud of the by-way into which they have strayed . . . the lady would drop in her passionate entreaty, but that Sally prevents her . . . . "Now, promise. You will never ask me anything more than the two words?"
>
> "Never! Never!"
>
> "You will never put them to a bad use, if I say them?"
>
> "Never! Never!"
>
> "Walter Wilding." (110)

40. Ibid., pp. 45, 184.
41. Dickens and Wills, "Received, A Blank Child," in *Charles Dickens' Uncollected Writings,* ed. Stone, 2:460.

This initial trangression is compounded by a second one twelve years later, when Walter Wilding's mother returns to the foundling to identify and claim her son, asking a female attendant which of the boys is Walter Wilding. Though the woman tells her that she is not allowed "to tell names to visitors" (111), she accepts the mother's bribe and places her hand on Walter's shoulder. The "Overture" ends with the mother offering the boy sweetmeats and asking him if he is "well and happy." She adopts Walter soon afterward, identifies herself as his mother five years later, and establishes him in trade.

Although Dickens refers to Wilding's mother as a woman "deceived" and "betrayed" (115), he does not relate the tale of her victimization as one of the foundling's petitioners. Instead, he tells a story of female transgression, representing women who repeatedly violate the rules to gain (or provide) forbidden knowledge. Rather than recounting the seduction and betrayal of Wilding's mother by her lover, Dickens obscures the circumstances surrounding her fall, using imagery that holds her responsible for her own "defilement": "As her footprints crossing and recrossing one another have made a labyrinth in the mire, so may her track in life have involved itself in an intricate and unravellable tangle" (108). A streetwalker of sorts, Wilding's mother exhibits none of the signs of moral direction required by the foundling, having "strayed" into "an empty street without a thoroughfare" (110).

In his "Overture," Dickens recasts the standard foundling tale of a woman's seduction as a story of female transgression, and he uses his portions of act 1 to dramatize the subversive meaning of such behavior and its damaging effect on the illegitimate son. Though grateful and content, Walter Wilding is often "confused" in his thinking and suffers from seizures and loss of consciousness. Wilding's illness is not diagnosed, but Dickens suggests that it stems from his parentless state at the foundling, from which his mother ostensibly rescued him:

> "'Honour,' said Mr. Wilding, sobbing as he quoted from the Commandments, 'thy father and thy mother, that thy days may be long in the land.' When I was in the Foundling . . . I was at such a loss how to do it, that I apprehended my days would be short in the land. But I afterwards came to honour my mother deeply, profoundly. And I honour and revere her memory." (116)

We soon gather, however, that it is the presence of a "supposed mother," coupled with the absence of a father, that leaves Wilding impaired. Learning from Sally Goldstraw that the woman he considers his mother had mistaken him for her biological son, also named Walter Wilding at the foundling but adopted earlier by another woman, he grows old before his time. "His body stoop[s], his step los[es] its elasticity," and his mind becomes "cloudy" (159) as he is forced out of existence by the loss of identity he suffers because of his adoptive mother's mistaken claims. "It is impossible that I can ever be myself again," he tells his new partner, "for, in fact, I am not myself":

> "Not yourself?"
> "Not what I supposed myself to be," said Wilding.
> "What, in the name of wonder, *did* you suppose yourself to be that you are not? . . . I may ask without impertinence, now that we are partners."
> "There again!" cried Wilding, leaning back in his chair, with a lost look at the other. "Partners! I had no right to come into this business. It was never meant for me. My mother never meant it should be mine. I mean, his mother meant it should be his—if I mean anything—or if I am anybody." (132–33)

In *No Name*, Collins uses the illegitimacy of the Vanstone sisters to criticize patriarchy and the laws that make women "non-persons" in Victorian culture. But in Dickens's "Overture," a son rather than a daughter is deprived of his identity, and not by the laws of patriarchy but by a woman who falsely defines him in matriarchal terms, as the child of his mother. What Dickens ultimately represents as illegitimate in "No Thoroughfare" are not the children of unwed mothers but rather the claims of mothers to their children, and he reinforces this point by excluding biological mothers from his cast. His characters include a host of maternal surrogates—Sally Goldstraw and Madame Dor, for example—but none whose relations to their children are defined as "natural" (116).

While discrediting maternal claims, Dickens more generally disparages female autonomy and women who assume the prerogatives of men. The gender transgressions of Walter's adoptive mother connect her to the professional women represented by Dickens in act 1; these self-supporting and domineering spinsters and widows appear at Walter's door, applying for the job of housekeeper:

> There were the buccaneering widows who came to seize him, and who griped umbrellas under their arms, as if each umbrella were he, and each griper had got him. There were towering maiden ladies who had seen better days, and who came armed with clerical testimonials to their theology. . . . There were professional housekeepers, like non-commissioned officers, who put him through his domestic exercise, instead of submitting themselves to catechism. (122)

Like noncommissioned officers, these professional women have risen from the ranks, but Dickens does not endorse their promotion from the private to the public sphere. Instead, he devotes much of his remaining narrative to putting "towering maidens" back in their proper place and promoting the value of feminine submission.

The first attempt to restore patriarchy is made by Wilding himself in Dickens's opening chapters. Never having known "a father of [his] own," he "wish[es] to be a father to all in [his] employment" (116) and outlines his plans for establishing his "patriarchal family" (156) and "sit[ting] at the head of the table at which the people in [his] employment eat together" (117–18). However, Wilding is, at best, an impaired father figure. Although he assumes his place at the head of the table, he grows confused while sitting there and becomes ever more dependent on Sally Goldstraw rather than his partner, whose efforts to aid him prove futile. The former foundling nurse and accomplice of his adoptive mother presides over his deathbed scene, as the would-be patriarch is infantalized under her "care":

> At length, . . . Walter Wilding took to his bed, and his housekeeper became his nurse . . . .
> "The old child-feeling is coming back upon me, Sally. The old hush and rest, as I used to fall asleep."
> After an interval he said, in a placid voice, "Please kiss me, Nurse," and, it was evident, believed himself to be lying in the old Dormitory. As she had been used to bend over the fatherless and motherless children, Sally bent over the fatherless and motherless man. (159–60)

As in such *Household Words* articles as "Wolf-Nurses," Dickens associates maternal care with a child's regression. Recalling the child stolen and adopted by the "wolf-nurse" in the *Household Words* article of that title, Wilding proves unable to develop without a father and takes his name and bearing from his "wild" mother, as Dickens describes her in his "Overture" (109). After Wilding's death, however, Vendale domesticates the "wild" women of "No Thoroughfare." Yet his triumph, as Dickens represents it, is muted in ways that signal the failure of male community in the story and is even more heavily qualified by Collins's variations on Dickens's themes. Before Vendale is betrayed by Obenreizer and marries Marguerite, Collins's second act intervenes, casting doubt on the perils that beset the English hero and providing a version of the tale that Victorians associated with the Foundling Hospital—the story of a woman's victimization.

Collins refers to the "ruin" of daughters in act 2 (164) but he focuses on their economic and legal rather than their sexual vulnerability, reconceiving Dickens's depiction of "lost" women to criticize their dependence on men. In his earliest draft of act 2, Collins identifies Obenreizer as a swindler but one who cheats "poor widows" as well as his own employers. Marguerite's companion, Madame Dor, is among his victims, having trusted her financial securities to him. "Mon Dieu!" she exclaims to Vendale and Marguerite in Collins's manuscript, "I am a lost woman!"[42]

Collins does not retain this specific passage in his final version of the narrative, but his concern with the exploitation and dependency of women remains clear. In his "Overture" and portions of act 1, Dickens takes as his theme the dangerous autonomy of women, and Collins recurs to it in one or two of his own passages—when Sally Goldstraw expresses remorse at having broken the rules and helped Walter's adoptive mother, for example: "I allowed myself to forget my duty, and dreadful consequences, I am afraid, have followed from it . . . . I feel as if I was to blame—I feel as if I ought to have had more self-command" (127, 129). More frequently, however, Collins suggests that women are unduly restrained. In the marginal notes of his manuscript, he comments on the lack of independence allowed to young women in his supposedly "modern" day.[43] And in the published story, he takes the authority of the father figure to a nearly gothic extreme in portraying Obenreizer. "My ward defies me. My ward withdraws herself from my authority," Obenreizer complains in Collins's portion of act 4: "I will enforce it. I will make her submit herself to it" (215–16). "The law gives me authority to control my niece's actions," he tells those who wish "to set [her] free": "If you resist the law, I take her by force" (222–23, 226).

Obenreizer has no need to use force to control Marguerite, Collins implies, because the law allows him to treat her as a form of property to be sold to the highest bidder:

> "Come to the point," said Vendale. "You view this question as a question of terms. What are your terms?" . . .
> "On the day when you satisfy me, by plain proofs, that your income has risen to three thousand a year, ask me for my niece's hand, and it is yours." (175)

Despite Obenreizer's status as a foreigner, Collins uses him in much the same way that he uses Count Fosco in *The Woman in White:* as a grotesque mirror image of his English hosts. "I remember that I am writing in England," Fosco notes in his narrative, justifying his tyranny over his wife, "I remember that I was married in England—and I ask, if a woman's marriage-obligations, in this

42. Wilkie Collins, autograph manuscript of "No Thoroughfare." The Pierpont Morgan Library, New York. MA 1021.
43. Ibid.

country, provide for her private opinion of her husband's principles? No! They charge her unreservedly, to love, honour, and obey him."[44] Like Fosco, Obenreizer expresses his admiration for English laws in a way that suggests their injustice. In bargaining with Vendale for his niece, Obenreizer simply follows the "English . . . principle of pounds, shillings, and pence" (164) and proves to be Vendale's double as well as his foil: "We have had our little skirmish—we have really been wonderfully clever on both sides," Obernreizer tells Vendale once their bargain is made. "Well played, Mr. Vendale! You combine the foreign quickness with the English solidity. Accept my best congratulations" (176–77).

In his portions of "No Thoroughfare," as in *The Woman in White,* Collins uses the villain to question the distinction between English justice and foreign barbarism, particularly in regard to the treatment of women. Rather than pursuing this investigation, Dickens emphasizes the otherness of Obenreizer in act 3, defining an imperiled English manhood against its "savage" Swiss counterpart and representing a failure in male community.

II

Writing to Collins on 23 August, Dickens tells him that he has "done the overture." He then outlines his "general idea" for the rest of the story, proposing that they "culminate" it

> in a wintry flight and pursuit across the Alps. Let us be obliged to go over—say the Simplon Pass—under lonely circumstances, and against warnings. Let us get into all the horrors and dangers of such an adventure under the most terrific circumstances, either escaping from, or trying to overtake (the latter, the better, I think) some one, on escaping from, or overtaking, whom, the love, prosperity, and Nemesis of the story depend. There we can get Ghostly interest, picturesque interest, breathless interest of time and circumstance, and force the design up to any powerful climax we please. (Pilgrim, 11:413)

To Philip Collins, Dickens's letter reveals the "common tastes" of an otherwise great writer—his unfortunate penchant for stage melodrama, with its villainous crimes, flights, and pursuits.[45] But it points to Dickens's interest in another popular genre as well—the accounts of daring Alpine adventure published in the

---

44. Wilkie Collins, *The Woman in White,* ed. Harvey Peter Sucksmith (1972; reprint, Oxford University Press, 1980), p. 570.

45. Philip Collins, *Dickens and Crime* (Bloomington: Indiana University Press, 1968), pp. 1–2.

1850s and 1860s and associated with the exploits of the London-based Alpine Club. In drawing on this material, Dickens associates his Christmas Number with an extensive collection of narratives in which manly character is revitalized and manhood inspired—in which English mountaineers, at once patriarchs and imperialists, band together to conquer a savage, feminine land.

Dickens himself experienced the manly regimen of Alpine adventure in the company of Collins and Augustus Egg, when the three men traveled to Switzerland together in October 1853. Writing to Burdett-Coutts, Dickens regaled her with tales of his "intrepidy" as a mountaineer, drawing on the ideological meaning of Alpine adventure as it was commonly understood by Victorians:

> We went on to Geneva and so to Chamounix, which, at this time of the year . . .
> is far more primitive and interesting than as one usually sees it. We went up to the
> Mer de Glace through pretty deep snow . . . came down again . . . and crossed to
> Martigny. These achievements (with a variety of gymnastic exercises with a pole,
> superadded) I performed on foot, to the infinite satisfaction of the Guides, who
> pronounced me "A strong Intrepid," and were of opinion that I ought to ascend
> Mont Blanc next summer. I told them in return that it had become such a nui-
> sance in my country that there was some idea of authorizing Paxton to take it
> down and re-erect it at Syndenham. (Pilgrim, 7:171)

For Dickens, as for his compatriots, the Alps testify to the Englishmen's strength, providing them with a vast and rugged terrain in which to perform their "gymnastic exercises" and prove themselves "intrepid." Frequently compared to the Arctic regions explored by Franklin, the Swiss Alps were considered a largely unknown and perilous territory to be charted and conquered, a "wild" landscape suggesting "moral savagery."[46] In describing Mont Blanc as merely another Crystal Palace that Joseph Paxton might disassemble and reerect for the enjoyment of friends back home, and in commending the engineering feats of his countrymen among the Alps in *All the Year Round,* Dickens flaunts the technological prowess of the English, which will domesticate the Swiss "wilds."[47]

While the Alpine peaks are represented as savage, so too are those living in the valleys. John Murray's *Handbook for Travellers in Switzerland* (1862), the most

---

46. John David Forbes, "Pedestrianism in Switzerland," *Quarterly Review* 101 (1857): 316; John Tyndall, *Hours of Exercise in the Alps* (New York: D. Appleton, 1872), p. 81.

47. As various *All the Year Round* articles note, English engineers, funded by English capital, built a mountain railroad through the Alps in the 1860s, using their advanced technology to pierce a tunnel through Mont Cenis. See, for example, "Earth. In Two Chapters. Chapter II," *All the Year Round* 12 (31 December 1864): 486–89.

popular Victorian guidebook to the region, notes that among the Alps, "man appears . . . in his most degraded and pitiable condition." Afflicted by "the maladies of *goitre* and *cretinism*," he is "a creature who may almost be said to rank a step below a human being."[48] English travelers often described the condition of these "ape-like" creatures—"distorted, mindless beings, more like brutes than men."[49] Their view was reinforced by the racial theories of Frederic Troyon, whose archeological discoveries were exhibited at Lausanne's Museum of Natural History in the 1850s. As a writer explains in "Subterranean Switzerland," published by Dickens in 1859, the "primitive" artifacts unearthed by Troyon in and around the Swiss lakes suggested that Switzerland was originally inhabited by Oriental peoples, a "pigmy race" whose features were "Hindoo-like" in structure. While the dwellings of the ancient Swiss resemble those currently seen "on the half-quaggy, inundating rivers and channel-pools of China," the "fragments of pottery" found in Lake Moosseedorf resemble "the vases . . . still used by the Hindoos and other Indian people."[50]

In traveling to Switzerland at mid-century, Dickens and his countrymen imagined themselves journeying to a savage region with ties to the East, a land they were destined to chart and develop. At the same time, they saw themselves banding together to conquer a female territory, since "nowhere else does Nature show herself in a wilder or more savage guise."[51] Typically, Alpine explorers speak of the mountains as "virgin peaks" to be "taken."[52] Their language helps to explain the celebrated power of mountaineering to revitalize patriarchy and "change totally, and in one short summer, the character of delicately brought-up and unadventurous youths."[53] So, too, does the recurring analogy between mountaineering and military assault, drawn by John Forbes, for example, in "Pedestrianism in Switzerland" (1857). "Perhaps the nearest ap-

48. [John Murray], *Handbook for Travellers in Switzerland, and the Alps of Savoy and Piedmont*, 9th ed. (London: John Murray, 1862), p. lxv. The cause of these afflictions among the Swiss—iodine deficiency—was not understood until the turn of the century.

49. Edward Whymper, *Scrambles Amongst the Alps in the Years 1860–69* (London: John Murray, 1871), pp. 299–300.

50. "Subterranean Switzerland," *All the Year Round* 2 (5 November 1859): 29. Similarly, "Grandfather Blacktooth," *All the Year Round* 12 (10 September 1864): 111–15, describes the "Chinese aspect" of the "Alpine hunter" (113).

51. "Grandfather Blacktooth," 111.

52. After the first ascent of the Matterhorn in July 1865, for example, a writer in the London *Times* referred to Mont Cervin as "the last virgin summit" in the region of Zermatt to "resist . . . the efforts of man" (21 July 1865, 10).

53. Forbes, "Pedestrianism," 287. As David A. Robertson notes, both Englishmen and Americans believed that the Alps produced the manly metamorphosis that Forbes describes. See "Mid-Victorians amongst the Alps," in *Nature and the Victorian Imagination*, ed. U. C. Knoepflmacher and G. B. Tennyson (Berkeley: University of California Press, 1977), pp. 113–36.

proach to a [military] campaign with which the ordinary civilian has a chance of meeting," Alpine adventure strengthens men by simulating "the privation and risk of the battlefield" and reinforces homosocial bonds by requiring the gentleman climber to rely on his lowborn guide:

> His trust—after God—must be in the humble, hardy fellow, whom in other circumstances he might treat as an inferior, but whom now a community of interests and perils renders a friend indeed; whose counsels are to be regarded, whose experience is to be valued, whose steps are to be followed; nay, with whom he may be willing and thankful to lie down as familiarly as with a brother in the exposed cleft on the hill-side, where necessity may compel him to pass the night, and by the communication of mutual warmth hinder both from freezing.[54]

In Dickens's portions of "No Thoroughfare," Englishmen stand badly in need of the manly regeneration and community of which Forbes and others speak. Dramatizing the threat posed to the "patriarchal establishment" by independent women and their maternal claims, Dickens depicts the physical and mental degeneration of the would-be father figure, Walter Wilding, whose infantilization and death bring act 1 to a close. As if to reverse this process, Dickens sends his surviving English hero on a dangerous expedition through the Swiss mountains, where Vendale pits himself against a savage and feminine terrain. But he does so with disappointing results. Rather than reinvigorating Vendale and providing the "community of interests and perils" that makes possible the cross-class brotherhood that Forbes envisions, his Alpine adventure proves nearly fatal and dramatizes yet another failed relationship between men, as Obenreizer turns traitor, attacks the Englishman, and leaves him for dead.

In the collaborative works, conceptions of racial difference often serve to resolve class conflict, perhaps most notably in "The Perils of Certain English Prisoners," when private Davis combines with his officers to defeat their native foes. But Obenreizer is both a peasant and a savage as Dickens represents him, and his attack on Vendale conflates class resentment with racial antipathy, leaving the men no common ground. A "low-born drudging Swiss peasant" (143) who has slowly risen to respectability, Obenreizer resents the English gentleman who "takes" Switzerland on the grand tour, and he contrasts the deprivations of his own "sordid childhood" with the luxuries of Vendale's (138–39). Driven, too, by "the animosity of a fierce cunning lower animal" for its civilized male hunter (190), Obenreizer recalls the "Hindoo-like" Swiss described by Frederic Troyon—more specifically, the rebellious sepoys described in

54. Forbes, "Pedestrianism," 287.

mutiny literature. "Lithe and savage" (195), "a black-haired young man . . . through whose swarthy skin no red glow ever shone" (139), Obenreizer seems devoted and subservient to the Englishman yet betrays him when he least expects it, just as Christian George King does the colonists in Dickens's portions of "The Perils." Drugged by his peasant guide, Vendale imagines himself in perilous situations that recall the earlier collaborative works—as if he were "belated on the steppes of Russia" or "shipwrecked in an open boat at sea" (196). But in "No Thoroughfare," Dickens replays such scenes with a difference, without affirming a bond between men. Whereas Wardour is heroically transformed and saves rather than murders Aldersley on the frozen deep, and Davis fights side by side with those he thought "fine gentlemen" in the colony of Silver-Store, Obenreizer leaves Vendale to die in a frozen gulf, in the midst of an Alpine storm.

In what is undoubtedly Dickens's most striking deviation from the earlier pattern, it is left to a daring woman to rescue the fallen Englishman in act 3 of the Christmas Number. "Without asking anybody's advice or permission" (224), Marguerite secretly follows Vendale and Obenreizer to Switzerland, accompanied by Joey Ladle. Overtaking the two Swiss guides who have set out to find Vendale, and who suspect that he and Obenreizer have come to harm, Marguerite demonstrates her mountaineering knowledge and skill. The first to spot Vendale on a shelf of ice, she takes charge of the rescue operation while Ladle loses consciousness and the guides remain largely inactive, "sickened" by the sight of the body below. Dickens structures the sentences in his description to emphasize her action and agency: "She girded herself with a cord under the breast and arms, she formed it into a kind of jacket, she drew it into knots, she laid its end side by side with the end of the other cord, she twisted and twined the two together, she knotted them together, she set her foot upon the knots, she strained them, she held them for the two men to strain at" (210). "Guiding herself down the precipitous icy wall with her hand" (210), Marguerite arrives at Vendale's side, keeps him warm, and helps to hoist him out of the ravine.

Dickens's characterization of the daring and skilled Marguerite can be seen to signal a change in his attitude toward women, perhaps under Collins's influence: "Conceivably, Dickens was beginning to share Collins's admiration for strong, active women," Sue Lonoff argues in discussing "No Thoroughfare."[55] Underlying Dickens's praise of Marguerite, however, is his sense of the dangers she poses to men. Just as Sally Goldstraw infantalizes Walter Wilding in nursing him, so Marguerite ministers to Vendale yet threatens to

55. Sue Lonoff, "Charles Dickens and Wilkie Collins," *Nineteenth-Century Fiction* 35 (September 1980): 160.

usurp his place, recalling the "towering maidens" and "wild" women derided by Dickens earlier in the Christmas Number as well as the female climbers ridiculed in mountaineering literature. Emphasizing that Alpine expeditions are not "calculated for females" in *The Story of Mont Blanc*, Albert Smith criticizes the bravado of Mlle. d'Angeville, the second woman to ascend that peak: "When on the summit, [she] made the guides lift her up on their shoulders, that she might say she had been actually higher than anybody else."[56] "Foreign Climbs," an article Dickens published in 1865, reminds us that the valleys and lakes are the proper region for women in Switzerland, not the mountain peaks and passes, where wives and daughters are all-too-apt to lose their footing and are "picked up afterwards a mangled mass."[57]

Performing the dangerous Alpine feats that are part of a "masculine education,"[58] Marguerite seems to supplant her future husband in the very act of saving him. Unlike Mlle. d'Angeville, however, who climbs Mont Blanc to prove herself superior to men, Marguerite submits to their control and better judgment. Despite her endurance, prowess, and strength, she introduces herself to the guides as a prospective wife and mother, assuming a subservient position and inviting a show of force:

> "Let me go with you, for the love of God! One of those gentlemen is to be my husband . . . . If any mischance should have befallen him, my love would find him, when nothing else could. On my knees, dear friends of travellers! By the love your dear mothers had for your fathers! . . . Watch my hands. If they falter or go wrong, make me your prisoner by force." (208, 210)

In Dickens's "Overture," the unwed mother of Walter Wilding tries to get "down upon her knees in the foul mud," begging Sally Goldstraw to "listen to [her] prayer"; Sally then reminds her that "prayers are to be put up to the Good Father of All, and not to nurses and such" (109). A second female supplicant, Marguerite assumes the same posture as Wilding's mother but implores paternal rather than maternal figures for aid and does so "for the love" of fathers, both human and divine. Marguerite's significance in this scene—in effect, her recognition of patriarchy's claims—is reinforced by the details Dickens provides about her girlhood. Because her mother dies in childbirth, Marguerite is dissociated from the maternal; she is raised and provided for by a single father rather

---

56. Albert Smith, *The Story of Mont Blanc* (New York: G. P. Putnam, 1853), pp. 145, 126. A friend of Dickens, Smith described his Alpine adventures in *Household Words*.
57. "Foreign Climbs," *All the Year Round* 14 (2 September 1865): 135–36.
58. Forbes, "Pedestrianism," 288.

than a single mother (143). Her situation thus inverts and corrects that of Walter Wilding.

In act 4, Dickens transforms the female mountaineer into a submissive bride, dependent on her husband. While Dickens's "Overture" and his portions of act 1 are marked by the absence or incapacity of father figures, his final chapter endows a maimed Vendale with new strength. Called out from the church in Brieg soon after his wedding ceremony, Vendale learns from the Swiss guides that Obenreizer has been killed by an avalanche and protects his bride from the sight of the mangled corpse. Although Marguerite exhibits the bravery and skill of a mountaineer before her marriage and takes action at a time when her squeamish male companions do not, she is now the delicate bride who "must not see" (232) what the men around her observe. "Do not look round, my darling, for a reason that I have," her husband tells her when they leave the church, "turn[ing] his head" to view what she cannot (233). Accepting Vendale's protection, Marguerite asks no awkward questions but simply does what her husband says, going where he leads her, although "unconscious why" (230).

Having lost one male partner and been betrayed by another, Vendale forms a different kind of union at the conclusion of "No Thoroughfare," one generally relegated to the margins of the collaborative stories and represented as second best. Nonetheless, Vendale's marriage to Marguerite serves its purpose, defusing the threat of female autonomy and devaluing the relation between mother and child. "I don't wish to deprive Madame Dor of her share in the embraces that are going on" (231), Mr. Bintrey asserts as the wedding party prepares to go to church, yet it is clear that Vendale's marriage will do just that. With her hands "clasped round the neck of the bride" (231), the maternal surrogate is forced to relinquish her daughter and recognize the claims of "true love" over the "natural claim" (135) of a mother to her children. With the defeat of the mother—a surrogate at best—Dickens brings his narrative to an end.

III

While Dickens devalues the claims of mother nature in "The Curtain Falls," Collins uses his portions of act 4 to question the authority of male culture—specifically, the power of fathers to legitimate. His two chapters of the act, particularly "The Clock-Lock," center on the character Maître Voigt—affectionately referred to by the people of Neuchâtel as "Daddy Voigt" (218)—a "fatherly" Swiss notary whose profession is emblematic of patriarchy; in a story about single mothers and their illegitimate sons, he legitimates and authenticates. "The Clock-Lock" opens with a passage that valorizes Voigt by associating his work with the pastoral—that is, with the cultivation or domestication of nature and hence with the ability of male culture to subdue the maternal "wilds." Whereas nature "rage[s] wildly" among the Swiss Alps, "insatiate for destruction" (204), she is both pleasant and productive in the notary's "oddly pastoral . . . office," under his control: "Goats browsed in the doorway, and a cow was within half-a-dozen feet of keeping company with the clerk . . . . According to the seasons of the year, roses, sunflowers, hollyhocks, peeped in at the windows. Maître Voigt's bees hummed through the office all the summer, in at this window and out at that, taking it frequently in their day's work, as if honey were to be made from Maître Voigt's sweet disposition" (213).

However, this idealized image of male cultivation and authority is missing from Collins's manuscript of "The Clock-Lock," and the passage may very well have been written and inserted into proofs by Dickens himself. This conjecture is supported, most obviously, by Collins's far-from-idealized portrait of Maître Voigt elsewhere in act 4. Despite the opening description of the "sweet" notary, Collins points to the absurdities of his logic (215) and implicates him in the abuses of patriarchal power. An old friend of Obenreizer's father, Voigt mistakenly legitimizes the villain, blindly defending Obenreizer's rights over Marguerite simply because he is his "father's son." "Courage, courage, my good fellow!" the notary tells him after he has been fired by his employers and defied by his ward: "You will begin a new life to-morrow morning in my office here. . . . I hate to see a man oppressed. I see you oppressed and I hold out my hand to you by instinct . . . . Your father sent me my first client . . . . Do I owe nothing to your father's son?" (214). A spokesman for the patrilineal and the debts owed to fathers, no matter how corrupt, Voigt assures Obenreizer that his "legal rights" over Marguerite are "absolutely unassailable," and counsels him to "be calm under [his] wrongs" (215–16).

As these ironies make clear, Collins was not likely to idealize "Daddy Voigt" at the outset of his chapter, and the conjecture that Dickens wrote the passage in question is supported by striking parallels between its account of the notary's "pastoral" office and one describing Dickens's own. In a letter to Annie Fields of May 1868, Dickens portrays the room in the Swiss Chalet in which he writes his fiction, "up among the branches of the trees"; its mirrors "reflect and refract in all kinds of ways the leaves that are quivering at the windows, and the great fields of waving corn, and the sail-dotted river . . . and the birds and butterflies fly in and out, and the green branches shoot in, at the open windows" (Letters, 3:650). The similarities between Voigt's office and that of Dickens, in which the natural world is mediated ("reflect[ed] and refract[ed]") by means of representation, suggests that the notary may be a more fitting persona for Dickens in "No Thoroughfare" than either of the partners who figure in it.

Indeed, Dickens's power to legitimate was brought home to both him and Collins during their exchange over Reade's *Griffith Gaunt,* with Dickens explaining what he would—and would not—"pass" as the editor of *All the Year Round.* From the start of his editorial career, Dickens conceived of himself as one who grants legitimacy to works of fiction—hence his comparison between *Household Words* and the Foundling Hospital, where authors, like unwed mothers, leave their "children" without a name (Pilgrim, 6:44). Despite his rise in professional status and the acknowledgment of his authorship in *All the Year Round,* Collins, too, remained keenly aware of Dickens's authority to legitimate but for obvious reasons was wary of that process as well. From Collins's perspective, Dickens's periodicals were less a haven for the illegitimate offspring of wayward contributors than a harem where writers were expected to submit to Dickens's will. Thus in negotiating his payment for *The Moonstone* in May 1867, before he and Dickens began working on the Christmas Number, Collins compared his idea for his new work to a virginal girl whose value was as yet undetermined, yet who would be sold to *All the Year Round.*[59] As long as Dickens acted as Collins's editor and publisher, "passing" and purchasing his "literary commodit[ies],"[60] their collaboration could not be considered a partnership but would be characterized by partial agreements, compromises, and resistance on Collins's part.

This point is borne out by the dramatic adaptation of the Christmas Number, written by Collins after Dickens left for America in November 1867 and described by a London *Times* reviewer as "an entirely original production."[61] Reinventing the story in Dickens's absence, Collins transformed the published text into a critique of English power and privilege. Describing the genesis of the play in his "Recollections of Charles Fechter" (1882), Collins explains that it "requir[ed] such new presentation of some of the persons of the story as almost involved the re-creating of them."[62] This "re-creation" is nowhere more apparent than in his characterization of Obenreizer, whom Collins now represents as a tragic figure.

In their first appearance on stage, Obenreizer and Marguerite resemble a couple engaged to be married; Collins introduces them as they are "house-

59. ALS to W. H. Wills, 13 May 1867. The Pierpont Morgan Library, New York. *The Letters of Wilkie Collins,* 2:287.
60. Ibid.
61. *Times* (London), 27 December 1867; quoted in Pilgrim, 11:520 n. 3.
62. Collins, "Recollections of Charles Fechter," p. 163.

hunting" in London, and Obenreizer treats Marguerite "tenderly": "She shall have a home replete with gratified wishes!" he proclaims.[63] Unable to compete with Marguerite's wealthy English suitor, Obenreizer is robbed of the woman he loves and compelled to steal in order to buy the lavish gifts that he hopes will "outshine" those of his rival (33, 19). He appears a sympathetic and vulnerable figure while the Englishman seems callous and over privileged. "Ah! this miserable luxury—this hollow show! Has Marguerite any idea of what this splendor costs me?" Obenreizer asks. "He forces me to it" (18), Obenreizer says, buying Marguerite jewels with the money he has embezzled, a crime for which Collins supplies the thief with a justifiable motive.

Rather than highlighting Obenreizer's savage aggression—what Dickens terms "the animosity of a fierce cunning lower animal" (190)—Collins places him on the defensive in the dramatic adaptation. In Dickens's narrative, the "swarthy" guide brandishes a dagger, wounding Vendale with it; in the play, Obenreizer is rejected by Marguerite in favor of Vendale and feels as if he has received a "knife . . . wound" (20). Reluctant to use violence, he hopes to retrieve his forged receipt from Vendale "without crime" (31). During their Alpine conflict, he never assaults Vendale and loses consciousness along with the Englishman; instead of escaping to Neuchâtel, as he does in the Christmas Number, he too is found "lying in the snow by the edge of the precipice" by Marguerite and the guides (34). Supplanted by the Englishman in Marguerite's affections and unwilling to be disgraced in her eyes, Obenreizer commits suicide in Collins's last scene. Having swallowed poison, he "sadly tak[es] Marguerite's hand" in the final moments of the play, bidding her "farewell": "So ends the dream of my life!" (39).

Two months before Collins wrote the dramatic adaptation, as the collaborators were working on their respective portions of the Christmas Number, Dickens sensed that their aims were diverging, particularly in regard to the English hero. To Dickens, Collins appeared to be "in some danger of making [Vendale] rather foolish or contemptible in the eyes of the readers" (Pilgrim, 11:451). In his adaptation, Collins does, indeed, make Vendale seem contemptible at times and Obenreizer heroic, ennobling the figure Dickens represents as savage and animalistic. Dickens's story about the dangers of female autonomy and the rehabilitation of English manhood had now become Obenreizer's tragedy. As the "synopsis" of the play notes, "the interest all concentrates on the central figure—Obenreizer—a character superbly played by

63. Charles Dickens [sic] and Wilkie Collins, No Thoroughfare. A Drama, in Five Acts and a Prologue. As First Performed at the New Adelphi Theatre, London, Under the Management of Mr. Benj. Webster, and the Direction of Mrs. Alfred Mellon, December 26th, 1867, De Witt's Acting Plays, Number 14 (New York: Robert M. De Witt, n.d.), p. 17; subsequent references to No Thoroughfare. A Drama are cited parenthetically in the text.

Mr. Fechter" (40). Not surprisingly, Dickens lacked enthusiasm for the new work, which he read in portions mailed to him by Collins. Despite the "glorious tidings of the Xmas No." that Wills sent to him in December, Dickens was "not sanguine about the play": "I don't see it, as I read it. It may be my mood, or my anxiety, or I know not what else; but I don't see it rush on to its end in a spirited manner" (Pilgrim, 11:528). "The Play is done *with great pains and skill*. But I fear it is too long," Dickens told Collins on Christmas Eve: "I greatly doubt its success" (Pilgrim, 11:520).

Even after the play proved successful, Dickens's feelings about it did not change, and a tone of displeasure underlies his account of its warm reception, particularly the acclaimed performance of Fechter in what had become the starring role. Writing to James Fields on 15 January 1868, Dickens tells his American friend that he "knew that Fechter would tear himself to pieces rather than fall short, but . . . was not prepared for his contriving to get the pity and sympathy of the audience out of his passionate love for Marguerite": "Although the piece is well cast and well played, my letters tell me that Fechter is so remarkably fine as to play down the whole company. The Times, in its account of it, said that 'Mr. Fechter' (in the Swiss mountain scene, and in the Swiss Hotel) 'was practically alone upon the stage'" (*Letters*, 3:604). Writing to Fields again on 15 May, after having "seen No Thoroughfare twice," his opinion of the play remains mixed at best: "Excellent things in it, but it drags to my thinking" (*Letters*, 3:647). Conceding that it "really *is* a success" in a letter to Georgina Hogarth, Dickens is left claiming that the adaptation would have been even *more* successful had he managed it himself: "I could have done wonders to it, in the way of screwing it up sharply and picturesquely, if I could have rehearsed it" (*Letters*, 3:600).

As Catherine Peters notes in discussing *No Thoroughfare*, Dickens "seems to have resented Wilkie's and Fechter's London triumph, achieved against his predictions and without his help" (*King*, 290). But if the play showed what Collins could accomplish without him, it also underscored Dickens's inability to control the meaning and effect of their collaborations. Considering the liberties taken by Collins in "re-creating" the 1867 Christmas Number for the stage, it is not surprising that "No Thoroughfare" proved to be their last joint effort. When Collins chose to work with Fechter on his next drama, *Black and White* (1869), Dickens seemed only too glad to be left to his own devices. Having decided to "abandon" the collaborative Numbers of *All the Year Round* after the publication of "No Thoroughfare," Dickens explained his decision to Wills, complaining that such works, even at their best, offered only a "shadowy" approach to a "congruous whole" (*Letters*, 3:661): "I have invented so many of these Christmas Nos.," he tells Wills in July 1868, "and they are so profoundly unsatisfactory after all with the introduced stories and their want of cohesion or originality, that I fear I am sick of the thing" (*Letters,* 3:659–60). The explanation Dickens offered to James Fields was less politic in tone and pointed more directly to his sense of being drowned out by Collins: "My reason for abandoning the Christmas number was, that I became weary of having my own writing swamped by that of other people" (*Letters,* 3:677).

In the winter of 1867–68, as *No Thoroughfare* was playing to appreciative audiences, Dickens's desire to control the meaning of works associated with his name was exacerbated by the role Collins was temporarily playing—that of visiting editor. As Collins told his mother in November 1867, his "very minutes are counted" since he is not only "finishing the 3rd act of the play" and "correcting The Moonstone for its first appearance" but also "conducting All the Year Round."[64] Although Dickens expressed "delight" at the news that Wills and Collins were "getting on together" at the office (Pilgrim, 11:490), he also wanted to determine what they did and did not publish while he was abroad: "Remember that no reference, however slight is to be made to America in any article whatever, unless by myself," Dickens warned Wills in a memorandum. "Remember that the same remark applies to the subject of the Fenians" (Pilgrim, 11:474).

In discussing Collins's brief editorial role at *All the Year Round,* which coincided with the serialization of *The Moonstone,* Hyungji Park expresses disappointment that little seemed to change in the journal during Dickens's absence: "In a unique instance in *AYR* for any writer other than Dickens, Collins was reading, editing and selecting the articles that could influence his audience's reading experience of his novel," yet the journal remained as palatable to middle-class readers as ever, its commentary on politically charged issues "oblique" at best.[65]

Even as visiting editor, however, Collins found his ability to shape the journal strictly limited—not only by Wills but by Dickens, determined to supervise his subordinates from the other side of the Atlantic. As Dickens's memorandum makes clear, Collins and Wills were not to publish articles on politically sensitive subjects, and Dickens's letters from America show that he was carefully watching and responding to their editorial decisions, sending them material for the journal, and telling them when to publish it: "I have received 3 Nos. of A.Y.R. all good," Dickens assured Wills in December, but went on to warn

64. Wilkie Collins to Harriet Collins, 26 November 1867; quoted by Peters, *King of Inventors,* pp. 287–88.

65. Hyungji Park, "'The Story of Our Lives': *The Moonstone* and the Indian Mutiny in *All the Year Round,*" in *Negotiating India in the Nineteenth-Century Media,* ed. Douglas M. Peers and David Finkelstein (New York: St. Martin's Press, 2000), pp. 102, 101.

him to "be extremely chary of using those Mugby Junction stories" (Pilgrim, 11:506). "I enclose a curious article . . . on the Poison of the Rattlesnake. You may publish it in A.Y.R. *any day after the 20th March*" (*Letters,* 3:627). "In making up A.Y.R. try to bring the matter closer down to the foot of the last page of the No. And for the love of Heaven no more of those Xmas Railway stories" (Pilgrim, 11:522).

Dickens's continued scrutiny of Collins and the constraints placed on him at *All the Year Round* help to explain Collins's decision to work with others in the late 1860s—advising Reade on the serial novel *Put Yourself in His Place* (1869–70) as well as its dramatic adaptation and collaborating with Fechter on the melodrama *Black and White,* first performed at the Adelphi in March 1869. Written in the wake of the Jamaica Insurrection and the trial of Governor Eyre, criticized for his repressive measures in putting down revolt among ex-slaves in 1865, *Black and White* is set on the island of Trinidad in 1830 but criticizes conceptions of racial difference still current in the 1860s. In its most radical moments, the play treats racial identity as a cultural construct rather than a biological fact; midway through the plot, the hero, a French count, is revealed to be the son of a slave woman raped by a colonist and hence himself the property of his father's heir. Forcibly separated from the woman he loves and sold to an English plantation owner, Count de Leyrac is only freed by the discovery of a long-lost paper of manumission, and Collins uses his enslavement and liberation to undermine the categories "black" and "white," and to suggest that the grounds of racial difference are arbitrary and shifting.

In *The Moonstone,* Collins anticipates his treatment of race relations in *Black and White,* although he approaches the subject in a more circumspect way. Working within the parameters of *All the Year Round,* Collins relegates his most blatant criticism of imperial practices to a frame narrative, for example. Nonetheless, Dickens found Collins's novel too radical for his tastes. While he did not publish a statement distancing himself from *The Moonstone,* as he had with one of Reade's novels, he harshly criticized it in a private letter to Wills and set out to rework it in his own novel of empire building, *The Mystery of Edwin Drood.*

CHAPTER 6

Crimes of the Empire, Contagion of the East:

The Moonstone and *The Mystery of Edwin Drood*

Toward the end of June 1867, as their plans for "No Thoroughfare" took shape, Dickens heard Collins read the first three numbers of his new novel *The Moonstone* and went "minutely through the plot of the rest to the last line." Writing to Wills on 30 June, Dickens expresses his approval of Collins's new work, which began running in *All the Year Round* in January 1868:

> Of course it is a series of "Narratives," and of course such and so many modes of action are open to such and such people; but it is a very curious story—wild, and yet domestic—with excellent character in it, great mystery, and nothing belonging to disguised women or the like. It is prepared with extraordinary care, and has every chance of being a hit. It is in many respects much better than any thing he has done. (Pilgrim, 11:385)

Despite his implicit criticism of what he sees as the standard elements of Collins's fiction ("of course . . . of course"), Dickens is enthusiastic about this "wild . . . yet domestic" story. But his enthusiasm is short lived. Writing to Wills one year later, as the serialization of *The Moonstone* was drawing to a close, Dickens tells his subeditor that he agrees with him about the novel: "The construction is wearisome beyond endurance, and there is a vein of obstinate conceit in it that makes enemies of readers" (*Letters,* 3:660).

Dickens's final and harsh reaction to *The Moonstone* has led critics and biographers to conclude that a personal rift divided the two writers in the years immediately preceding Dickens's death. "In view of [Dickens's] earlier opinion of the same novel . . . it is hard to suppress a notion that personal animosity entered into the matter," Kenneth Robinson argues.[1] This animosity is often attributed to Dickens's growing hostility toward Charles Collins, who had married Kate Dickens in 1860, and whose ill health, rumored impotence, and financial difficulties made him a less-than-ideal son-in-law. Thus William M. Clark represents Collins as "forced to choose between Charles Dickens and his brother" and claims that his decision "meant a growing estrangement from one of his oldest and dearest friends."[2]

At the same time, critics note, Dickens was increasingly put off by Collins's unorthodox domestic arrangements, which included not only Caroline Graves but, as of the mid-1860s, Martha Rudd as well. "It was perhaps Wilkie's affairs that were 'wearisome beyond endurance,'" Catherine Peters remarks (King, 311). As early as March 1861, Dickens expressed reservations about each member of the Collins family, as his letter to Esther Elton Nash reveals:

> Katie and her husband have come home; but how long they may remain at home is unknown. . . . There are no "Great Expectations" of perspective [sic] Collinses. Which I think a blessed thing. . . . Old Mrs. Collins dined here last Sunday week, and contradicted everybody upon every subject for five hours and a half, and was invariably Pig-headed and wrong. So I was very glad when she tied her head up in a bundle and took it home . . . .
>
> Wilkie . . . has made his rooms in Harley Street, very handsome and comfortable. We never speak of the (female) skeleton in that house, and I therefore have not the least idea of the state of his mind on that subject. I hope it does not run in any matrimonial groove. I can imagine similar cases in which that end is well and wisely put to the difficulty. But I can *not* imagine any good coming of such an end in this instance. (Pilgrim, 9:388–89)

While some critics place Dickens's reaction to *The Moonstone* in the context of these strained family relations, conjecturing that they came to a head in 1868, others attribute Dickens's distaste for Collins's novel to professional jealousy. Catherine Peters suggests that Dickens "turned against" *The Moonstone* because it was more popular than his own works, "even beating the success of *Great Expectations*" (King, 310–11), and Sue Lonoff observes that Dickens "had seen his admiring protégé develop into . . . a rival competing for the public's attention with considerable success" and "could hardly have avoided feelings of competition, perhaps even feelings of resentment against a younger writer who was still in his prime."[3] Similarly, Michael Hollington believes that Dickens was

1. Kenneth Robinson, *Wilkie Collins: A Biography* (New York: Macmillan, 1952), p. 215.
2. William M. Clarke, *The Secret Life of Wilkie Collins* (Chicago: Ivan R. Dee, 1991), pp. 127, 138.
3. Sue Lonoff, "Charles Dickens and Wilkie Collins," *Nineteenth-Century Fiction* 35 (September 1980): 162–63.

made "suddenly jealous" by the successes of *The Moonstone* and the dramatic adaptation of "No Thoroughfare," and expressed his hostility in the portrait of John Jasper, who presumably kills his young rival in *The Mystery of Edwin Drood*.[4]

Yet Dickens's criticism of *The Moonstone* and his more fully developed response to it in *Edwin Drood* can also be understood in the broader context of the collaborative relationship—as the last and most acrimonious in a series of exchanges that began nearly two decades before. Although Dickens initially praised *The Moonstone,* basing his judgment on its opening numbers and a plot synopsis, the effect of the novel may have struck him quite differently once it was actually written and serialized, particularly since its concluding section drew "tears" for the Hindu characters, as Geraldine Jewsbury noted in her 1868 *Athenaeum* review:

> The "epilogue" of *The Moonstone* is beautiful. It redeems the somewhat sordid detective element, by a strain of solemn and pathetic human interest. Few will read of the final destiny of *The Moonstone* without feeling the tears rise in their eyes as they catch the last glimpse of the three men, who have sacrificed their cast[e] in the service of their God, when the vast crowd of worshippers opens for them, as they embrace each other and separate to begin their lonely and never-ending pilgrimage of expiation. The deepest emotion is certainly reserved to the last.[5]

Furthermore, Dickens's initial praise of *The Moonstone* in June 1867 preceded his experience of writing "No Thoroughfare" with Collins and then watching his collaborator adapt the story for the stage. Collins's "re-creation" of the 1867 Christmas Number may well have intensified Dickens's disapproving sense of the younger writer's autonomy as well as his more radical political sympathies. In his dramatic adaptation of "No Thoroughfare," Collins makes a hero of the figure Dickens represented as a "swarthy" and treacherous native, just as he "re-serves" the "deepest emotion" (in Jewsbury's words) for the Hindus in *The Moonstone*. Read in this context, *The Mystery of Edwin Drood* reveals not only Dickens's "intense rivalry" with Collins,[6] but also his desire to rework Collins's

---

4. Michael Hollington, "'To the Droodstone,' or, from *The Moonstone* to *Edwin Drood* via *No Thoroughfare*," *QWERTY* 5 (1995): 141. Hollington compares the "thematic patterns" in "No Thoroughfare," *The Moonstone,* and *Edwin Drood,* considers "identity and difference" in the three works, and contrasts the "cyclical" and modernist structure of Dickens's last novel with Collins's "linear" narrative, with the 1867 Christmas Number serving as "a middle term" (142, 148).

5. [Geraldine Jewsbury], *Athenaeum* (25 July 1868): 106; *Wilkie Collins: The Critical Heritage,* ed. Norman Page (London: Routledge & Kegan Paul, 1974), pp. 170–71.

6. Jerome Meckier, *Hidden Rivalries in Victorian Fiction: Dickens, Realism, and Revaluation* (Lexington: University Press of Kentucky, 1987), p. 93.

vision of empire and race relations to a more conservative end. With some justification, Collins's critique of imperialism has itself been criticized in recent years as overly qualified and indirect in its indictment of the British. Nonetheless, Dickens's response to the novel reminds us that such judgments are relative; by the standards of the 1860s, *The Moonstone* could indeed be seen as a work that challenged prevailing attitudes toward the empire and its "swarthy" subjects.[7]

I

Early in 1858, less than a year after the Indian sepoys began to rebel against the British, Collins contributed an article on the mutiny to *Household Words;* "A Sermon for Sepoys" was published on 27 February. It is unclear whether Collins volunteered to write on the mutiny or whether Dickens asked him to do so; in either case, the subject was not new to him. Only two months before, in his portion of the 1857 Christmas Number, Collins had represented the imprisonment and escape of English colonists from "native" pirates, in a story loosely based on the mutiny and intended by Dickens to celebrate British "heroics" in India.

Like his chapter in "The Perils of Certain English Prisoners," "A Sermon for Sepoys" looks ahead to Collins's representation of British India in *The Moonstone* and clearly distinguishes his views on the subject from those of Dickens. In "The Perils," Collins alters the tone of Dickens's opening chapter, deflating its high seriousness, and he models the pirate captain on dandified

7. John R. Reed was the first critic to discuss Collins's critique of imperialism in *The Moonstone* at any length. In "English Imperialism and the Unacknowledged Crime of *The Moonstone*," *Clio* 2 (June 1973): 281–90, Reed points to "England's imperial depredations" as Collins represents them, asserting that "the Indian priests are heroic figures, while the representatives of Western Culture are plunderers" (286, 283). Reed notes that Collins sets his main narrative in 1849, the year in which the British forcefully annexed the Punjab, and that Ablewhite is murdered in the vicinity of the East India Company offices. In *Wilkie Collins and His Victorian Readers: A Study in the Rhetoric of Authorship* (New York: AMS Press, 1982), Sue Lonoff places Collins's critique of empire in *The Moonstone* in the context of the Eyre controversy (pp. 178–79). Patrick Brantlinger addresses Collins's attitude toward empire very briefly and is more tentative in his assessment of *The Moonstone* as "perhaps . . . anti-imperialist" (*Rule of Darkness: British Literature and Imperialism, 1830–1914* [Ithaca, N.Y.: Cornell University Press, 1988], p. 295 n. 19). Tamar Heller briefly contrasts Collins's "reservations about imperialism" with Dickens's support of it and suggests that Dickens's harsh criticism of *The Moonstone* may have stemmed from the authors' disagreement on imperial issues (*Dead Secrets: Wilkie Collins and the Female Gothic* [New Haven, Conn.: Yale University Press, 1992], pp. 190–91 n. 8). The critical debate over the imperial politics of *The Moonstone* is ongoing; for a full discussion of this debate, see the section on "Collins and Empire" (pp. 298–303) in Lillian Nayder, "Wilkie Collins Studies: 1983–1999," *Dickens Studies Annual* 28 (1999): 257–328.

British officers rather than on treacherous sepoy leaders; in so doing, he provides an alternative reading of the origins of the revolt. In "A Sermon for Sepoys," Collins again questions prevailing responses to the rebellion but by proposing an alternative *solution* to the conflict.

As Patrick Brantlinger notes in his study of mutiny literature, British writing about India before 1857 generally suggested that the natives "might be helped to progress in the scale of civilization" but denied these "hopeful though obviously ethnocentric possibilities" after the sepoy revolt, depicting the Indians as inherently violent and superstitious.[8] Yet Collins not only believes the mutineers can be reformed; he feels that reformers should look to oriental rather than Western ideals in accomplishing this goal. Instead of preaching to the rebellious Indians from a Christian text, he draws his sermon from one of their own—from the lesson delivered to the seventeenth-century Muslim emperor Shah Jehan ("the wise, the bountiful, the builder of the new city of Delhi") by the wise man Abbas:

> The more gifts you have received, the better use it is expected you will make of them. Although the All-Powerful alone can implant virtue in the human heart, it is still possible for you, as the dreaded representative of authority, to excite to deeds of benevolence, even those who may have no better motive for doing good, than the motive of serving their own interests . . . . Spread the example, therefore, of your own benevolence, beyond the circle of those only who are wise and good . . . and fortify your mind with the blessed conviction that the life you will then lead, will be of all lives the most acceptable in the eyes of the Supreme Being.[9]

In delivering this lesson, an oriental parable of the talents, and in representing benevolent and charitable Muslims with "human hearts," Collins dissociates himself from Dickens, who expressed the desire to "exterminate the Race upon whom the stain of the late cruelties rested" when writing to Angela Burdett-Coutts and Emile de la Rue about the mutiny (Pilgrim, 8:459, 473). Whereas Dickens writes of a race "stain[ed]" with "cruelties," whose members have "disfigured the earth with . . . abominable atrocities" (Pilgrim, 8:473), Collins suggests that the Indians are as capable of moral goodness as the British.

Although Dickens did not record his reaction to "A Sermon for Sepoys," his response is suggested by a second article on the mutiny that he published one month later, perhaps intending it to answer Collins—George Craig's

---

8. Brantlinger, *Rule of Darkness*, p. 200.
9. [Wilkie Collins], "A Sermon for Sepoys," *Household Words* 17 (27 February 1858): 247.

"Blown Away!" Condemning the "savages of Cawnpore and Delhi," Craig describes the execution of two mutineers blown from cannons by the British. While this "spectacle . . . may be denounced by a class of Englishmen, as cruel and inhuman," Craig writes, "they ought, before condemning, to pause and reflect on the enormity of the crime, which the men who were executed had projected."[10]

"Blown Away!" is designed to resolve whatever doubts *Household Words* readers may have had about the proceedings of the British in putting down the revolt, and it justifies the extreme measures taken to punish the rebellious "savages," in part, by using poetic language to describe grisly acts. Yet Craig's description of the execution, which reduced the bodies of the mutineers to "little particles of a crimson colour . . . falling, thick as snow-flakes . . . over the plain," also illustrates the savagery of the British, who used means that Craig concedes are "barbarous and horrible" to produce this "snow shower."[11] Although acts of retaliation against the Indians were largely ignored, suppressed, or represented as "excesses of heroism" in the British press,[12] there were those who found the British no better—or even worse—than the sepoys. "The European troops have become fiends when opposed to natives," an officer stationed in Benares told the London *Times* in 1857, a comment quoted by Karl Marx in the *New York Daily Tribune*. Marx catalogued a host of atrocities committed by British officers against the Indians, arguing that the criminality of the sepoys merely reflected that of the English themselves. "However infamous the conduct of the sepoys, it is only the reflex, in a concentrated form, of England's own conduct in India, not only during the epoch of the foundation of her Eastern Empire, but even during the last ten years of a long-settled rule . . . . There is something in human history like retribution; and it is a rule of historical retribution that its instrument be forged not by the offended, but by the offender himself."[13]

The theme of Hindu retribution is central to *The Moonstone* and conveys Collins's sense that the Indians rather than the British were on the defensive in 1857: "The Moonstone will have its vengeance yet on you and yours!" a dying

10. [George Craig], "Blown Away!" *Household Words* 17 (17 March 1858): 348, 350.
11. Ibid., 350, 348.
12. Brantlinger, *Rule of Darkness*, p. 201.
13. Karl Marx, "The Indian Revolt," *New York Daily Tribune* (16 September 1857); *The Portable Karl Marx*, ed. Eugene Kamenka (Harmondsworth: Penguin, 1983), pp. 351–52. As Brantlinger observes, Marx was not alone in using the mutiny to criticize British conduct in India. Although his political aims differed sharply from those of Marx, Disraeli also attributed the sepoy revolt to colonial practices of which he disapproved: the "forcible destruction of native authority," the "disturbance of the settlement of property," and the "tampering with the religion of the people" (quoted by Brantlinger, *Rule of Darkness*, p. 202).

Brahmin warns the English officer who steals the sacred diamond in Collins's prologue.[14] Collins's decision to begin his novel with an account of British violence in 1799, during the siege of Seringapatam, has been seen as evasive by some critics, perhaps most notably by Deirdre David. In her view, Collins merely provides us with "a fable of individual brutality" in his opening scene, one intended to define the aims and methods of Victorian imperialists against those of their corrupt eighteenth-century predecessors.[15] Yet in opening *The Moonstone* with the 1799 siege, which gave the British their foothold in India, Collins, like Marx, traces the mutiny back to an originary crime and suggests that the later violence of the sepoys is "only the reflex . . . of England's own conduct in India."[16]

In *The Moonstone,* eleven different narrators tell the story of a sacred Hindu diamond that is stolen and restolen four times in the course of the narrative. Englishmen commit three of these four thefts. The central plot of the novel is set in England nine years before the mutiny, in 1848–49, but the prologue opens in Seringapatam half a century earlier, shortly before and after the British siege. During the looting that follows the British victory, John Herncastle, an English officer, steals the Moonstone from its three Brahmin guards and murders them. He then brings the gem to England, bequeathing it to his niece Rachel Verinder. On 21 June 1848, the night that Rachel receives the Moonstone, it is stolen by the man she loves, her first cousin Franklin Blake; Blake is acting under the influence of opium, which has been secretly administered to him, and remains ignorant of his crime for much of the novel. On that same night, the Exeter Hall philanthropist Godfrey Ablewhite, another cousin who is pressed for funds, steals the Moonstone from Blake. A year later, the three Brahmins who have followed the gem from India to England (and who are descendents of its original guards) steal it from Ablewhite and murder him. The novel ends with a ceremony celebrating the restoration of the Moonstone to its Indian shrine, which is observed by Mr. Murthwaite, an English authority on India.

Collins's aims in constructing this plotline are suggested, in part, by his manner of reworking the historical materials on which he based his novel. As a

14. Wilkie Collins, *The Moonstone,* ed. J. I. M. Stewart (1966; reprint, Harmondsworth: Penguin, 1986), p. 37; subsequent references to *The Moonstone* are cited parenthetically in the text.

15. Deirdre David, *Rule Britannia: Women, Empire, and Victorian Writing* (Ithaca, N.Y.: Cornell University Press, 1995), p. 18.

16. Jaya Mehta makes a related point in discussing *The Moonstone:* "In substituting the Storming of Seringapatam for the Mutiny," she argues, "Collins chooses . . . an event in which British aggression and rapacity had encountered some public criticism," and he "presents an inverted parallel to what the British regarded as the notorious Sieges of Cawnpore, Delhi, Lucknow, and Agra, allowing the reader to read the illegitimacy of empire into the antecedents of the unmentioned Mutiny" ("English Romance; Indian Violence," *Centennial Review* 39, 4 [fall 1995]: 620).

source for his description of the siege of Seringapatam, Collins used Theodore Hook's biography of General David Baird, which casts the British imperialists in a heroic light. Hook contrasts the murderous cruelty of the Muslim ruler Tippoo with "the gallant conduct" of the British troops, "already chronicled in the annals of fame": "Let it never be forgotten in this great contest, who were, in fact, the oppressors," Hook asserts.[17] Collins, by contrast, makes no mention of Tippoo's cruelty, portraying the lawlessness of the British troops instead. Hook notes that the British pillaged the Muslim treasury after the siege and that a private in the British Army murdered Tippoo "in cold blood" and plundered the corpse. But he appends the following qualifier in a footnote: "Let us hope the man was a Sepoy."[18] Collins leaves little room for such "hopes" in his own account of the plundering.[19]

Indeed, Collins proves more interested in excusing than indicting Indian violence in *The Moonstone*. Of the four central crimes committed in the novel, he mitigates only one—that of the Brahmins. Redefining the nature of their crime in his epilogue, Collins explains its significance in Hindu rather than Christian terms; they are not guilty of theft and murder but have forfeited their caste in the service of their god.[20] The epilogue is narrated by Mr. Murthwaite, who has disguised himself as a Hindu, and his heightened and lyrical description of the diamond's restoration encourages us to think of the Brahmins as martyrs; they are purified, not punished, at the end of the novel: "The god had commanded that their purification should be the purification by pilgrimage. On that night, the three men were to part. In three separate directions, they were to set forth as pilgrims to the shrines of India. Never more were they to rest on their wanderings, from the day which witnessed their separation, to the day which witnessed their death" (526). As Jewsbury's 1868 *Athenaeum* review makes clear, Victorian readers found such passages "beautiful" and accepted Collins's redefinition of the Brahmins' crimes as sacrifices, sympathizing with "the three men . . . [who] begin their lonely and never-ending pilgrimage of expiation" in the epilogue.

17. Theodore Edward Hook, *The Life of General, the Right Honourable Sir David Baird, Bart.*, 2 vols. (London: Bentley, 1832), 1:102, 217.

18. Ibid., 1:217.

19. As Catherine Peters notes, Collins also ignored the information provided to him by John Wyllie of the Indian Civil Service, who referred him to the letters of Captain Hugh Wheeler and told him of the "barbarism" of the Hindus, with their "primitive ethics" (quoted by Peters, *King*, p. 291).

20. Sue Lonoff makes this point in discussing what she sees as the growing sympathy for the Brahmins in *The Moonstone*, noting that their portrait is "emancipated" for its time. In her view, the epilogue and prologue "reverse and correct" the racist view of the Indians provided in the "inner story"; they are "selfless devotees," while the English are "devious and criminal" (*Wilkie Collins and His Victorian Readers*, pp. 223–25).

Collins invites no such sympathy for Herncastle and Ablewhite, whose crimes represent the military, economic, and moral trespasses of the British Empire. Collins repeatedly refers to John Herncastle as "the Honourable John" (63, 66), the nickname for the East India Company; in so doing, he suggests that Herncastle's crimes are not those of a wayward and brutal individual—a black sheep whose upright relations have "closed the[ir] doors . . . against him" (63). They are, instead, representative of British economic policy in the years leading up to the Indian Mutiny.[21]

In the years preceding the mutiny, Dickens published articles critical of British practices in India—among them, "The Honourable John"—and Collins may have had such articles in mind when creating his own "Honourable John" in *The Moonstone*. The personified figure of the East India Company described in *Household Words* is a landed gentleman who "commit[s] many vagaries" on his "vast property" and cares little for "the prosperity of his estate."[22] Not only does he keep his farms in "wretched condition" and abuse his native tenants; he acquires his estate by robbing the natives of their land:

> At various periods in his career, Honourable John possessed himself of large tracts of land belonging to native proprietors, on various conditions, and under different pretexts. . . . In taking possession of the lands assigned to him for farming purposes, [Honourable John] seized a great quantity of personal property not included in the bargain, and resolutely refused to give it up. Letter after letter was written to him on the subject of these robberies; but he invariably had the meanness to shuffle out of any reply. . . . So bad has my friend's conduct become, that his former admirers and supporters have been seriously thinking of taking all power of doing mischief out of his hands.[23]

Like this figure, "the Honourable John" of *The Moonstone* is a man of "low . . . principles" who robs Indians of their property.[24] But Collins compounds what is represented in *Household Words* as his "obstinate perseverance in wrong-doing,"[25] adding murder to the list of his crimes.

21. For a useful history of the East India Company, see Brian Gardner, *The East India Company: A History* (New York: Dorset Press, 1971). Although a joint stock company, "Honourable John" was, in Macaulay's words, "entrusted with the sovereignty of a large population, the disposal of a larger clear revenue, the command of a larger army than are under the direct management of the Executive Government of the United Kingdom" (quoted by Gardner, *East India Company,* p. 203). After the Indian Mutiny, rule of the colony passed to the British government; the company was finally dissolved in 1874.

22. [John Capper], "The Honourable John," *Household Words* 7 (30 July 1853): 516–17.

23. Ibid., 517, 518.

24. Ibid., 517.

25. Ibid., 518.

Collins uses Ablewhite in much the same way that he uses Herncastle—to dramatize the ability of whites to make the most (financially) of their colonial possessions. A speaker at Exeter Hall (89), the center of England's missionary movement, Ablewhite invalidates the claim that empire building serves a moral end. Unlike "the Christian Hero" (239) he is made out to be by his admirer, Miss Drusilla Clack, Ablewhite embezzles from the trust fund of his ward and keeps a mistress in an expensive suburban villa. He does not convert the heathen but steals their sacred gem in the hope of paying off his debts. Traveling to Amsterdam, he makes the necessary arrangements to have the diamond "cut into separate stones" and thus transformed from a sacred object into "a marketable commodity" (512–13).

Unlike Herncastle and Ablewhite, however, the third English thief, Franklin Blake, is provided with an alibi of sorts. As the mystery of *The Moonstone* unfolds, we learn that Blake stole the diamond from Rachel Verinder under the influence of opium, secretly administered to him by Dr. Candy, who hoped to convince Blake of its medicinal qualities. Before Dr. Candy can "acknowledge the trick that he had played" (435), he falls ill, and it is left to his assistant, Ezra Jennings, a character of mixed race, to discover that Blake "took the Diamond, in a state of trance, produced by opium" and is thus "guiltless, morally speaking, of the theft" (435, 441). "Under the stimulating influence [of opium]," Jennings tells Blake,

> any apprehensions about the safety of the Diamond which you might have felt during the day . . . would impel you into practical action to preserve the jewel— would direct your steps, with that motive in view, into the room which you entered—and would guide your hand to the drawers of the cabinet, until you had found the drawer which held the stone . . . . Later, as the sedative action began to gain on the stimulant action, you would slowly become inert and stupified. Later still you would fall into a deep sleep. When the morning came, and the effect of the opium had been all slept off, you would wake up as absolutely ignorant of what you had done in the night as if you had been living at the Antipodes. (442–43)

Not only does Blake steal the diamond unconsciously; he does so to "preserve" it, out of concern for its "safety." Returning to his room with the Moonstone, still in an opium trance, Blake hands it to Ablewhite: "Take it back, Godfrey, to your father's bank. It's safe there—it's not safe here" (510).

In providing Blake with this alibi for his theft, Collins becomes an apologist for empire in the eyes of some critics; in effect, he proves willing to make excuses for the robberies that brought the English their Indian possessions. Collins offers a scientific rather than a political explanation of Blake's act, Ronald R.

Thomas argues, and represents the Englishman as "the victim of his physiological reaction to the foreign body of the opium." In so doing, Collins "obscures the memory of the brutal political crime by which the gem was attained in the first place."[26] Describing "Blake's unconsciousness" in similar terms, Jaya Mehta sees it as one of several "gaps, silences, blanks, and amnesias" that enable Collins's characters to forget "the illegitimacy of empire," while Tamar Heller notes the connection between Blake's "unconscious" motive for taking the diamond—to ensure its safety—and "the rationalization of imperialism as 'the white man's burden,' protecting people who presumably cannot take care of themselves."[27] As Heller goes on to observe, this rationalization is provided by Jennings, a "half-caste" who pointedly declines to describe his own experience of colonial oppression. To Heller, Jennings's silence on the subject of empire as well as his request to be buried with his writings suggest Collins's own "self-censorship" in writing *The Moonstone,* his desire "to muffle [his] unconventional tendencies in order to . . . win the approval of [his] audience."[28]

But as both Heller and Mehta concede, Collins reveals as much as he suppresses in representing Blake's theft and invites us to question "the rationalization of imperialism" at the same time that he provides it. As Mehta expresses the point, Blake's action does not simply obscure Herncastle's original crime but "replays" it to a critical end, by suggesting "the violation that is colonialism" through the "trope of conquest-as-rape."[29] In his narcotic trance, Blake steals a sacred Hindu diamond but also the most precious jewel of the woman he hopes to marry, and thus his act conflates empire building with sexual violation. Rachel's anxiety over the safekeeping of her jewel, its association with the moon, and her sense of shame and rage after it has been stolen, call attention to Collins's sexual subtext, as does the central piece of evidence in the case: a stained nightgown.[30] Reinforcing the analogy between Rachel's violation and

---

26. Ronald R. Thomas, "Minding the Body Politic: The Romance of Science and the Revision of History in Victorian Detective Fiction," *Victorian Literature and Culture* 19 (1991): 238–39. Elsewhere, Thomas characterizes *The Moonstone* as a novel that conflates "sexual desire" with "British colonial domination" and that uses Blake's "missing dream" to examine the process of psychological and political repression and recovery, with Jennings as "a prototype of the psychoanalyst" who "exposes the duplicity of an imperial policy that presents itself as innocent." See *Dreams of Authority: Freud and the Fictions of the Unconscious* (Ithaca, N.Y.: Cornell University Press, 1990), pp. 203–5, 212.

27. Mehta, "English Romance," 620–21; Heller, *Dead Secrets,* p. 146.

28. Heller, *Dead Secrets,* p. 162.

29. Mehta, "English Romance," 646.

30. A number of critics have discussed the sexual subtext of *The Moonstone,* often from a psychoanalytic perspective. See, for example, Lewis A. Lawson, "Wilkie Collins and *The Moonstone,*" *American Imago* 20 (1963): 61–79; Charles Rycroft, "The Analysis of a Detective Story," in *Imagination and Reality: Psychoanalytical Essays, 1951–1961* (London: Hogarth Press, 1968), pp. 114–28; and Albert D. Hutter, "Dreams, Transformations, and Literature: The Implications of Detective Fiction," *Victorian Studies* 19 (December 1975): 181–209. As Hutter puts it, "what is stolen from Rachel is both the actual gem and

the rape of India, Collins describes his heroine in the same terms as the Hindus: to the English, the Indians appear "swarthy," "lithe," "supple," and "cat-like" (324, 326); after her diamond is stolen, Rachel appears "dark," "fierce," and "lithe and supple . . . as a young cat" (190). In her staunch desire for "independence" (87), furthermore, and her anger at Blake, Rachel exhibits a resistance that recalls the Indian Mutiny itself. Her characterization ties the subjugation and rebellion of Englishwomen to those of colonized peoples.[31]

Identifying Blake as the man who threatens Rachel Verinder with sexual violation, Collins turns one of the central myths of mutiny literature on its head.[32] In contrast to Dickens's first chapter of "The Perils," in which Miss Maryan implores Gill Davis to kill her before she can be raped by the mutineers, Rachel is figuratively assaulted by the English hero of *The Moonstone,* and the three Indians falsely accused. "The poor ill-used Indians have been most unjustly put in prison," Blake acknowledges soon after the Moonstone disappears: "They are as innocent as the babe unborn. My idea that one of them was hidden in the house, has ended, like all the rest of my ideas, in smoke. It's been proved . . . to be simply impossible" (119).

Having conquered Rachel Verinder, Blake makes his connection to empire building more explicit by leaving England to "wander . . . in the East" (339). But his ties to the empire—and its criminality—are also suggested by the role that opium plays in his act of theft. Although Ronald Thomas describes opium as a "foreign body" in discussing Blake's behavior, Collins's original readers

---

her symbolic virginity" (201). Sue Lonoff concurs, "recalling the Victorian maxim that a young girl's virginity is her most precious possession, and the statement in the Prologue that the diamond's luster waxes and wanes on a lunar cycle" (*Wilkie Collins and His Victorian Readers,* p. 210). William M. Burgan discusses the sexual symbolism of the Moonstone as well, but in the context of Masonic ritual, Hindu belief, and Victorian representations of Siva, god of time, generation, and justice. See "Masonic Symbolism in *The Moonstone* and *The Mystery of Edwin Drood,*" *Dickens Studies Annual* 16 (1987): 257–303.

31. As Heller argues, "The parallels Collins draws between the two thefts of the diamond—the first in India, the second in England—demonstrate the interpenetration of the realms of empire and domesticity by showing how the hierarchies of gender and class that undergird British culture replicate the politics of colonialism" (*Dead Secrets,* p. 144).

32. Mehta notes that "black-on-white rape, an inexhaustible staple of Anglo-Indian fiction and imperial ideology after the 1857 uprising[,] . . . is figuratively recast by Collins as the theft of an English woman's 'jewel'—not by three lurking Indian men, as the reader is led to suspect, but by a man of her own race" ("English Romance," 646). Hyungyi Park downplays this crucial point in her reading of *The Moonstone* as "a monitary tale in which the danger of Indian sexuality is speculatively imported into the country mansions of Victorian society with devastating results" ("'The Story of Our Lives': *The Moonstone* and the Indian Mutiny in *All the Year Round,*" in *Negotiating India in the Nineteenth-Century Media,* ed. David Finkelstein and Douglas M. Peers [New York: St. Martin's Press, 2000], p. 89). For a detailed analysis of the rape narrative generated by the Indian Mutiny, see Nancy L. Paxton, "Mobilizing Chivalry: Rape in British Novels about the Indian Uprising of 1857," *Victorian Studies* 36, 1 (fall 1992): 5–30.

were more likely to think of the drug as the most lucrative cash crop produced in British India and its most controversial one as well. At a time when the British demand for Chinese goods greatly outweighed the Chinese demand for British products, this contraband commodity enabled the British to correct their trade imbalance. Produced in India and transported on ships licensed by the East India Company, opium was smuggled into China by the British in violation of imperial edict, in exchange for the goods that were in such great demand at home. When the Chinese began to enforce their policies in the late 1830s, the British government intervened. Easily defeated in the first Opium War, the Chinese were forced to cede Hong Kong to the British in 1842, to open four additional ports for foreign trade, and to allow the Western smugglers to carry on the opium trade unmolested. After a second China war concluded in 1860, the importation of opium was legalized by the Treaty of Tientsin.[33]

Victorians often debated the ethics of the opium trade, and it was used by critics of empire to illustrate the hypocrisy of the British, who assumed a posture of moral superiority over Hindus and Muslims in India while promoting the moral corruption of the Chinese. "The Company claimed to itself the high prerogative of being the guardian of the laws, and the preservers of the morals of the people over whom they ruled," the M.P. for Sheffield complained in 1833, as politicians discussed the company's China trade monopoly; yet

> they cultivated opium for no other purpose than for smuggling it into China, against the laws and edicts of the empire . . . poisoning the health, and destroying the morals of the people of that country. It was painful to think what a vast amount of evil had been already created by this trade . . . the whole guilt of which rested with the Company, as it was they who furnished the opium from India, and their supercargoes at Canton who licensed the smugglers in China, so that the beginning and the end of this illicit and contraband trade was theirs.[34]

Although the company lost its monopoly in 1833, the opium trade was not abolished until 1917, and it continued to stir debate over the ethics of empire throughout the Victorian period.[35]

33. The East India Company held a monopoly on the opium trade from 1773 to 1833, after which it participated in the trade indirectly, by licensing those who grew the drug in India and sold it to the Chinese. In 1849, when the action of *The Moonstone* is set, opium provided the company with well over £3 million in annual revenue. On the subject of the opium trade and the Opium War, see Michael Greenburg, *British Trade and the Opening of China: 1800–42* (Cambridge: Cambridge University Press, 1951); Christopher Hibbert, *The Dragon Wakes: China and the West, 1793–1911* (New York: Harper and Row, 1970); and Arthur Waley, *The Opium War through Chinese Eyes* (Stanford, Calif.: Stanford University Press, 1958).

34. Hansard's Parliamentary Debates, 3d series, 356 vols. (London: Wyman, 1830–1891), 18:770.

35. See Bruce Johnson, "Righteousness before Revenue: The Forgotten Moral Crusade against the Indo-Chinese Opium Trade," *Journal of Drug Issues* 5 (fall 1975): 304–26.

In the 1850s and 1860s, the controversy surrounding the opium trade made its way into the columns of Dickens's periodicals, in various articles critical of British policy toward the Indians and the Chinese. "It will suffice if Mr. Bull exalts his horns the least part of an inch in triumph over what he has been doing," Henry Morley facetiously remarks in an 1852 *Household Words* article reviewing John F. Davis's *China, During the War and Since the Peace* (1852):

> The government of China has been beaten and beggared, but if its wits be bright-ened, what of that? For an Asiatic state to be well thrashed by Europeans must conduce greatly to its future good, and to the total prospects of humanity.
>
> Taking that matter, however, on its own ground, we are disposed to doubt whether the evil of the Chinese war will lead to so much good as our conceit in the character of Europeans caused us to imagine. No wonders have happened in the way of commerce with the external world, and the internal state of China, since the war, and in consequence of the war, seems to have become utterly wretched.[36]

The articles Dickens published on the opium trade after the mutiny are much more circumspect in their criticism than Morley's; asserting their neutrality, they "steer . . . clear between the merchant-bias on the one hand, and the mis-sionary bias on the other."[37] Nonetheless, they "present the arguments on both sides of the opium question," including the view of those who see "opium chests" as "Pandora-boxes whence much mischief flies out to trouble the Oriental world"; who criticize the "tyranny" of the company over the Indian ryot, or peasantry, forced to cultivate opium rather than other crops; and who represent "the opium trade as a source of evil" to the Chinese.[38]

In *The Moonstone,* Blake is not a merchant who profits from the opium trade but a gentleman who unwittingly ingests the drug. However, he is associated with corrupt imperial practices, since he delivers the Moonstone to Rachel Verinder for "the Honourable John" and steals it himself, and Collins suggests that, in ingesting opium, the Englishman is, in effect, getting a taste of his own medicine. Collins develops this point by repeatedly speaking of "the vengeance of . . . opium" in the novel (447, 462) and connecting the drug and its "fright-ful" effects (447) with the theme of retribution against the English; as the dying Brahmin tells Herncastle in the prologue, "the Moonstone will have its vengeance yet on you and yours" (37).

36. [Henry Morley], "China with a Flaw in It," *Household Words* 5 (3 July 1852): 369.

37. [George Dodd], "Opium: Chapter the First. India," *Household Words* 16 (1 August 1857): 105.

38. Ibid., 104, 106; and [George Dodd], "Opium: Chapter the Second. China," *Household Words* 16 (22 August 1857): 184.

However, the damaging effects of opium are most keenly felt by Jennings, whose mixed racial background and colonial origins associate him with the Hindus in the novel and whose sufferings evoke those endured by the Indian ryot forced to cultivate the drug and the Chinese addicts encouraged to consume it. Despite Jennings's praise of opium as "that all-potent and all-merciful drug" (430), which he takes for "an incurable internal complaint" (429), the "palliative" proves worse than the disease, and he finds himself faced with "the dreadful alternative between the opium and the pain" (483).[39]

Jennings's praise of opium, despite the "horror" he associates with it (430), and his dedication to Blake, whom he proves "guiltless, morally speaking, of the theft of the Diamond" (441), have led some critics to conclude that he serves to justify imperial rule. For example, David compares Jennings to the "Babu," an English-educated Indian trained as a civil servant and "produced by the empire for its maintenance and reproduction." In her view, Collins uses Jennings to illustrate the "acquiescence" of the subaltern to his own subordination and hence to "resolve" the problem of native rebellion in a way that fulfills imperial "desires."[40] Similarly, Heller notes that Jennings identifies with the imperialists rather than the colonized, despite his mixed racial background, speaking of "our colonies." In Heller's view, Jennings "contains his subversive energy," becoming "a kind of Friday who serves the upper-class Blake."[41]

Yet such readings overlook the ironies of Collins's novel, particularly its revisionary treatment of *Robinson Crusoe* and Defoe's portrait of the ideal native servant, ever-grateful to his English master. Indeed, it is one of Collins's central ironies that Gabriel Betteredge, a primary narrator and the steward at the Verinder estate, valorizes Defoe's idyll of empire building and mistakenly reads Crusoe's colonial experiences as a prototype for his own. Revering *Robinson Crusoe* as if it were his bible, Betteredge consistently acts on its authority, having found it "[his] friend in need in all the necessities of this mortal life" (41). Defoe's novel proves particularly useful to Betteredge because it gives him a convenient way to "read" the three Indians who appear at the Verinder estate—as if they were the cannibals who arrive on Crusoe's island and who inspire fear and moral self-righteousness. Betteredge refers to Crusoe's terror of

39. As Barry Milligan points out, Jennings's physical features, particularly his hair ("still of . . . deep black" on the top of the head, but "turned completely white" on the sides [Collins, *Moonstone*, p. 371]), "serves as a metaphor not only for the mixing of black and white but more pointedly for the *colonization of black by white*." Milligan argues that Jennings's "lament of having progressed 'from the use of opium to the abuse of it' and of 'feeling the penalty at last'" can be read as a political allegory: "Jennings's 'internal complaint' and his recourse to opium echo the ills and palliatives of British India." See *Pleasures and Pains: Opium and the Orient in Nineteenth-Century British Culture* (Charlottesville: University Press of Virginia, 1995), p. 75.

40. David, *Rule Britannia*, pp. 33, 142, 147.

41. Heller, *Dead Secrets*, pp. 158–59.

the "savage wretches" in describing his own fear of the "heathenish" Brahmins (82), and although Blake reminds him that "the Indians . . . originally owned the jewel" (72), Betteredge sees them as a set of "murdering thieves" who have "invaded" the "quiet English house" he helps to maintain in their criminal quest for "Miss Rachel's lawful property" (67, 109, 73).

In his influential reading of *The Moonstone,* D. A. Miller identifies Betteredge as Collins's spokesman, as a narrator who embodies the "collective cognition" of the novel and voices the norms shared by the community. Miller describes what he sees as "the plain dealing" of Betteredge's "self-presentation" and the "unproblematic" nature of his language: "His narrative may not tell us 'the whole truth,' but it can be relied upon to tell us 'nothing but the truth.'" Miller notes that Betteredge "treats *Robinson Crusoe* like an oracle," yet he dismisses this trait as an idiosyncracy that does little or nothing to discredit the authority of the "faithful retainer."[42]

But in dismissing Betteredge's view of *Robinson Crusoe* in this way, Miller misconstrues Collins's intentions. The uses to which Betteredge puts Defoe's novel are central to Collins's conception of this narrator, and they provide the measure of his *un*reliability. While Betteredge reads the actions of the Brahmins through the eyes of Robinson Crusoe, Collins subverts Defoe's distinction between civilized Englishmen and dark-skinned savages, in part by treating the Brahmins' faith with the seriousness that Defoe accords only to Christian belief. While Defoe ridicules the heathenism of Friday, for whom "old Benamuckee" is god,[43] Collins reveals the religious hypocrisy of the Evangelical movement, to which his most corrupt characters belong. He further blurs the racial polarities of Defoe's novel by casting the Brahmins as the kind masters of a young English boy. In Defoe's novel, Crusoe adopts the young native Friday, saving his life and teaching him Christianity; in *The Moonstone,* the Brahmins adopt an English boy, rescuing him from a life of poverty and teaching him their own "catechism" (51).

The Indians appear at the Verinder estate in the guise of strolling conjurors, accompanied by their servant, "a little delicate-looking light-haired English boy" (49). Warned off the premises, they put the boy into a clairvoyant trance, first pouring an inklike substance into the palm of his hand: "When the Indian said, 'Hold out your hand,' the boy shrunk back, and shook his head, and said he didn't like it. The Indian, thereupon, asked him (not at all unkindly), whether he would like to be sent back to London, and left where they had

---

42. D. A. Miller, *The Novel and the Police* (Berkeley: University of California Press, 1988), pp. 45, 53–54.

43. Daniel Defoe, *Robinson Crusoe,* ed. Angus Ross (1965; reprint, Harmondsworth: Penguin, 1985), p. 218.

found him, sleeping in an empty basket in a market—a hungry, ragged, and forsaken little boy. This, it seems, ended the difficulty" (50). The Indians use the English boy for their own purposes—to foresee the arrival of Blake and the Moonstone in Yorkshire—but they do not "ill-use" him, despite suspicions to the contrary (49). In fact, they treat the boy better than do his fellow Englishmen, who allow such children to live in marketplaces and sleep in baskets. Furthermore, they show considerably more benevolence toward this English native than Englishmen show toward Indians. Whereas the English kill and loot in storming Seringapatam, the Indians who "invade" England save the "hungry, ragged, and forsaken" child from the wilds of London.

In *The Moonstone,* Collins uses the image of the English Friday to question and invert the idea of imperial mastery but also to reveal what myths of empire building obscure—the connection between race relations in the colonies and class relations at home. At one point in his narrative, Betteredge equates his services with those of Defoe's Friday; refusing to assist Sergeant Cuff with his investigation, he hopes that he has, in effect, left the detective "without a man Friday to keep him company" (207). But the English steward generally likes to think of himself as a Crusoe figure, comparing his experiences with those of the English colonist and overlooking his ties to the native servant.[44] However, Collins develops the connection that Betteredge ignores, reworking *Robinson Crusoe* so that the faithful retainer plays the part of both Crusoe *and* Friday. In so doing, Collins reminds his readers that working-class Englishmen may be masters in India but remain servants at home.

While Betteredge plays the part of Crusoe in his dealings with the Indians, he plays the part of Friday in his dealings with Lady Verinder. Like Friday, who gladly learns to call Crusoe "Master" and willingly "swear[s] to be [his] slave for ever,"[45] Betteredge belongs to Lady Verinder, moving with her from her father's home to that of her husband when she marries, having been "more than fifty years in her service" when his narrative begins (42, 44). Friday will go nowhere without his master: "no wish Friday there, no master there," he tells Crusoe.[46] Betteredge expresses the same loyalty, although in better English: "It was all one to me where I went, so long as my mistress and I were together" (42). On those rare occasions when Betteredge speaks of class differences and the privileges of his social superiors, he does so in jest, expressing pity for the members of the idle class rather than resentment toward them:

44. Betteredge reads his own experiences through Crusoe's on at least five occasions; see pp. 39, 45, 110, 233, and 519.

45. Defoe, *Robinson Crusoe,* p. 207.

46. Ibid., p. 227.

Gentlefolks in general have a very awkward rock ahead in life—the rock ahead of their own idleness. . . . It often falls heavy enough, no doubt, on people who are really obliged to get their living, to be forced to work for the clothes that cover them, the roof that shelters them, and the food that keeps them going. But compare the hardest day's work you ever did with the idleness that splits flowers and pokes its way into spiders' stomachs, and thank your stars that your head has got something it *must* think of, and your hands something that they *must* do. (84–85)

However, none of Betteredge's working-class companions share his thankfulness, and most resent those belonging to the leisure class. Revealing the pitfalls of identifying with one's masters, Collins brings Betteredge into conflict with others from his class, whose anger provides a striking contrast to his willing servitude. "All the hard work falls on my shoulders in this house," the kitchen maid Nancy complains to the steward (53), a sentiment shared by the second housemaid, Rosanna Spearman, whose deformed shoulder bears witness to the truth of Nancy's claim and who is judged to be "monstrous" by Betteredge because of her social aspirations, her love for Blake, a gentleman, and her disrespect for her upper-class rival (80). "Suppose you put Miss Rachel into a servant's dress, and took her ornaments off—?" Rosanna asks in the suicide note she writes to Blake. "It can't be denied that she had a bad figure; she was too thin. But who can tell what the men like? And young ladies may behave in a manner which would cost a servant her place . . . . I can't expect you to read my letter, if I write it in this way. But it does stir one up to hear Miss Rachel called pretty, when one knows all the time that it's her dress does it, and her confidence in herself" (363).

As her letter reveals, Rosanna channels her class resentment into sexual jealousy, directing it at Rachel Verinder rather than at Blake. But her resentful friend and fellow cripple, Lucy Yolland, does not. On the contrary, Lucy's rage conflates the inequities of the class system with those of patriarchy and is aimed at Blake in his dual role as man and gentleman, as Betteredge recounts:

"Where's the man you call Franklin Blake?" says the girl, fixing me with a fierce look, as she rested herself on her crutch.

"That's not a respectful way to speak of any gentleman," I answered. "If you wish to inquire for my lady's nephew, you will please to mention him as Mr. Franklin Blake."

She limped a step nearer to me, and looked as if she could have eaten me alive. "*Mr.* Franklin Blake?" she repeated after me. "Murderer Franklin Blake would be a fitter name for him . . . . Where is he?" cries the girl, lifting her head from the crutch, and flaming out again through her tears. Where's this gentleman that I mustn't speak of, except with respect? Ha, Mr. Betteredge, the day is not far off

when the poor will rise against the rich. I pray Heaven they may begin with *him*."
(226–27)

Like Rosanna Spearman, Lucy Yolland is characterized by a deformity that embodies her class injury (163) but that also recalls the "one defect" that
Betteredge perceives in her social superior, Rachel Verinder: the desire for female autonomy (87). While Rachel desires to think for herself, resents her dependence on Blake, and learns that men marry for "selfish and mercenary ends"
(318), Lucy hopes to escape from these injustices by moving to London with
Rosanna, where they could "live . . . together like sisters," without the interference of men: "Oh! if she had only thought of the men as I think, she might
have been living now!" (226–27). Also like Rachel, Lucy resembles the Indians
who seek independence from the British, her call for revolution an echo of their
own. Describing Lucy as a man-eater as well as a man hater—"as if she could
have eaten [him] alive"—Betteredge implicitly compares her to the savages
who intrude on Crusoe's island and the Hindus who "invade" his own.

In *The Moonstone,* Collins leaves it to his female Fridays to resent and resist
their subordination to their masters. In so doing, he distances himself from their
call for revolution but also acknowledges their twofold oppression as women
and as workers. When Rachel, like Lucy, speaks "so spitefully, so savagely, with
such an extraordinary outbreak of ill-will toward Mr. Franklin," that she appears unladylike in Betteredge's eyes, he feels "ashamed of [her] for the first
time in [his] life" (138). Yet what is more shameful, Collins suggests here and
elsewhere, is the social state that "pass[es] itself off as civilized" while dehumanizing the majority of its members on the grounds of their gender and / or
their class.[47] "Life means dirty work, small wages, hard words, no holidays, no
social station, no future," Collins writes of his English maid of all work in "Laid
Up in Lodgings," describing a downtrodden female servant whose portrait
would seem shocking even in "a book about a savage country": "No state of
society which composedly accepts this, in the cases of thousands, as one of the
necessary conditions of its selfish comforts, can pass itself off as civilized, except
under the most audacious of all false pretenses."[48]

Collins's social criticism is not always this pointed. As Heller and Mehta note,
Collins qualifies and contains much of what seems radical in *The Moonstone,*
placing his most subversive figures on its margins and reinscribing gender norms
when Rachel Verinder marries Blake, even though he is the man who steals

---

47. Wilkie Collins, "Laid Up in Two Lodgings," *Household Words* 13 (7 and 14 June 1856): 481–86
and 517–23; republished as "Laid Up in Lodgings," in *My Miscellanies,* vol. 20 of *The Works of Wilkie
Collins,* 30 vols. (New York: AMS Press, 1970), p. 121.
48. Ibid., pp. 121, 123.

her "jewel." While we cannot determine who was responsible for many of the editorial decisions made at *All the Year Round* as *The Moonstone* was being serialized in Dickens's absence, the novel was contextualized in a way that, at times, lent credence to Betteredge's views by valorizing Britain's possession of India: representing it, for example, as a "jolly" place for Englishmen "fond of outdoor sports."[49] The weekly issue in which Betteredge asserts that the Indians are "murdering thieves" and describes their "tigerish quickness" (109, 106) also includes an article entitled "My First Tiger," which recounts the adventures of a British "shooting-party" in Bengal, depicts a Muslim guide "frantic with rage" in his pursuit of the wounded animal, and represents India itself as a land designed for the pleasure and profit of Englishmen.[50]

Yet the counterpoint between such representations of the empire and those in *The Moonstone,* particularly in its narrative frame, underscores Collins's critical aims in writing the novel. Although his methods are sometimes indirect and his criticism conveyed through irony, he questions racist assumptions about Indians at the same time that Betteredge voices them and exposes England's "false pretenses" to civilization as a country that tolerates its own forms of savagery. *The Moonstone* thus develops the subject of Collins's "Highly Proper," an article against which Dickens put Wills on his guard. "Where is Doctor Livingstone?" Collins asks in this article, equating English class prejudice with African heathenism: "Here are the heathen about us, somewhere or other in this country, and no Society for the Propagation of the Gospel At Home, to find them out."[51]

II

In the England of *Edwin Drood,* Dickens's characters also discover that there are "heathen about us." Yet their discovery reveals a different set of concerns on Dickens's part and more clearly points to the dangers of imperial decline than the criminality of empire building. As if to confirm and deepen Betteredge's fears of Eastern invasion, Dickens writes a novel that anticipates the imperial gothic fiction of the 1880s and 1890s and that represents the threat of racial "contagion" from without England as well as racial degeneration within. Like later narratives of reverse colonization, *Edwin Drood* suggests that England's decline may be a punishment for imperial crimes, yet foregrounds the dangers

---

49. "My First Tiger," *All the Year Round* 19 (1 February 1868): 178.
50. Ibid., 179.
51. [Wilkie Collins], "Highly Proper!" *Household Words* 18 (2 October 1858): 362.

posed to English civilization by savage races as well as the need to defend against them.[52]

Left half finished at Dickens's death, *Edwin Drood* centers on the disappearance of an imperialist-in-the-making and addresses the theme of empire and crime in several ways: through the ambitions of Edwin Drood, whose plans to "go engineering into the East" and "to wake up Egypt a little" are forestalled by his presumed death;[53] through the experiences of Helena and Neville Landless, twins from Ceylon, the latter of whom is widely suspected of Drood's murder, despite the allegiance of Reverend Crisparkle, the minor canon of Cloisterham cathedral, and Mr. Tartar, a former naval officer; through the characterization of John Jasper, Drood's uncle, an opium-addicted choirmaster whom Dickens apparently planned to unmask as Drood's murderer; and through the plight of Rosa Bud, who (with Drood's consent) dissolves their long-standing engagement to be married and is secretly yet relentlessly pursued by Jasper.

Whereas Collins went "minutely through the plot" of *The Moonstone* with Dickens before that novel was written, Dickens did not tell Collins of his plans for *Edwin Drood,* instead confiding them to John Forster. In his biography, Forster explains that Dickens intended to end the novel with Jasper's arrest and confession, highlighting the divided consciousness of the murderer, who had killed his nephew out of sexual jealousy:

> The last chapters were to be written in the condemned cell, to which his wickedness, all elaborately elicited from him as if told of another, had brought him. Discovery by the murderer of the utter needlessness of the murder for its object, was to follow hard upon commission of the deed; but all discovery of the murderer was to be baffled till towards the close, when, by means of a gold ring which had resisted the corrosive effects of the lime into which he had thrown the body, not only the person murdered was to be identified but the locality of the crime and the man who committed it. . . . Rosa was to marry Tartar, and Crisparkle the sister of Landless, who was himself, I think, to have perished in assisting Tartar finally to unmask and seize the murderer.[54]

Although critics occasionally dispute Forster's claims and continue to speculate about the intended plotline of the novel, his account of Dickens's plans for

---

52. For a discussion of imperial gothic fiction and reverse colonization narratives, see Brantlinger, *Rule of Darkness*, pp. 227–53; and Stephen D. Arata, "The Occidental Tourist: *Dracula* and the Anxiety of Reverse Colonization," *Victorian Studies* 33, 4 (summer 1990): 621–45.

53. Charles Dickens, *The Mystery of Edwin Drood*, ed. Arthur J. Cox (1974; reprint, Harmondsworth: Penguin, 1982), pp. 50, 96; subsequent references to *Edwin Drood* are cited parenthetically in the text.

54. John Forster, *The Life of Charles Dickens*, ed. J. W. T. Ley (New York: Doubleday, Doran, 1928), p. 808.

Edwin Drood are partly confirmed by Luke Fildes, its original illustrator. When Fildes asked Dickens about the significance of Jasper's long black scarf, having already sketched the character in a black tie, he was told that the scarf was necessary because "Jasper strangles Edwin Drood with it."[55] In light of Fildes's report, Howard Duffield and Edmund Wilson, among other critics, surmise that Dickens conceived of Jasper as a Thug, a member of the Indian cult devoted to the worship of Kali.[56] Best known for their ritualized strangulations of travelers, the Thugs were suppressed by the British in the 1830s and 1840s and their cult eradicated. Their murderous practices were given fictional form by Dickens's acquaintance, Captain Philip Meadows Taylor, an Indian Army officer and *Household Words* contributor whose popular novel, *Confessions of a Thug* (1839), was reissued in 1858.

Whether or not Dickens intended to unmask Jasper as a Thug, he connects the choirmaster to the Orient in his opening chapter. In a scene that conflates the East with East London, Dickens places Jasper in an opium den run by the haggard Englishwoman, "Princess Puffer," helping to shape the conventions of the opium den narratives that were popularized in the late 1860s and 1870s— tales of social exploration among the orientalized dangers of the imperial metropolis.[57] In his striking first paragraph, Dickens represents Jasper's opium dream and the "scattered consciousness" that "fantastically piece[s] itself together":

55. Luke Fildes, "The Mysteries of Edwin Drood," *Times Literary Supplement* (3 November 1905): 373.

56. Howard Duffield was the first critic to identify Jasper as a Thug. See "John Jasper—Strangler," *Bookman* (February 1930): 581–88. Edmund Wilson elaborates on Duffield's reading in "Dickens: The Two Scrooges," in *The Wound and the Bow* (Cambridge, Mass.: Houghton Mifflin, 1941), pp. 3–85. In "John Jasper and Thuggee," *Modern Language Review* 72 (July 1977): 526–37, Wendy S. Jacobson re-examines the arguments of Duffield and Wilson and explains what she sees as their improbability, despite the scattered references to Thuggee throughout Dickens's periodicals, including some examples in which the Thug is "anglicized" ("John Jasper," 527). See also Jacobson's *Companion to The Mystery of Edwin Drood* (London: Allen & Unwin, 1986). William Burgan notes that the cover of the monthly numbers of *Edwin Drood* includes a female figure that resembles Kali. Like Jacobson, Burgan provides a useful summary of the critical debate over Thuggee in Dickens's novel, but concludes that "if Jasper is not literally a Thug," he can be considered one "emblematically" ("Masonic Symbolism," 296). For a brief account of Thuggee and its suppression by the British, see James Morris, *Heaven's Command: An Imperial Progress* (New York: Harcourt Brace Jovanovich, 1973), pp. 71–85.

57. See, for example, "Lazarus, Lotus-Eating," published by Dickens in *All the Year Round* 15 (12 May 1866): 421–25; "East London Opium Smokers," *London Society* 14 (1868): 68–72; and "In An Opium Den," *Ragged School Union Magazine* 20 (1868): 198–200. As Virginia Berridge notes, "descriptions of opium smoking as a domestic phenomenon began only in the 1860s," "part . . . of the general fashion for investigation of 'darkest England' and East London in particular," with Dickens's account "mark[ing] the beginning of a more melodramatic presentation of the subject" than was provided in earlier narratives. See "East End Opium Dens and Narcotic Use in Britain," *London Journal* 4, 1 (1978): 3–28. For a discussion of opium den narratives and their conventions, see Timothy L. Carens, "Restyling the Secret of the Opium Den," in *Reading Wilde: Querying Spaces* (New York: Fales Library, 1995), pp. 65–75.

An ancient English Cathedral town? How can the ancient English Cathedral town be here! The well-known massive grey square tower of its old Cathedral? How can that be here! There is no spike of rusty iron in the air, between the eye and it, from any point of the real prospect. What IS the spike that intervenes, and who has set it up? Maybe, it is set up by the Sultan's orders for the impaling of a horde of Turkish robbers, one by one. It is so, for cymbals clash, and the Sultan goes by to his palace in long procession. Ten thousand scimitars flash in the sunlight, and thrice ten thousand dancing-girls strew flowers. Then, follow white elephants caparisoned in countless gorgeous colors, and infinite in number and attendants. Still, the Cathedral tower rises in the background, where it cannot be, and still no writhing figure is on the grim spike. Stay! Is the spike so low a thing as the rusty spike on the top of a post of an old bedstead that has tumbled all awry? Some vague period of drowsy laughter must be devoted to the consideration of this possibility. (37)

In *The Moonstone,* "the spiritualized intoxication of opium" (442) leads Blake to steal the Hindu diamond, an act that conflates imperial and sexual violation, and that provides an ironic commentary on the alleged protection extended to wives by their husbands, and to India by "the Honourable John." Jasper's dream, too, connects opium use with sex and violence but relies on and reinforces familiar stereotypes of the Orient, its transgressive pleasures and dangers, to do so: hence the references to sultans, scimitars, dancing-girls, and Turkish robbers impaled on spikes.[58] In *The Moonstone,* Collins ridicules those who blame the transgressions of the English on Eastern scapegoats—Miss Clack, for example, who sees Ablewhite as a saintly figure and the Hindus as emblems of sin, and draws a moral maxim from her error: "When the Christian hero of a hundred charitable victories plunges into a pitfall that has been dug for him by mistake, oh, what a warning it is to the rest of us to be unceasingly on our guard! How soon may our own evil passions prove to be Oriental noblemen who pounce on us unawares!" (241). Yet Dickens orientalizes Jasper's "evil passions" in his opening scene, just as he does Jasper's opium consumption, eliding England's responsibility for the trade.

58. Primarily concerned with conceptions of the self (the "human consciousness") in Victorian detective fiction, Ronald R. Thomas also compares Blake's dream to Jasper's, arguing that the latter reveals "a deeper skepticism" about "communal order" and human identity than the former (*Dreams of Authority*, pp. 218–19). In Thomas's view, the psychological conflicts of both novels are represented in political terms—by means of political plots in which imperial transgressions are repressed and at least partially recovered. To Thomas, *Edwin Drood* reveals Dickens's ambivalence about imperialism: "the mixture of pride and guilt that accompanied the late nineteenth-century expansion of the British Empire" (*Dreams of Authority,* p. 231).

Whereas Blake swallows opium in the form of laudanum—a familiar, English product rather than a "foreign body"—Jasper smokes it like a "Chinaman," and Dickens describes its effects as atavistic, as the English characters in the opium den go native. Under the influence of the drug, both the choirmaster and his English supplier come to resemble their savage bedfellows—a Chinaman and a Lascar:

> [Jasper] rises unsteadily from the bed . . . and looks with repugnance at his three companions. He notices that the woman has opium-smoked herself into a strange likeness of the Chinaman. His form of cheek, eye, and temple, and his color, are repeated in her. Said Chinaman convulsively wrestles with one of his many Gods, or Devils perhaps, and snarls horribly. The Lascar laughs and dribbles at the mouth. The hostess is still . . . .
>
> As he watches the spasmodic shoots and darts that break out of her face and limbs, like fitful lightning out of a dark sky, some contagion in them seizes upon him: insomuch that he has to withdraw himself to a lean arm-chair by the hearth—placed there, perhaps, for such emergencies—and to sit in it, holding tight, until he has got the better of this unclean spirit of imitation.
>
> Then he comes back, pounces on the Chinaman, and, seizing him with both hands by the throat, turns him violently on the bed. The Chinaman clutches the aggressive hands, resists, gasps, and protests. (38–39)

In a chapter he initially titled the "Prologue," and that recalls the narrative frame of *The Moonstone,* Dickens portrays an Englishman's act of violence against an Eastern figure—in this case, a "Chinaman" rather than an Indian—who "clutches the aggressive hands, resists, gasps, and protests" in self-defense. Represented in the context of opium consumption, Jasper's violence against the protesting "Chinaman" calls to mind English aggression against the Chinese in the Opium Wars, as criticized in articles that Dickens himself published on the "thrashing" of the "Asiatic state" by England.[59] Yet in *Edwin Drood,* Dickens attributes Jasper's violence to his corruption by opium and the East: his "unclean spirit of imitation." Rather than revealing the aggression of English imperialists or the crimes committed by "the Honourable John," Jasper's behavior mirrors that of Easterners who "wrestle" with their "Devils," "snarl . . . horribly," and "dribble . . . at the mouth."

In *The Moonstone,* the discovery that Blake, like his far-from-"honourable" uncle, has stolen the Hindu diamond is followed by a second revelation, when Sergeant Cuff unmasks Ablewhite in the public house where he lies dead.

---

59. [Morley], "China with a Flaw," 369.

Dressed as a "swarthy" sailor with "a noticeably dark complexion" and "a bushy black beard," and initially mistaken for "a spy in the service of the Indian conspiracy" (487, 495), Ablewhite is killed before he can leave London for Amsterdam, where he plans to have the Moonstone cut into separate stones and marketed. Ablewhite masquerades as an Oriental in stealing the diamond, but he is caught in the act, and Collins uses his disguise and unmasking to criticize the ploy used by his own characters, who blame the Indians for the crimes the English have themselves committed. When Cuff removes Ablewhite's black wig and beard and "wash[es] off his complexion" (502), he exposes the whiteness of the thief, an English philanthropist rather than an Indian spy.

In *Edwin Drood,* however, Dickens uses the very strategy that Collins exposes by unmasking Ablewhite. He orientalizes his English villain,[60] and his success in doing so is reflected in the various solutions to the novel that critics have proposed, most of which look to the East to account for Drood's murder. In what is perhaps the best-known solution, Duffield and Wilson claim that Dickens conceived of Jasper as a worshipper of Kali; like a Thug, Jasper leads a double life, treats his prospective victim with great kindness, and prepares a burial place before committing murder; he observes omens and describes his victim as a "fellow traveller," using key terms from "the vocabulary of the Stranglers."[61] Disputing this reading, Charles Forsyte notes that the Thugs did not attack Europeans and operated only within India, where they worked in groups. But having concluded that Drood is "a most unlikely victim for a Thug," Forsyte then looks to Egypt rather than England to solve what he terms the "exotic mystery in *Edwin Drood,*" arguing that the murderous Jasper is Drood's resentful half-brother, part English and part Egyptian.[62] His argument extends and revises that of Felix Aylmer, who points to one of the proposed titles for the novel, "The Mystery in the Drood Family," and claims that Dickens planned to identify Jasper as the son of a Muslim woman and as Drood's protective half brother, devoted to saving him from Eastern assassins in an Egyptian blood feud.[63] Despite the variations among these solutions, and regardless of their plausibility, each one reflects and extends a single strategy on Dickens's part: the displacement of crime and criminality from West to East.

Having made his English villain into an Oriental of sorts, Dickens invokes the sexual myths of mutiny novels and opium den narratives in representing

---

60. In comparing *Edwin Drood* and *The Moonstone,* Meckier makes the opposite claim—that Jasper is "a thoroughly English murderer." His logic is based on the assumption that Dickens must model Jasper on Ablewhite in order to "rewrite" *The Moonstone* (*Hidden Rivalries,* p. 180).

61. Duffield, "John Jasper," 584–86.

62. Charles Forsyte, *The Decoding of Edwin Drood* (New York: Charles Scribner's Sons, 1980), p. 26.

63. Felix Aylmer, *The Drood Case* (New York: Barnes and Noble, 1965), p. 44.

Jasper's persecution of Rosa Bud: the threatened violation of Englishwomen at the hands of oriental men. In pursuing Rosa, Jasper exhibits the sexual force of the rebellious sepoys in mutiny fiction but also the "vampirelike" mastery attributed to "Chinese opium masters" in tales of English opium dens.[64] In *The Moonstone,* Collins debunks such myths by revealing that Blake rather than the Hindus stole Rachel Verinder's jewel; as Blake's violation of his future wife suggests, Englishwomen are imperiled by their own menfolk and the privileges their husbands enjoy, not by swarthy and lascivious savages. Furthermore, because Rachel is allied with the Hindus in her looks and her anger, her violation points to the British rape of India as well. But in *Edwin Drood,* Dickens dissolves this alliance by characterizing Rosa as hostile to all things Eastern—to "Arabs, and Turks, and Fellahs, and . . . the Pyramids" (59)—and by creating two heroines, one English and one Oriental, only the first of whom is imperiled by Jasper's "fierce extreme of admiration" (229). Defining the vulnerability and innocence of Rosa against the "ferocity" and "power" of Helena Landless (94) as well as the "wickedness" of Jasper (228), Dickens rejects Collins's analogy between oppressed Englishwomen and colonized peoples.

Like the mutiny narratives discussed by Nancy L. Paxton, *Edwin Drood* "mobilizes chivalry" in the Englishwoman's defense. "Soiled" by Jasper, Rosa is "cleaned from the stain of . . . impurity by appealing to the honest and true" (234). She turns to those "chivalric" Englishmen who defend her with the "stoutness" of their "knight-errantry" (236, 241) and whose virtues appear uniquely English: the muscular Christianity of Crisparkle, for example, and the bravery and cleanliness of the naval Tartar.[65] Specimens of English manhood at its best, these figures not only protect Rosa from oriental contagion but also enable Dickens to defend the empire from the kind of criticism leveled against it by Collins.

64. Milligan discusses the reputed sexual powers and "hypnotic charisma" of the "Chinese opium master," comparing them to those of Jasper (*Pleasures and Pains,* p. 108). Eve Kosofsky Sedgwick draws the comparison between Jasper and du Maurier's Jewish Svengali in her discussion of Dickens's novel and what she sees as its imperial "discourse of homophobia" (226 n. 5, 182). In Sedgwick's view, Dickens is more concerned with the threat of "male rape" in *Edwin Drood* than he is with the threatened violation of the English heroine (182). See "Up the Postern Stair: *Edwin Drood* and the Homophobia of Empire," in *Between Men: English Literature and Male Homosocial Desire* (New York: Columbia University Press, 1985), pp. 180–200. Like both Milligan and Sedgwick, Fred Kaplan discusses Jasper's "eros of domination," which he associates with the powers of mesmerism. See *Dickens and Mesmerism: The Hidden Springs of Fiction* (Princeton, N.J.: Princeton University Press, 1975), pp. 165–215.

65. As Donald E. Hall explains, the phrase "muscular Christianity" dates from an 1857 review of Charles Kingsley's *Two Years Ago* and describes an ideal of manhood based on "physical strength, religious certainty, and the ability to shape and control the world around oneself," often in the service of empire (introduction, *Muscular Christianity: Embodying the Victorian Age,* ed. Donald E. Hall [Cambridge: Cambridge University Press, 1994], p. 7).

In *The Moonstone,* the English hero violates the woman he loves in the course of protecting her, reenacting the British rape of India, but in *Edwin Drood,* Dickens's heroes serve as models of benevolent domination.[66] In naming his retired naval lieutenant "Tartar," Dickens obliquely refers to the damaging effects of the first Opium War on the Chinese, as described by English historians and reiterated in *Household Words:* the weakening of the Tartar dynasty, whose rulers were considered moderates—"more reasonable enemies" than the Ming mandarins.[67] Yet Dickens's Tartar provides a reassuring image of England's military might; far from "cannonading" Orientals in an excessive show of strength,[68] he befriends Neville Landless; and although he collects exotic artifacts on his tours of duty, they are not, like the Moonstone, the "fortune[s] of war" (68) but "curiosities" ("birds, fishes, reptiles, arms, articles of dress, shells, seaweeds, grasses") that reveal his scientific interests and his classifying skills rather than his imperial greed and violence (248). Similarly, Crisparkle counters Collins's image of Ablewhite, training rather than exploiting the "heathen" through the exercise of his muscular Christianity.[69] "Hitting out from the shoulder with the utmost straightness" during his boxing practice, Crisparkle proves himself both morally and physically fit to train Neville in the ways of civilization, and only "soft-hearted benevolence beam[s] from his boxing-gloves" (78).[70]

66. Suvendrini Perera discusses the connections between "imperial" and "masculine" power in a chapter on "the complicated imperial and sexual tensions" of *Edwin Drood,* tensions she believes result in "narrative inconclusiveness." Her analysis of the disavowals and displacements of imperial wrongdoing in *Edwin Drood* is compelling, but she misrepresents *The Moonstone* by claiming that it revived "interest in 'thuggee'" in the 1860s and by speaking of Collins's Hindus as a "gang of sinister Indian stranglers" derived from Meadow Taylor's work. In fact, the Indians in Collins's novel never strangle anyone. See *Reaches of Empire: The English Novel from Edgeworth to Dickens* (New York: Columbia University Press, 1991), pp. 107, 113.

67. [Morley], "China with a Flaw," 370. Dickens's understanding of China's internal affairs was based, in part, on Sir John Francis Davis's *China, During the War and Since the Peace,* 2 vols. (London: Longman, Brown, Green, and Longmans, 1852), which was reviewed in *Household Words.* Davis discusses the repeated attempts of representatives of the Ming dynasty to expel the Tartars from power (2:182–219).

68. [Henry Morley], "Our Phantom Ship. China," *Household Words* 3 (28 June 1851): 325.

69. For Collins, the Victorian cult of athleticism suggested the affinity between Englishmen and "the savage and the brute," allowing his countrymen "to excuse all that is violent and brutish in [their] national acts" (*Man and Wife,* ed. Norman Page [Oxford: Oxford University Press, 1995], p. 68). The primitivism of the university athlete, Geoffrey Delamayn, is a central concern in *Man and Wife,* which began running in *Cassell's Magazine* in January 1870, three months before the first number of *Edwin Drood* was published. As some critics suggest, Dickens may have conceived of Crisparkle in response to Delamayn as well as Ablewhite. See Robert Ashley, "*Man and Wife:* Collins, Dickens, and Muhammad Ali," *Wilkie Collins Society Journal* 5 (1985): 5–9.

70. In his reading of *Edwin Drood,* David Faulkner argues that Dickens "deconstructs" Crisparkle's muscular Christianity and "Anglo-Saxon vigor and virtue," pointing to what he sees as the connections between the minor canon and the orientalized Jasper. Although the novel seems to oppose "Orient and Occident," Faulker claims, "the gulf between home and abroad is always already bridged" ("The

Uniting benevolence with strength, Christian morality with muscle, Crisparkle also provides a foil to the self-styled philanthropist of *Edwin Drood*, Luke Honeythunder, a critic of empire whom Dickens models on the radical M.P. John Bright.[71] One of the most outspoken figures on the "Jamaica Committee," Bright and his fellow committee members were criticized by Dickens for their "platform-sympathy with the black—or the native, or the devil—afar off, and [their] platform indifference to our own countrymen at enormous odds in the midst of bloodshed and savagery" (Pilgrim, 11:115). Bright called for the criminal conviction of Governor Eyre after the Jamaica Insurrection, and Dickens uses Honeythunder to ridicule the pacifism of those who condemned the use of force against "the native, or the devil," while advocating the punishment of Englishmen such as Eyre: "You were to abolish military force, but you were first to bring all commanding officers who had done their duty, to trial by court martial for that offense, and shoot them" (85).

To the extent that Dickens himself criticizes Britain's imperial practices and acknowledges the wrongs inflicted on colonized peoples in *Edwin Drood*, he does so through his characterization of the Landlesses, newly arrived in England from Ceylon. Dickens first presents the brother and sister through the "rough mental notes" of Crisparkle:

> An unusually handsome lithe young fellow, and an unusually handsome lithe girl; much alike; both very dark, and very rich in color; she of almost the gipsy type; something untamed about them both; a certain air upon them of hunter and huntress; yet withal a certain air of being the objects of the chase, rather than the followers. Slender, supple, quick of eye and limb; half shy, half defiant; fierce of look; an indefinable kind of pause coming and going on their whole expression, both of face and form, which might be equally likened to the pause before a crouch, or a bound. (84–85)

Like Betteredge's impression of the Indians in *The Moonstone*, Crisparkle's description of the Landlesses draws on stereotypes of the catlike Oriental; "lithe," "dark," and "fierce" in appearance, they are compared to jungle animals, ready to "crouch" or "bound." But Crisparkle's "notes" also suggest that the Landlesses are on the defensive, and their surname as well as their personal history point to the dispossession of the colonized.

Confidence Man: Empire and the Deconstruction of Muscular Christianity in 'The Mystery of Edwin Drood,'" in *Muscular Christianity*, ed. Hall, pp. 175, 180, 182).

71. On the connection between Honeythunder and Bright, see Perera, *Reaches of Empire*, pp. 115–16; and K. J. Fielding, "Edwin Drood and Governor Eyre," *Listener* (25 December 1952): 1083–84.

Recalling the Indians described in such articles as "The Honourable John," Neville and Helena appear to have been robbed of their lands. As Barry Milligan notes, their deprivations and sufferings under the parentage of a "cruel" and "grinding" stepfather suggest the oppression of those governed by the "tyrannical stepparent, England."[72] Young children when their mother died, they "have had a wretched existence," Neville tells Crisparkle. "We lived with a stepfather," "a miserly wretch, who grudged us food to eat, and clothes to wear" (88):

> I have had, sir, from my earliest remembrance, to suppress a deadly and bitter hatred. This has made me secret and revengeful. I have been always tyrannically held down by the strong hand. This has driven me, in my weakness, to the resource of being false and mean. I have been stinted of education, liberty, money, dress, the very necessaries of life, the commonest pleasures of childhood, the commonest possessions of youth. This has caused me to be utterly wanting in I don't know what emotions, or remembrances, or good instincts—I have not even a name for the thing, you see!—that you have had to work upon in other young men to whom you have been accustomed. (90)

In this passage, Dickens comes closest to endorsing the view of those critics of empire who saw the Indian Mutiny as an act of retaliation for political wrongs, not as an example of the innate treachery of Orientals. Neville "unspeakably shock[s]" Crisparkle by telling his tutor that he "might have killed" his stepfather had the "cruel brute" not died, yet his catalog of injuries leaves the minor canon feeling "less severe" toward his new pupil and largely justifies Neville's anger (88), as does his experience of racial discrimination in England. Neville is told by a patronizing Drood that he is "no judge of white men"—an "insulting allusion to his dark skin" (102)—and the mayor of Cloisterham, Mr. Sapsea, judges Neville to be guilty of Drood's murder on racial grounds, asserting that "the case had a dark look; in short (and here his eyes rested full on Neville's countenance), an Un-English complexion" (188). Drawing on the inflamatory rhetoric used to demonize the rebellious sepoys, Jasper speaks of Neville's "demoniacal passion," "strength in . . . fury," and "savage rage" (132), stirring up the racism of his fellow townspeople in order to frame Neville for a murder he himself has (presumably) committed.

Yet Neville no sooner recounts his experience of oppression in Ceylon than he disavows its political implications, invoking the motif of Eastern contagion to explain his vengeful and violent tendencies. Although Dickens allies the

72. Milligan, *Pleasures and Pains*, p. 107.

Landlesses with those colonized in the East and refers to their "imperceptibly acquired mixture" of "Oriental blood" in his number plans for the novel,[73] Neville suggests that he has somehow "contracted" his otherness from the natives, along with the ferocity associated with it: "I have been brought up among abject and servile dependents, of an inferior race, and I may easily have contracted some affinity with them. Sometimes, I don't know but that it may be a drop of what is tigerish in their blood" (90). Whether his racial origins are Anglo-Saxon, "Oriental," or some "mixture" of the two, Neville has "contracted" or been transfused with "tigerish" qualities in the East and, like Jasper, exhibits symptoms of its pathology, a diagnosis that mitigates our sense of England's imperial wrongdoing.

Dickens's use of Ceylon rather than India as the origin of the Landlesses has the same effect, enabling him to sidestep the allegations of criminality and misrule leveled against England for its role in the Indian Mutiny and the opium trade. In *Edwin Drood,* Dickens not only depicts a Chinese opium smoker but refers to the tea imported from China to England in exchange for opium and enjoyed at home by Reverend Crisparkle and his mother: a "Superior Family Souchong" (82).[74] Yet the colony in which the British produced the opium they exchanged for this tea goes unmentioned in the novel. In Ceylon, coffee rather than opium profited the empire.

Unlike India, furthermore, Ceylon was a colony in which the harsh treatment of natives had long been accepted as a necessary feature of the British administration, since the Kandyans were represented as an unusually troublesome race, in a continual state of insurrection. Indeed, the example of Ceylon and the harsh measures taken there to put down native revolt were cited by Governor Eyre in defending his own actions in Jamaica.[75] As described in *Ceylon: An Account of the Island* (1859) by Sir James Emerson Tennent, civil secretary to the colony from 1845 to 1850, Ceylon was a land where the need for martial law, and the desire for "retribution" and "vengeance" on the part of the British, appeared self-evident.[76] A friend of Dickens and an *All the Year Round* contributor, Tennent notes that in the years preceding the Indian Mutiny, the Kandyans plotted against or violently resisted British authority on at least nine

73. "Appendix A: Dickens's Notes and Number Plans," *The Mystery of Edwin Drood*, p. 286.

74. As Morley explains in "Our Phantom Ship. China," Souchong is "the best black tea" gathered during the main harvest on the Chinese plantations; exported to England, where it "comes into our pots," it is an integral component of the opium trade (328).

75. See Stella Swain, "Narrative and Legality: Charles Dickens' *The Mystery of Edwin Drood*," *New Formations* 32 (autumn–winter 1997): 77–90, esp. 87 n. 57.

76. Sir James Emerson Tennent, *Ceylon: An Account of the Island, Physical, Historical, and Topographical,* 5th ed., 2 vols. (London: Longman, Green, Longman, and Roberts, 1859), 2:84.

occasions, beginning with the "lamentable massacre" of British troops in 1803. His list of native troubles in Ceylon includes "the formidable rebellion of 1817," "agitations" in 1820, 1823, and 1824, arrests and trials for treason in 1830, 1835, and 1843, and the "formidable rising of the Kandyans" in 1848.[77]

In using Ceylon as the colonial backdrop for his novel, Dickens implicitly justifies the use of harsh and controversial measures to defend the empire, a defense that seems all the more necessary in light of Drood's intended destination—Egypt—a country that evoked anxieties about the potential decline of British hegemony in the late 1860s. Although Dickens sets the action of his novel in the 1840s, Drood's description of "triumphs of engineering skill" that "are to change the whole condition of an undeveloped country" (96, 59) had a topical and ironic resonance for Dickens's original readers. The Suez Canal opened the year before *Edwin Drood* was published, in 1869, an event represented in the English press as a humiliation for Queen Victoria: "The Queen of England has opened the Holborn Viaduct, and the Empress of France is going to open the Suez Canal."[78] Despite Drood's pride in the engineering "triumphs" he plans to achieve in Egypt, the French rather than the English constructed the Suez Canal, which was believed to threaten British control of trade to the East and to provide the Russians as well as the French with better access to India.[79] Compounding fears of imperial decline in the 1860s with evidence of England's own colonization in antiquity, Dickens uses the history of Cloisterham, and the waves of invasion to which its scattered ruins bear witness, to remind his readers that the English were once a conquered people and could become so again: "Cloisterham . . . was once possibly known to the Druids by another name, and certainly to the Romans by another, and to the Saxons by another, and to the Normans by another" (51).[80]

77. Ibid., 2:74, 93–94.

78. Quoted in C. A. Bayly, ed., *Atlas of the British Empire* (New York: Facts on File, 1989), p. 138.

79. Dickens's interest in the Suez Canal dates from 1850, when he published an article on "that little neck of land which lies between the head of the Red Sea and the Gulph of Gaza, in the Mediterranean" ([William Weir and W. H. Wills], "Short Cuts Across the Globe: The Isthmus of Suez," *Household Words* 1 [11 May 1850]: 167). He kept a close eye on France's imperial affairs throughout the 1850s and 1860s, and published numerous articles on French colonies and activities in the East.

80. Dickens describes the subjugation and resistance of the ancient English to foreign conquest in his opening chapters of *A Child's History of England,* and he published various articles on the subject as well. See, for example, "Rome and Turnips" (*All the Year Round* 1 [14 May 1859]: 53–58), which describes excavations of Roman artifacts and structures at Wroxeter, and recounts the period in which "strong Rome, possessing England as a province, ground our corn and ate our oysters with a hearty appetite" (53). Similarly, "Latin London" (*All the Year Round* 3 [5 May 1860]: 78–81) represents the sack of London by the Danes, describes the era before that city was "dignified with the name of a colony," and notes that Rochester was known to the Romans as "Durobrivae on the Madus" (79).

Indeed, the savage condition of numerous English characters in *Edwin Drood*, particularly those of the working class, suggests that their reversion to a subject race is already underway. Dickens satirizes Honeythunder for confusing Britons with "natives" in his scheme for "making a raid on all the unemployed persons in the United Kingdom . . . and forcing them, on pain of prompt extermination, to become philanthropists" (85). Yet Dickens himself describes English agricultural workers as "Bedouins" who "invade" Cloisterham (225), refers to the stonemason Durdles as a "gipsy" (68), and represents Deputy, the ragged boy who works as "man servant" at the Travellers' Twopenny, as "a little savage" and "brother to Peter the Wild Boy" (72–73).

A figure drawn from Dickens's own experiences of urban policing, the "Wild Boy" of *Edwin Drood* recalls the "Deputies" he describes in his *Household Words* article "On Duty with Inspector Field," ragged figures who assist the police in their inspections of London's cheap lodging houses yet who themselves need to be colonized and converted by the authorities, as do their fellow lodgers. Thus Inspector Field begins his nightly tour of duty in the British Museum, among "the Elgin marbles" and "cat-faced Egyptian giants," but protects the British Empire from the fate of Egypt or Greece by turning next to Whitechapel and St. Giles, where he storms and conquers the slums, empowered by Lord Shaftsbury's Common-Lodging Houses Act.[81] As Dickens told Sir John Bowring, the former governor of Hong Kong, he gathered material for the opium den scenes in *Edwin Drood* while accompanying the police on such a mission: "The opium smoking I have described, I saw (exactly as I have described it, penny ink-bottle and all) down in Shadwell this last autumn. A couple of the Inspectors of Lodging-Houses knew the woman and took me to her as I was making a round with them to see for myself the working of Lord Shaftesbury's Bill" (*Letters,* 3:775). With her oriental features and her opium addiction, Princess Puffer is modeled on the Englishwoman Dickens refers to in this letter and known as "Lascar Sal."[82] But she also resembles a host of Englishmen and Englishwomen characterized by their otherness in Dickens's narratives of social exploration, particularly his accounts of the "street expedi-

---

81. [Charles Dickens], "On Duty with Inspector Field," *Household Words* 3 (14 June 1851): 265. Enid Gauldie devotes a chapter to the Lodging Houses Acts in her history of working-class housing. She explains that the Common-Lodging Houses Act (1851), revised in 1853, gave police the right "to enter lodging houses, inspect their sanitary provisions and ask questions about the numbers staying there" (245). In 1853 alone, over 3,300 of London's lodging houses were under inspection. See *Cruel Habitations: A History of Working-Class Housing, 1780–1918* (New York: Harper and Row, 1974), pp. 239–50.

82. See Philip Collins, "Inspector Bucket Visits the Princess Puffer," *Dickensian* 60 (May 1964): 88–90.

tions" he published in *All the Year Round* and collected in *The Uncommercial Traveller.*[83]

Like Collins, Dickens represents working-class savages in his novel of empire. However, his portraits suggest the dangers of racial degeneration among the English poor, not the dehumanizing effects of the class system.[84] Dickens's concern that imperial decline could originate in the English slums dates from the 1850s, when he began publishing articles on the subject in his periodicals, and it remained a recurring theme. In "Touching Englishmen's Lives" (1866), for example, the Roman Empire, in its decline and fall, provides a possible antecedent for the British:

> Comparisons have often been drawn between the Roman and the British empires, and the question asked: Will Britain lose its strength and fade away, as Rome faded? That it is natural that every nation should have its periods of youth, of maturity, and of decay, the records of ancient nations would lead us to infer. It would seem, too, that foremost amongst the great causes of national destruction and decay have ever been over-conquest . . . and over-crowding—by which [a nation's] vitality becomes lessened, because its men decay at home. In the first case it is left unprotected, and a prey to other nations; in the second, it becomes enervated, diseased, and festers into discontent, rebellion, and anarchy; so that while in the one instance it is destroyed by others, in the other it becomes its own destroyer.[85]

In his letters describing the Indian Mutiny and the Jamaica Insurrection, Dickens holds treacherous savages responsible for the perils that threaten the empire, drawing an insuperable boundary between "New Zealanders and Hottentots" and "men in clean shirts at Camberwell" (Pilgrim, 11:116); the

83. In the 1850s and 1860s, Dickens frequently wrote and published articles on the "undiscovered country" within London, narratives in which he and his contributors "explored a strange world" within the metropolis, traveling "among a labyrinth of dismal courts and blind alleys" ([Charles Dickens], "The Uncommercial Traveller," *All the Year Round* 2 [10 March 1860]: 464–65), in a "heathen" territory that requires "conversion to Christianity" by sanitary reformers and philanthropic societies ([Henry Morley], "Conversion of a Heathen Court," *Household Words* 10 [16 December 1854]: 410). Dickens explored "the worst haunts of the most dangerous classes" as early as 1842, when he, Forster, and Daniel Maclise took Longfellow on an "expedition" to the East End and the Borough, escorted by two police officers. See Forster, *Life of Charles Dickens*, pp. 278–79.

84. As Anthony S. Wohl notes, fears of racial decline among the urban poor were expressed as early as the 1850s, because of recruitment problems during the Crimean War. See *Endangered Lives: Public Health in Victorian Britain* (London: J. M. Dent, 1983), p. 331. For a discussion of the interrelation of racial and class identities in *Edwin Drood*, which reveals Dickens's lost faith in social transformation through work and education, see Tim Dolin, "Race and the Social Plot in *The Mystery of Edwin Drood,*" in *The Victorians and Race*, ed. Shearer West (Aldershot, U.K.: Scolar Press, 1996), pp. 84–100.

85. "Touching Englishmen's Lives," *All the Year Round* 15 (30 June 1866): 582.

English, however poor, will always prove superior to dirty, ignorant, and unruly primitives, Dickens argues. Yet his portrait of the illiterate English private in "The Perils of Certain English Prisoners" undermines the distinction between working-class Englishmen and uneducable natives, as do the descriptions of East End savages in the articles collected as *The Uncommercial Traveller* and in *Edwin Drood*. In these works, as in "Touching Englishmen's Lives," imperial decline begins "at home," among those who live in the wilderness of East London and degenerate into members of a pack or tribe.

Charting the devolution of England in "On An Amateur Beat," for example, Dickens imagines the geologists of a future age discovering and interpreting the marks left in the mud by "wretched" and "wolfish" slum children, the offspring of an imperial nation whose people will by then have become extinct.[86] Recounting his travels "eastward of London" in "A Small Star in the East," a region in which "many thousands (who shall say how many?) of the English race" undergo "degeneracy, physical and moral," Dickens describes "a wilderness of dirt, rags, and hunger. A mud-desert, chiefly inhabited by a tribe from whom employment has departed," yet who "propagate their wretched race."[87] Developing his sense of these "labourers" as racial others, Dickens speaks of their degeneration into English Bushmen; the wife of an unemployed boilermaker is "toning down towards the Bosjesman colour," as is the wife of a coal porter, whom Dickens also sees "degenerating to the Bosjesman complexion."[88]

In expressing his anxieties over the racial degeneration of the English poor, Dickens places particular emphasis on the darkening skin color of working-class women. He includes portraits of working-class men in "A Small Star in the East," yet only their wives, who find work when their husbands cannot, "degenerat[e] to the Bosjesman complexion." In drawing this gender distinction, Dickens anticipates the arguments of late Victorian eugenists who attributed the decline of the British Empire to female emancipation and "maternal inadequacy."[89] Although he sounds facetious when describing Rosa Bud as one of "the future wives and mothers of England" (93), Dickens conceives of female purity and fertility as crucial resources for the nation—hence the subtitle of

---

86. Charles Dickens, "On An Amateur Beat," *All the Year Round*, n.s., 1 (27 February 1869): 300–303; *The Uncommercial Traveller and Reprinted Pieces* (1958; reprint, Oxford: Oxford University Press, 1968), p. 347.

87. Charles Dickens, "A Small Star in the East," *All the Year Round*, n.s., 1 (19 December 1868): 61–66; *Uncommercial Traveller*, pp. 320, 319.

88. Ibid., p. 324.

89. Anna Davin, "Imperialism and Motherhood," *History Workshop* 5 (1978): 10, 13–14. In 1904, Davin notes, J. W. Taylor warned the assembled members of the British Gynaecological Society that "shrinking from maternity" placed the British in "danger of race-suicide" (quoted by Davin, "Imperialism," 17).

"The Perils of Certain English Prisoners," which identifies Englishwomen as imperial "treasure." In *Edwin Drood,* both Jasper and Princess Puffer go native, taking on a "strange likeness of the Chinaman" (38). Yet as Milligan points out, Jasper contracts his oriental likeness from his "hostess," whom Dickens identifies as "the immediate source of contagion."[90] Modeled, in part, on the East End prostitutes of "Tiger Bay," she promises to "mother" her customers (266) yet shares her bed with them, spreading illness among them. The last of Dickens's female primitives, Princess Puffer differs from Collins's more admirable female Fridays in her degeneracy and transmits Eastern contagion as if it were a venereal disease.

90. Milligan, *Pleasures and Pains,* p. 97. Milligan discusses the connection between *Edwin Drood* and the Contagious Diseases Act (1864), and the ways in which "stereotypes of dangerous East End women merge with familiar misegenation anxieties" in Dickens's representations. See *Pleasures and Pains,* pp. 96–102. Similarly, Susan Meyer discusses the tie between the sexual and the racial degeneracy of Princess Puffer in the opening pages of *Imperialism at Home: Race and Victorian Women's Fiction* (Ithaca, N.Y.: Cornell University Press, 1996).

Conclusion

"This Unclean Spirit of Imitation":
Dickens and the "Problem" of Collins's Influence

A mystery novel, *Edwin Drood* is also a novel of imitations and parodies, one in which a host of characters model themselves on—and sometimes mock—their betters. Self-important and socially ambitious, Cloisterham's mayor strives to become the "Fetch" of the Dean, "studying his original in minute points of detail" (148). He "'dresses at' the Dean," and "has been bowed to for the Dean, in mistake" (62), while Miss Brobity, the woman who admires and marries the mayor, adopts his rhetorical style in the "dictation-exercizes" she gives to her pupils (64). Conversely, the irreverent schoolgirls at Miss Twinkleton's Seminary for Young Ladies parody masculine behavior; they pretend "to be their brothers"—and also Edwin Drood—when dancing at Rosa's birthday ball (56), and Miss Ferdinand "clap[s] on a paper moustache," comically reenacting the struggle between Neville Landless and Drood, with the help of Miss Giggles (109). Imitation enables characters to emulate or mock those placed above them, but it can also mark their social descent. Thus Jasper exhibits the "unclean spirit of imitation" with which the novel opens, modeling himself on his opium-smoking inferiors and signaling his racial degeneration and downward mobility (39).

For generations of Dickens critics, the "unclean spirit of imitation" that pollutes John Jasper became a symbol of Dickens's own, as the "master" of English fiction unwisely modeled himself on his artistic inferior, Wilkie Collins, and became a mere "mechanician" in consequence. In an essay published soon after Dickens's death, A. W. Ward expresses the regret that Dickens "attempted plots of extreme intricacy" in his later works, "under the influence of Mr. Wilkie Collins's example":

In the preface to his *Tale of Two Cities,* . . . [Dickens] informs us he first conceived the main idea when he was acting with his friends and children in Mr. Wilkie Collins's drama of the *Frozen Deep;* yet the tale itself is one of the very few of Mr. Dickens's works which require an effort in the perusal. The master of humour and pathos, the magician whose potent wand, if ever so gently moved, exercises effects which no one is able to resist, seems to be toiling in the mechanician's workshop, and yet never attains to a success beyond that of a more or less promising apprentice.[1]

Like the choirmaster who goes slumming in *Edwin Drood* and is "sullied" by those he imitates (*Edwin Drood,* 39), "the master of humour and pathos" becomes a lowly workshop apprentice when influenced by Collins, an inferior writer skilled at constructing intricate plots but unable to endow them with the "magic" of literary genius.

Over the next fifty years, the image of Dickens, brought low by imitating Collins, became a staple of criticism about the two novelists. Thus J. W. T. Ley, author of *The Dickens Circle* (1918) and editor of Forster's *Life of Dickens* (1928), claimed that the "lowly" Collins ("not a creative artist at all") "drove [Dickens] to [the] mere laboriousness" of producing "intricately conceived and skilfully unravelled mysteries"—"a prostitution of his genius": "Collins would have spoiled [Dickens] if that had been possible, would have converted—or perverted—him into little more than a story-manufacturer."[2] Influenced, in turn, by such views of Dickens's "perversion" at Collins's hands, editors of the collaborative stories did what they could to purify them—by omitting Collins's portions. "A number of the stories, both in *Household Words* and *All the Year Round,* were written in collaboration with Wilkie Collins," Margaret Lane concedes, introducing the *Christmas Stories* in volume 11 of the Oxford Illustrated Dickens, "a practical arrangement but not a happy one, for Dickens was not the man to run well in double harness":

The elaborately contrived plot, at which Collins was adept, was cramping to the natural play of [Dickens's] fancy and humour; even those chapters which are known to have belonged to Dickens alone read as though they were written under constraint. The two men spared no pains over the collaboration, going down into the country together to gather material whenever it seemed necessary, enduring the miseries of bad hotels in a diligent search for a substitute for inspiration. "We had stinking fish for dinner," Dickens wrote from Bideford, where they had gone

1. A. W. Ward, *Charles Dickens: A Lecture* (Manchester: 1870); *Dickens: The Critical Heritage,* ed. Philip Collins (New York: Barnes and Noble, 1971), pp. 537–38.
2. J. W. T. Ley, "Wilkie Collins's Influence upon Dickens," *Dickensian* 20 (1924): 67, 68.

to seek local colour for *A Message from the Sea,* "and have been able to drink nothing, though we have ordered wine, beer, and brandy-and-water. There is nothing in the house but two tarts and a pair of snuffers." These were not the conditions which suited him, though one has the impression that it was the presence of Collins rather than the stinking fish which spoiled the prospect. Left to himself, Dickens made brilliant capital out of the squalid vicissitudes of inns and travelling.[3]

Accordingly, the editor of the collaborative works in this Oxford volume leaves Dickens "to himself" and thus prevents Collins from "spoil[ing] the prospect." Following the 1871 Charles Dickens Edition, published by Chapman and Hall, the volume presents "The Seven Poor Travellers" as a story "in three chapters" rather than seven, for example,[4] and "The Perils of Certain English Prisoners" as a story in two rather than three. "The second chapter . . . was not written by Dickens," the editor of "The Perils" explains, leaping from the first to the third chapter of the story without naming its coauthor.[5]

Yet for the writer who prided himself on being inimitable, the decision to imitate Collins signaled his mastery over his junior collaborator, not his subordination to an inferior. Rather than marking a loss of "potency," as A. W. Ward claims, such imitations helped to symbolize it, placing Dickens apart from and above those whose alleged imitations of his own style were seen as necessarily imperfect and "slavish."[6] Corresponding with an ailing Collins in October 1862, Dickens offers to fill in for his contributor if necessary, claiming to be able to write "so like" Collins that, were he to author portions of *No Name,* "no one should find out the difference":

> Write to me at Paris, at any moment, and say you are unequal to your work, and want me, and I will come to London straight and do your work. I am quite confident that, with your notes and a few words of explanation, I could take it up at any time and do it . . . . Don't make much of this offer in your mind—it is nothing—except to ease it. If you should want help, I am as safe as the Bank. The trouble would be nothing to me, and the triumph of overcoming a difficulty—

3. Margaret Lane, introduction, *Christmas Stories,* Oxford Illustrated Dickens, 21 vols. (1956; reprint, Oxford: Oxford University Press, 1987), 11:vii–viii.
4. *Christmas Stories,* Oxford Illustrated Dickens, 11:69.
5. Ibid., 11:192.
6. When Dickens edited the writings of his contributors, G. A. Sala recalls in *Things I Have Seen and People I Have Known,* the "tropes, illustrations, and metaphors" he interpolated into their stories and articles "led to their being taunted with being slavish imitators of their leader" (quoted by P. D. Edwards, *Dickens's 'Young Men': George Augustus Sala, Edmund Yates and the World of Victorian Journalism* [Aldershot, U.K.: Ashgate, 1997], p. 12).

great. Think it a Xmas No., an Idle apprentice, a Lighthouse, a Frozen Deep. I
am as ready as in any of those cases to strike in and hammer the hot iron out.
(Pilgrim, 10:142)

Dickens no doubt intended to put Collins at ease in making this offer, despite
his own sense of coming "triumph" at replacing the younger novelist. But as
Mary Poovey argues, it effectively put Collins in his place, suggesting that he
was expendable—"not . . . an individual, much less a 'genius,' but . . . just one
instance of labor, an interchangeable part subject to replacement in case of failure."[7] Whereas Ley argues that Collins threatened to "pervert" Dickens
"into . . . a story-manufacturer," Poovey reminds us that this is precisely what
Dickens *was* as the editor and publisher of Collins's fiction.

Although the Oxford Illustrated edition of the *Christmas Stories* remains in
print, the view of the collaborative relationship that it promotes in its introduction and its editorial practices has been challenged in recent years, due to
broad changes in the field of literary studies as well as the efforts of certain critics and editors to write Collins back into the stories he helped create. The distinction between literary technicians who craft plot and literary masters who
create character has been undermined by critiques of literary value and discussions of literary modes of production, as has the image of the literary genius
writing masterpieces in isolation. Influenced by such movements as feminism
and new historicism, critics are now more likely to consider the ideological
work that literature performs than to make claims about its intrinsic and time-
less value, and thus sensation novels, like other popular subgenres of English
fiction, have become a focus of Victorian scholarship, a change that has helped
to reverse Collins's fortunes and bring many of his works back into print.

At the same time, critics such as Lonoff and Heller have challenged the long-
standing view of Collins and his allegedly harmful influence on Dickens. These
critics consider the ways in which Collins benefited his mentor and was himself harmed by the influence of Dickens, who taught him "how to cater to his
readers," "withheld the encouragement that might have fortified [him] in his
battles with the censors," and pressured him to compromise his political principles in writing for *Household Words* and *All the Year Round*.[8] Although critics
traditionally date Collins's artistic decline from 1870, attributing it to the loss of
the guide who held in check his melodramatic excesses and radical zeal, Lonoff

7. Mary Poovey, *Uneven Developments: The Ideological Work of Gender in Mid-Victorian England*
(Chicago: University of Chicago Press, 1988), pp. 104, 230 n. 19.
8. Sue Lonoff, "Charles Dickens and Wilkie Collins," *Nineteenth-Century Fiction* 35 (September
1980): 156–57; Tamar Heller, *Dead Secrets: Wilkie Collins and the Female Gothic* (New Haven, Conn.:
Yale University Press, 1992), pp. 92–93.

suggests that Collins may, in fact, have been liberated by Dickens's death, freed to develop "important aspects of his talent": his candid treatment of female sexuality, for example.[9]

"Everything connected with *his* writing is part of the literary history of England," Collins bitterly remarked of Dickens in 1873, when responding to Chapman's request that he write himself out of the collaborative works—that he lay claim to his own contributions to "No Thoroughfare" so that they could be dropped from future editions. Declining to cooperate, Collins instead describes how he and Dickens wrote "side by side at two desks in [Dickens's] bedroom at Gad's Hill" and "as nearly as possible *halved* the work."[10] Resisting his exclusion from "the literary history of England," Collins himself rewrites it, providing Chapman with an image of equity and partnership that was rarely, if ever, achieved in his working relationship with Dickens. Few critics would now deny Collins a place in English literary history. Yet we can only realize his significance to that history in the fullest sense by questioning images of equity between himself and Dickens, particularly those the collaborators themselves provided, and examining the editorial practices—both Victorian and modern—that make certain writers disappear.[11]

9. Lonoff, "Dickens and Collins," 156.

10. Quoted by Frederic G. Kitton, *The Minor Writings of Charles Dickens* (London: Elliot Stock, 1900), p. 173.

11. As Gill Gregory notes, Dickens's female collaborators remain the least visible of all. Whereas the 1961 Methuen edition of "The Wreck of the Golden Mary" restored the interpolated tales of White, Fitzgerald, and Parr, it "jettisoned" Procter's poem and described the 1856 Christmas Number as a story that "came from the hands of two great novelists" (quoted by Gregory, *The Life and Work of Adelaide Procter: Poetry, Feminism and Fathers* [Aldershot, U.K.: Ashgate, 1998], p. 229).

Works Cited

Ashley, Robert P. "Wilkie Collins and the Dickensians." *Dickensian* 49 (1953): 59–65.

Baker, William. "Wilkie Collins, Dickens, and *No Name*." *Dickens Studies Newsletter* 11 (June 1980): 49–52.

Barker-Benfield, G. J. "The Spermatic Economy: A Nineteenth-Century View of Sexuality." In *The American Family in Social-Historical Perspective,* edited by Michael Gordon. 2d ed. NewYork: St. Martin's Press, 1978. 374–402.

Barnett, Correlli. *Britain and Her Army, 1509–1970*. New York: William Morrow, 1970.

Barret-Ducrocq, Françoise. *Love in the Time of Victoria: Sexuality and Desire among Working-Class Men and Women in Nineteenth-Century London*. Translated by John Howe. Harmondsworth: Penguin, 1991.

Baumgarten, Murray. "Seeing Double: Jews in the Fiction of F. Scott Fitzgerald, Charles Dickens, Anthony Trollope, and George Eliot." In *Between "Race" and Culture: Representations of "the Jew" in English and American Literature,* edited by Bryan Cheyette. Stanford, Calif.: Stanford University Press, 1996. 44–61.

Bayly, C. A., ed. *Atlas of the British Empire*. New York: Facts on File, 1989.

Beetz, Kirk. "Wilkie Collins and *The Leader*." *Victorian Periodicals Review* 15, 1 (spring 1982): 20–29.

Berridge, Virginia. "East End Opium Dens and Narcotic Use in Britain." *London Journal* 4,1 (1978): 3–28.

Blain, Virginia. Introduction to *No Name,* by Wilkie Collins. 1986. Reprint, Oxford: Oxford University Press, 1991. vii–xxi.

[Bourne, Henry Richard Fox]. "Hindoo Law." *Household Words* 18 (25 September 1858): 337–41.

Brannan, Robert Louis. Introduction to *Under the Management of Mr. Charles Dickens: His Production of "The Frozen Deep."* Ithaca, N.Y.: Cornell University Press, 1966. 1–90.

Brantlinger, Patrick. *Rule of Darkness: British Literature and Imperialism, 1830–1914*. Ithaca, N.Y.: Cornell University Press, 1988.

Bulwer-Lytton, Sir Edward, Bart. *Not So Bad As We Seem; or, Many Sides to a Character. A Comedy in Five Acts*. London: Chapman and Hall, 1851.

Bump, Jerome. "Parody and the Dickens-Collins Collaboration in *No Thoroughfare*." *Library Chronicle of the University of Texas at Austin* (1986): 38–53.

Burgan, William M. "Masonic Symbolism in *The Moonstone* and *The Mystery of Edwin Drood.*" *Dickens Studies Annual* 16 (1987): 257–303.

[Capper, John]. "The Honourable John." *Household Words* 7 (30 July 1853): 516–18.

[———]. "Law in the East." *Household Words* 5 (26 June 1852): 347–52.

[———]. "Off to the Diggings!" *Household Words* 5 (17 July 1852): 405–10.

Carr, Jean Ferguson. "Dickens's Theatre of Self-Knowledge." In *Dramatic Dickens,* edited by Carol Hanbery MacKay. New York: St. Martin's Press, 1989. 27–44.

Clarke, William M. *The Secret Life of Wilkie Collins.* Chicago: Ivan R. Dee, 1991.

Collins, Philip. *Dickens and Crime.* Bloomington: Indiana University Press, 1968.

Collins, Wilkie. *Antonina; or, the Fall of Rome.* Vol. 17 of *The Works of Wilkie Collins.* 30 vols. New York: AMS Press, 1970.

———. *Armadale.* Edited by Catherine Peters. 1989. Reprint, Oxford: Oxford University Press, 1991.

[———]. "The Cruise of the Tomtit." *Household Words* 12 (22 December 1855): 490–99.

———. "The Diary of Anne Rodway." In *Mad Monkton and Other Stories,* edited by Norman Page. Oxford: Oxford University Press, 1994. 129–64.

———. *The Frozen Deep.* Autograph manuscript. The Pierpont Morgan Library, New York. MA 81.

———. *The Frozen Deep.* In *The Frozen Deep and Other Stories.* 2 vols. London: Richard Bentley and Son, 1874. 1:2–220.

———. *The Frozen Deep: A Drama. In Three Acts.* London: C. Whiting, [1866].

———. "The Ghost in the Cupboard Room." Republished as "Blow Up with the Brig! A Sailor's Story." In *The Woman in White (Part Two) and Short Stories.* Vol. 2 of *The Works of Wilkie Collins.* 30 vols. New York: AMS Press, 1970. 541–58.

[———]. "Highly Proper!" *Household Words* 18 (2 October 1858): 361–63.

———. "The Incredible Not Always Impossible. To G. H. Lewes." *Leader* 3, 106 (3 April 1852): 328–29.

———. "A Journey in Search of Nothing." In *My Miscellanies.* Vol. 20 of *The Works of Wilkie Collins.* 30 vols. New York: AMS Press, 1970. 24–47.

———. "Laid Up in Lodgings." In *My Miscellanies.* Vol. 20 of *The Works of Wilkie Collins.* 30 vols. New York: AMS Press, 1970. 85–125.

———. *The Letters of Wilkie Collins.* 2 vols. Edited by William Baker and William M. Clark. London: Macmillan, 1999.

———. "Magnetic Evenings at Home. Letter I.—To G. H. Lewes." *Leader* 3, 95 (17 January 1852): 63–64.

———. "Magnetic Evenings at Home. Letter V.—To G. H. Lewes." *Leader* 3, 102 (6 March 1852): 231–33.

———. *Man and Wife.* Edited by Norman Page. Oxford: Oxford University Press, 1995.

———. *The Moonstone.* Edited by J. I. M. Stewart. 1966. Reprint, Harmondsworth: Penguin, 1986.

[———]. "Mrs. Bullwinkle." *Household Words* 17 (17 April 1858): 409–11.

———. *No Name.* Edited by Virginia Blain. 1986. Reprint, Oxford: Oxford University Press, 1991.

———. "No Thoroughfare." Autograph manuscript. The Pierpont Morgan Library, New York. MA 1021.

———. "The Ostler." In *Mad Monkton and Other Stories,* edited by Norman Page. Oxford: Oxford University Press, 1994. 105–28.

———. "A Petition to the Novel Writers." In *My Miscellanies.* Vol. 20 of *The Works of Wilkie Collins.* 30 vols. New York: AMS Press, 1970. 69–84.

———. "Picking Up Waifs at Sea." Republished as "The Fatal Cradle: Otherwise, the Heart-Rending Story of Mr. Heavysides." In *The Woman in White (Part Two) and Short Stories.* Vol. 2 of *The Works of Wilkie Collins.* 30 vols. New York: AMS Press, 1970. 477–510.

[———]. "A Sermon for Sepoys." *Household Words* 17 (27 February 1858): 244–47.

[———]. "A Shy Scheme." *Household Words* 17 (20 March 1858): 313–16.

——. "Wilkie Collins's Recollections of Charles Fechter." In *Charles Albert Fechter*, edited by Kate Field. 1882. Reprint, New York: Benjamin Blom, 1969. 145–73.

——. *The Woman in White*. Edited by Harvey Peter Sucksmith. 1972. Reprint, Oxford: Oxford University Press, 1980.

Course, A. G. *The Merchant Navy: A Social History*. London: Frederick Muller, 1963.

[Craig, George]. "Blown Away!" *Household Words* 17 (17 March 1858): 348–50.

Cross, Nigel. *The Common Writer: Life in Nineteenth-Century Grub Street*. Cambridge: Cambridge University Press, 1985.

David, Deirdre. *Rule Britannia: Women, Empire, and Victorian Writing*. Ithaca, N.Y.: Cornell University Press, 1995.

Davin, Anna. "Imperialism and Motherhood." *History Workshop* 5 (1978): 9–65.

Davis, Nuel Pharr. *The Life of Wilkie Collins*. Urbana: University of Illinois Press, 1956.

Defoe, Daniel. *Robinson Crusoe*. Edited by Angus Ross. 1965. Reprint, Harmondsworth: Penguin, 1985.

Dickens, Charles. *Bleak House*. Edited by Norman Page. 1971. Reprint, Harmondsworth: Penguin, 1985.

——. *A Child's History of England*. In *Holiday Romance and Other Writings for Children*, edited by Gillian Avery. London: J. M. Dent, 1995. 1–395.

——. *Christmas Stories*. Edited by Ruth Glancy. London: J. M. Dent, 1996.

——. *Christmas Stories*. Oxford Illustrated Dickens. 21 vols. 1956. Reprint, Oxford: Oxford University Press, 1987. Vol. 11.

——. *David Copperfield*. Edited by Trevor Blount. 1966. Reprint, Harmondsworth: Penguin, 1980.

——. "The Haunted House." ["The Mortals in the House," "The Ghost in Master B.'s Room," and "The Ghost in the Corner Room."] In *Christmas Stories*, edited by Ruth Glancy. London: J. M. Dent, 1996. 307–40.

——. "The Holly Tree Inn." ["The Guest," "The Boots," and "The Bill."] In *Christmas Stories*, edited by Ruth Glancy. London: J. M. Dent, 1996. 83–121.

——. "A House to Let." ["Over the Way," "Going into Society," and "Let at Last."] In *Christmas Stories*, edited by Ruth Glancy. London: J. M. Dent, 1996. 258–307.

——. *The Letters of Charles Dickens*. 3 vols. Edited by Walter Dexter. Bloomsbury: Nonesuch Press, 1938.

——. *The Letters of Charles Dickens*. Pilgrim Edition. 11 vols. to date. Edited by Madeline House, Graham Storey, and Kathleen Tillotson. Oxford: Clarendon Press, 1965–.

——. *Little Dorrit*. Edited by John Holloway. 1967. Reprint, Harmondsworth: Penguin, 1982.

[——]. "The Lost Arctic Voyagers." *Household Words* 10 (2 December 1854): 361–65.

[——]. "The Lost Arctic Voyagers." *Household Words* 10 (9 December 1854): 385–93.

——. *The Mystery of Edwin Drood*. Edited by Arthur J. Cox. 1974. Reprint, Harmondsworth: Penguin, 1982.

[——]. "The Noble Savage." *Household Words* 7 (11 June 1853): 337–39.

——. "Note." *All the Year Round* 10 (26 December 1863): 419.

——. "On An Amateur Beat." In *The Uncommercial Traveller and Reprinted Pieces*. 1958. Reprint, Oxford: Oxford University Press, 1968. 345–52.

[——]. "On Duty with Inspector Field." *Household Words* 3 (14 June 1851): 265–70.

——. "The Perils of Certain English Prisoners." [Chapters 1 and 3.] In *Christmas Stories*. Oxford Illustrated Dickens. 21 vols. 1956. Reprint, Oxford: Oxford University Press, 1987. 11:163–208.

——. *The Pickwick Papers*. Edited by Robert L. Patten. 1972. Reprint, Harmondsworth: Penguin, 1981.

——. "The Seven Poor Travellers." ["The First" and "The Road."] In *Christmas Stories*, edited by Ruth Glancy. London: J. M. Dent, 1996. 54–83.

——. "A Small Star in the East." In *The Uncommercial Traveller and Reprinted Pieces*. 1958. Reprint, Oxford: Oxford University Press, 1968. 319–30.

[——]. "Sucking Pigs." *Household Words* 4 (8 November 1851): 145–47.

——. *A Tale of Two Cities.* Edited by George Woodcock. 1970. Reprint, Harmondsworth: Penguin, 1980.

——. "Tom Tiddler's Ground." ["Picking Up Soot and Cinders," "Picking Up Miss Kimmeens," and "Picking Up the Tinker."] In *Christmas Stories,* edited by Ruth Glancy. London: J. M. Dent, 1996. 419–48.

[——]. "The Uncommercial Traveller." *All the Year Round* 2 (10 March 1860): 462–66.

Dickens, Charles, and Wilkie Collins. *The Frozen Deep: In Three Acts* (The Prompt-Book). In *Under the Management of Mr. Charles Dickens: His Production of "The Frozen Deep,"* edited by Robert Louis Brannan. Ithaca, N.Y.: Cornell University Press, 1966. 93–160.

——. "The Lazy Tour of Two Idle Apprentices." In *The Lazy Tour of Two Idle Apprentices and Other Stories.* London: Chapman and Hall, 1890. 3–104.

——. "No Thoroughfare." In *The Lazy Tour of Two Idle Apprentices and Other Stories.* London: Chapman and Hall, 1890. 107–233.

——. "The Perils of Certain English Prisoners." In *The Lazy Tour of Two Idle Apprentices and Other Stories.* London: Chapman and Hall, 1890. 237–327.

Dickens, Charles [sic], and Wilkie Collins. *No Thoroughfare. A Drama, in Five Acts and a Prologue. As First Performed at the New Adelphi Theatre, London, Under the Management of Mr. Benj. Webster, and the Direction of Mrs. Alfred Mellon, December 26th, 1867.* De Witt's Acting Plays. Number 14. New York: Robert M. De Witt, n.d.

[Dickens, Charles, and Wilkie Collins, with Henry F. Chorley (or Robert Buchanan), Charles Collins, Amelia B. Edwards, and Harriet Parr]. "A Message from the Sea." *All the Year Round.* Extra Christmas Number. 1860.

[Dickens, Charles, and Wilkie Collins, with Percy Fitzgerald, Harriet Parr, Adelaide Anne Procter, and James White]. "The Wreck of the Golden Mary." *Household Words.* Extra Christmas Number. 1856.

Dickens, Charles, and W. H. Wills. "Received, a Blank Child." In *Charles Dickens' Uncollected Writings from "Household Words," 1850–1859,* edited by Harry Stone. 2 vols. Bloomington: Indiana University Press, 1968. 2:455–65.

[Dixon, Edmund Saul]. "If This Should Meet His Eye." *Household Words* 4 (13 March 1852): 598–600.

[Dodd, George]. "Opium: Chapter the First. India." *Household Words* 16 (1 August 1857): 104–8.

[——]. "Opium: Chapter the Second. China." *Household Words* 16 (22 August 1857): 181–85.

Duffield, Howard. "John Jasper—Strangler." *Bookman* (February 1930): 581–88.

Edwards, P. D. *Dickens's 'Young Men': George Augustus Sala, Edmund Yates and the World of Victorian Journalism.* Aldershot, U.K.: Ashgate, 1997.

Faulkner, David. "The Confidence Man: Empire and the Deconstruction of Muscular Christianity in 'The Mystery of Edwin Drood.'" In *Muscular Christianity: Embodying the Victorian Age,* edited by Donald E. Hall. Cambridge: Cambridge University Press, 1994. 175–93.

Feltes, Norman N. *Modes of Production of Victorian Novels.* Chicago: University of Chicago Press, 1986.

Fildes, Luke. "The Mysteries of Edwin Drood." *Times Literary Supplement* (3 November 1905): 373.

Fildes, Valerie. *Wet Nursing: A History from Antiquity to the Present.* Oxford: Basil Blackwell, 1988.

Fitzgerald, Percy. "Charles Dickens in the Editor's Chair." *Gentleman's Magazine* 250 (1881): 725–42.

Forbes, John David. "Pedestrianism in Switzerland." *Quarterly Review* 101 (1857): 285–323.

"Foreign Climbs." *All the Year Round* 14 (2 September 1865): 135–37.

Forster, John. *The Life of Charles Dickens.* Edited by J. W. T. Ley. New York: Doubleday, Doran, 1928.

Forsyte, Charles. *The Decoding of Edwin Drood.* New York: Charles Scribner's Sons, 1980.

Gardner, Brian. *The East India Company: A History.* New York: Dorset Press, 1971.

Gauldie, Enid. *Cruel Habitations: A History of Working-Class Housing, 1780–1918.* New York: Harper and Row, 1974.

"Grandfather Blacktooth." *All the Year Round* 12 (10 September 1864): 111–15.

Green, Martin. *Dreams of Adventure, Deeds of Empire.* New York: Basic Books, 1979.

Gregory, Gill. *The Life and Work of Adelaide Procter: Poetry, Feminism and Fathers*. Aldershot, U.K.: Ashgate, 1998.

Grossman, Jonathan H. "The Absent Jew in Dickens: Narrators in *Oliver Twist, Our Mutual Friend*, and *A Christmas Carol*." *Dickens Studies Annual* 24 (1996): 37–57.

Grubb, Gerald. "Dickens' Editorial Methods." *Studies in Philology* 40 (1943): 79–100.

——. "Dickens' Influence as an Editor." *Studies in Philology* 42 (1945): 811–23.

Halberstam, Judith. "Technologies of Monstrosity: Bram Stoker's *Dracula*." *Victorian Studies* 36, 3 (spring 1993): 333–52.

Hall, Donald E. Introduction to *Muscular Christianity: Embodying the Victorian Age*. Cambridge: Cambridge University Press, 1994. 3–13.

[Hannay, James]. "The Blue-Jacket Agitation." *Household Words* 3 (5 April 1851): 36–41.

Hansard's Parliamentary Debates. 3d series. 356 vols. London: Wyman, 1830–1891.

[Harrold, Miss, and W. H. Wills]. "Chip: A 'Ranch' in California." *Household Words* 3 (9 August 1851): 471–72.

Heller, Tamar. *Dead Secrets: Wilkie Collins and the Female Gothic*. New Haven, Conn.: Yale University Press, 1992.

[Heraud, John Abraham]. "The North Against the South." *Household Words* 14 (6 September 1856): 190–92.

Hibbert, Christopher. *The Great Mutiny: India 1857*. New York: Penguin, 1980.

Higginson, Thomas Wentworth. *Women and Her Wishes; an Essay: Inscribed to the Massachusetts Constitutional Convention*. Boston: Robert F. Wallcut, 1853.

Hollington, Michael. "'To the Droodstone,' or, from *The Moonstone* to *Edwin Drood* via *No Thoroughfare*." *QWERTY* 5 (1995): 141–49.

Hook, Theodore Edward. *The Life of General, the Right Honourable Sir David Baird, Bart*. 2 vols. London: Bentley, 1832.

H[ornby], E[dward] J. "To Dr. Rae." *Times* (London), 3 November 1854, 7.

[Horne, Richard H.]. "Arctic Heroes: A Fragment of Naval History." *Household Words* 1 (27 April 1850): 108–9.

[——]. "A Digger's Diary." *Household Words* 8 (3 September 1853): 6–11.

Houston, Gail Turley. *Consuming Fictions: Gender, Class, and Hunger in Dickens's Novels*. Carbondale: Southern Illinois University Press, 1994.

"How to Make Money." *All the Year Round* 2 (3 December 1859): 125–28.

Hutter, Albert D. "Dreams, Transformations, and Literature: The Implications of Detective Fiction." *Victorian Studies* 19 (December 1975): 181–209.

Ingham, Patricia. *Dickens, Women and Language*. Toronto: University of Toronto Press, 1992.

Jacobson, Wendy S. "John Jasper and Thuggee." *Modern Language Review* 72 (July 1977): 526–37.

JanMohamed, Abdul R. "The Economy of Manichean Allegory: The Function of Racial Difference in Colonialist Literature." *Critical Inquiry* 12, 1 (autumn 1985): 59–87.

[Jewsbury, Geraldine]. Review of *The Moonstone*, by Wilkie Collins, in *Athenaeum* (25 July 1868). In *Wilkie Collins: The Critical Heritage*, edited by Norman Page. London: Routledge & Kegan Paul, 1974. 170–71.

Johnson, Edgar. *Charles Dickens: His Tragedy and Triumph*. 2 vols. New York: Simon and Schuster, 1952.

Kaplan, Fred. *Dickens: A Biography*. New York: Avon Books, 1988.

Kitton, Frederic G. *The Minor Writings of Charles Dickens*. London: Elliot Stock, 1900.

Koestenbaum, Wayne. *Double Talk: The Erotics of Male Literary Collaboration*. New York: Routledge, 1989.

Lane, Margaret. Introduction to *Christmas Stories*, by Charles Dickens. Oxford Illustrated Dickens. 21 vols. 1956. Reprint, Oxford: Oxford University Press, 1987. 11:v–ix.

[Lang, John]. "Wolf-Nurses." *Household Words* 6 (26 February 1853): 562–63.

"Latin London." *All the Year Round* 3 (5 May 1860): 78–81.

Lévi-Strauss, Claude. *The Raw and the Cooked.* Translated by John and Doreen Weightman. New York: Harper and Row, 1969.

Ley, J. W. T. "Wilkie Collins's Influence upon Dickens." *Dickensian* 20 (1924): 65–69.

Lonoff, Sue. "Charles Dickens and Wilkie Collins." *Nineteenth-Century Fiction* 35 (September 1980): 150–70.

———. *Wilkie Collins and His Victorian Readers: A Study in the Rhetoric of Authorship.* New York: AMS Press, 1982.

Loomis, Chauncey C. "The Arctic Sublime." In *Nature and the Victorian Imagination,* edited by U. C. Knoepflmacher and G. B. Tennyson. Berkeley: University of California Press, 1977. 95–112.

[Lynn, Eliza]. "Rights and Wrongs of Women." *Household Words* 9 (1 April 1854): 158–61.

Macauley, Thomas Babington. *The History of England from the Accession of James II.* 5 vols. Philadelphia: J. B. Lippincott, 1868.

Marx, Karl. "The Indian Revolt." *New York Daily Tribune* (16 September 1857). In *The Portable Karl Marx,* edited by Eugene Kamenka. Harmondsworth: Penguin, 1983. 351–55.

McClure, Ruth K. *Coram's Children: The London Foundling Hospital in the Eighteenth Century.* New Haven, Conn.: Yale University Press, 1981.

McGann, Jerome J. *The Beauty of Inflections: Literary Investigations in Historical Method and Theory.* Oxford: Clarendon Press, 1988.

Meckier, Jerome. *Hidden Rivalries in Victorian Fiction: Dickens, Realism, and Revaluation.* Lexington: University Press of Kentucky, 1987.

Mehta, Jaya. "English Romance; Indian Violence." *Centennial Review* 39, 4 (fall 1995): 611–57.

[Meredith, Louisa Anne]. "Shadows of the Golden Image." *Household Words* 15 (4 April 1857): 313–18.

Michie, Elsie B. *Outside the Pale: Cultural Exclusion, Gender Difference, and the Victorian Woman Writer.* Ithaca, N.Y.: Cornell University Press, 1993.

Miller, D. A. *The Novel and the Police.* Berkeley: University of California Press, 1988.

Milley, Henry J. W. "Wilkie Collins and 'A Tale of Two Cities.'" *Modern Language Review* 34 (1939): 525–34.

Milligan, Barry. *Pleasures and Pains: Opium and the Orient in Nineteenth-Century British Culture.* Charlottesville: University Press of Virginia, 1995.

[Morley, Henry]. "China with a Flaw in It." *Household Words* 5 (3 July 1852): 368–74.

[———]. "Chip: Highland Emigration." *Household Words* 5 (19 June 1852): 324–25.

[———]. "A Clouded Skye." *Household Words* 5 (17 April 1852): 98–101.

[———]. "Conversion of a Heathen Court." *Household Words* 10 (16 December 1854): 409–13.

[———]. "The Harvest of Gold." *Household Words* 5 (22 May 1852): 213–18.

[———]. "The Life of Poor Jack." *Household Words* 7 (21 May 1853): 286–88.

[———]. "Modern Human Sacrifices." *Household Words* 8 (11 February 1854): 561–64.

[———]. "Our Phantom Ship Among the Ice." *Household Words* 3 (12 April 1851): 66–72.

[———]. "Our Phantom Ship. China." *Household Words* 3 (28 June 1851): 325–31.

[———]. "Unspotted Snow." *Household Words* 8 (12 November 1853): 241–46.

[Morley, Henry, and Samuel Rinder]. "Sailors' Homes Afloat." *Household Words* 6 (19 February 1853): 529–33.

[Murray, John]. *Handbook for Travellers in Switzerland, and the Alps of Savoy and Piedmont.* 9th ed. London: John Murray, 1862.

[Murray, Mrs. Grenville]. "A Gun Among the Grouse." *Household Words* 6 (16 October 1852): 115–18.

"My First Tiger." *All the Year Round* 19 (1 February 1868): 177–80.

Nead, Lynda. *Myths of Sexuality: Representations of Women in Victorian Britain.* Oxford: Basil Blackwell, 1988.

"The New Mercantile Marine Act: Deputation to the Board of Trade." *Times* (London), 6 March 1851, 5.

Nunokawa, Jeff. "The Miser's Two Bodies: *Silas Marner* and the Sexual Possibilities of the Commodity." *Victorian Studies* 36, 3 (spring 1993): 273–92.

Oddie, William. "Dickens and the Indian Mutiny." *Dickensian* 68 (January 1972): 3–15.

Ortner, Sherry B. "Is Female to Male as Nature Is to Culture?" In *Women, Culture, and Society,* edited by Michelle Zimbalist Rosaldo and Louise Lamphere. Stanford, Calif.: Stanford University Press, 1974. 67–87.

Owen, Alex. *The Darkened Room: Women, Power and Spiritualism in Late Victorian England.* Philadelphia: University of Pennsylvania Press, 1990.

Palmer, William J. "Dickens and Shipwreck." *Dickens Studies Annual* 18 (1989): 39–92.

Park, Hyungji. "'The Story of Our Lives': *The Moonstone* and the Indian Mutiny in *All the Year Round.*" In *Negotiating India in the Nineteenth-Century Media,* edited by Douglas M. Peers and David Finkelstein. New York: St. Martin's Press, 2000. 84–109.

Patten, Robert L. *Charles Dickens and His Publishers.* Oxford: Clarendon Press, 1978.

Paxton, Nancy L. "Mobilizing Chivalry: Rape in British Novels about the Indian Uprising of 1857." *Victorian Studies* 36, 1 (fall 1992): 5–30.

Perera, Suvendrini. *Reaches of Empire: The English Novel from Edgeworth to Dickens.* New York: Columbia University Press, 1991.

Peters, Catherine. *The King of Inventors: A Life of Wilkie Collins.* Princeton, N.J.: Princeton University Press, 1991.

Peters, Laura. "'Double-dyed Traitors and Infernal Villains': *Illustrated London News, Household Words,* Charles Dickens and the Indian Rebellion." In *Negotiating India in the Nineteenth-Century Media,* edited by David Finkelstein and Douglas M. Peers. New York: St. Martin's Press, 2000. 110–34.

Poovey, Mary. *Uneven Developments: The Ideological Work of Gender in Mid-Victorian England.* Chicago: University of Chicago Press, 1988.

Pope-Hennessy, Una. *Charles Dickens.* New York: Howell, Soskin, 1946.

Rae, John, M. D. "Dr. Rae's Report." *Household Words* 10 (30 December 1854): 457–59.

——. "The Lost Arctic Voyagers." *Household Words* 10 (23 December 1854): 433–37.

——. "Report to the Secretary of the Admiralty." *Times* (London), 23 October 1854, 7.

——. "Sir John Franklin and His Crews." *Household Words* 11 (3 February 1855): 12–20.

Rance, Nicholas. *Wilkie Collins and Other Sensation Novelists: Walking the Moral Hospital.* Rutherford, N.J.: Fairleigh Dickinson University Press, 1991.

Reade, Charles. *Griffith Gaunt; or, Jealousy.* Boston: James R. Osgood, 1875.

Reed, John R. "English Imperialism and the Unacknowledged Crime of *The Moonstone.*" *Clio* 2 (June 1973): 281–90.

[Reeves]. "Promotion, French and English." *Household Words* 15 (24 January 1857): 90–92.

Roberts, Ann. "Mothers and Babies: The Wetnurse and Her Employer in Mid-Nineteenth-Century England." *Women's Studies* 3, 3 (1976): 276–93.

[Robertson, John]. "Scotch Coast Folk." *Household Words* 13 (5 July 1856): 585–90.

Robinson, Kenneth. *Wilkie Collins: A Biography.* New York: Macmillan, 1952.

"Rome and Turnips." *All the Year Round* 1 (14 May 1859): 53–58.

[Sala, George Augustus]. "Cheerily, Cheerily!" *Household Words* 6 (25 September 1852): 25–31.

——. *The Life and Adventures of George Augustus Sala.* 2 vols. New York: Scribner's, 1895.

[——]. "Numbers of People." *Household Words* 10 (21 October 1854): 221–28.

Schor, Hilary M. *Scheherezade in the Marketplace: Elizabeth Gaskell and the Victorian Novel.* Oxford: Oxford University Press, 1992.

Scott, Sir Walter. *Waverley.* Edited by Andrew Hook. 1972. Reprint, Harmondsworth: Penguin, 1986.

Sedgwick, Eve Kosofsky. *Between Men: English Literature and Male Homosocial Desire.* New York: Columbia University Press, 1985.

Slater, Michael. *Dickens and Women.* London: J. M. Dent, 1983.

Smith, Albert. *The Story of Mont Blanc*. New York: G. P. Putnam, 1853.

"Soldier's Law." *All the Year Round* 16 (28 July 1866): 55–58.

Solly, Henry Shaen. *The Life of Henry Morley, L. L. D.* London: Edward Arnold, 1898.

Squier, E. G. *The States of Central America; Their Geography, Topography, Climate, Population, Resources, Productions, Commerce, Political Organization, Aborigines, Etc., Etc.* New York: Harper and Brothers, 1858.

Sterrenburg, Lee. "Psychoanalysis and the Iconography of Revolution." *Victorian Studies* 19 (December 1975): 241–64.

Stone, Harry. *Dickens and the Invisible World: Fairy Tales, Fantasy, and Novel-Making*. Bloomington: Indiana University Press, 1979.

——, ed. *Charles Dickens' Uncollected Writings from "Household Words," 1850–1859*. 2 vols. Bloomington: Indiana University Press, 1968.

"Subterranean Switzerland." *All the Year Round* 2 (5 November 1859): 25–31.

Sutherland, John. Introduction and note on the text to *Armadale*, by Wilkie Collins. Harmondsworth: Penguin, 1995. vii–xxxiii.

——. *Victorian Novelists and Publishers*. Chicago: University of Chicago Press, 1976.

Swinburne, A. C. "Wilkie Collins." *Fortnightly Review* (1 November 1889). In *Wilkie Collins: The Critical Heritage*, edited by Norman Page. London: Routledge & Kegan Paul, 1974. 253–64.

[Talfourd, Thomas Noon]. "A Glimpse of the Cairngorm Mountains." *Household Words* 4 (4 October 1851): 40–45.

"Tape at the Horse Guards." *All the Year Round* 6 (6 March 1862): 568–72.

Tennent, Sir James Emerson. *Ceylon: An Account of the Island, Physical, Historical, and Topographical*. 5th ed. 2 vols. London: Longman, Green, Longman, and Roberts, 1859.

Thomas, Deborah A. *Dickens and the Short Story*. Philadelphia: University of Pennsylvania Press, 1982.

Thomas, Ronald R. *Dreams of Authority: Freud and the Fictions of the Unconscious*. Ithaca, N.Y.: Cornell University Press, 1990.

——. "Minding the Body Politic: The Romance of Science and the Revision of History in Victorian Detective Fiction." *Victorian Literature and Culture* 19 (1991): 233–54.

"Tom Tiddler's Ground: Extraordinary Proceedings in Wellington-Street." *Queen* 1, 16 (21 December 1861): 313–15.

"Touching Englishmen's Lives." *All the Year Round* 15 (30 June 1866): 582–85.

[Townsend, E., and Alexander Henry Abercromby Hamilton]. "Indian Recruits and Indian English." *Household Words* 16 (3 October 1857): 319–22.

Trodd, Anthea. "Collaborating in Open Boats: Dickens, Collins, Franklin, and Bligh." *Victorian Studies* 42, 2 (winter 1999–2000): 201–25.

Tyndall, John. *Hours of Exercise in the Alps*. New York: D. Appleton, 1872.

Ward, A. W. *Charles Dickens: A Lecture*. In *Dickens: The Critical Heritage*, edited by Philip Collins. New York: Barnes and Noble, 1971. 537–41.

[Weir, William, and W. H. Wills]. "Short Cuts Across the Globe: The Isthmus of Suez." *Household Words* 1 (11 May 1850): 167–68.

"Why We Can't Get Recruits." *All the Year Round* 14 (9 December 1865): 464–68.

Whymper, Edward. *Scrambles Amongst the Alps in the Years 1860–69*. London: John Murray, 1871.

"Wilkie Collins About Charles Dickens. (From a Marked Copy of Forster's 'Dickens')." *Pall Mall Gazette* (20 January 1890): 3.

[Wills, W. H.]. "One of Our Legal Fictions." *Household Words* 9 (29 April 1854): 257–60.

Index

Italicized numbers indicate pages with figures.

Index